FAMILY LEGAL VULNERABILITY

Family Legal Vulnerability

How Immigration Policy Shapes the
Lives of Latino College Students

Laura E. Enriquez, Zulema Valdez,
Annie Ro, Cecilia Ayón,
and Jennifer R. Nájera

NEW YORK UNIVERSITY PRESS
New York

NEW YORK UNIVERSITY PRESS
New York
www.nyupress.org

© 2026 by New York University
All rights reserved

Please contact the Library of Congress for Cataloging-in-Publication data.

ISBN: 9781479837342 (hardback)
ISBN: 9781479837373 (paperback)
ISBN: 9781479837403 (library ebook)
ISBN: 9781479837380 (consumer ebook)

This book is printed on acid-free paper, and its binding materials are chosen for strength and durability. We strive to use environmentally responsible suppliers and materials to the greatest extent possible in publishing our books.

The manufacturer's authorized representative in the EU for product safety is Mare Nostrum Group B.V., Mauritskade 21D, 1091 GC Amsterdam, The Netherlands. Email: gpsr@mare-nostrum.co.uk.

Manufactured in the United States of America

10 9 8 7 6 5 4 3 2 1

Also available as an ebook

CONTENTS

LIST OF FIGURES

PART I

Conceptualizing Family Legal Vulnerability

Introduction

*How Immigration Policy Threatens Families
and Undermines Students*

As an undocumented student approaching college graduation, Aiden Chacón was trying to be more optimistic. At age 15, he had become a beneficiary of the Deferred Action for Childhood Arrivals (DACA) program, but the executive action was rescinded and thrust into legal uncertainty during his senior year of high school, raising the specter of deportation to Mexico, a country he no longer remembered. As he put it, "Having DACA doesn't mean that it's guaranteed that I am allowed to be here." Years earlier, after graduating high school, he decided to commute to the University of California, San Diego from his mother's home to minimize the risks associated with crossing interior border enforcement checkpoints between San Diego and the rest of California. He struggled, he said, with "pessimistic thoughts." During his first year of college, he was placed on academic probation, "and it kind of just started tumbling down in my second and third year." He linked this to declining mental health: "I think that's something that affects your grades in a lot of ways, just because [you're] already having to deal with your own problems and then you have to worry about your status and whether you can or can't stay in this country. It's a lot to have on your plate." Using his temporary work authorization, Aiden was able to obtain a corporate internship, for which he received pay through a fellowship. But Aiden knew he was just one stroke of bad luck away from financial ruin. When he got COVID-19 twice in the same quarter, he lost out on four weeks of pay from the internship while he was in quarantine; he blew through his meager savings and had to ask his mom to help cover some of his bills. Then the director of the fellowship program he depended on for employment left the position. Aiden was soon without a job and the professional development it had offered. Other corporate internships turned him down, and Aiden believed this was because his prospective employers feared that he would ask them to sponsor him for an employment visa.

Aiden's story is a testament to how immigration status can compromise undocumented students' outcomes; however, digging deeper reveals that Aiden's experiences are situated within an important family context. Specifically, Aiden shared that his mom's undocumented status had limited her employment options to working under the table as a caretaker at a residential care home. Immigration officials had recently investigated the facility's employment records, and his mom felt like it was just a matter of time before "they either fire them or immigration comes and takes the people that they can." Given his mom's low income and job insecurity, Aiden felt it was essential that he work for money. He took on a second job in addition to his internship, further compromising his ability to excel at school. He also chose to live at home to minimize costs. Aiden's personal financial struggles were magnified in the larger context of his family's household economy. His academic difficulties were exacerbated by having to rush from one thing to the next to meet his financial commitments and continue commuting to his classes. He struggled to fit in time to study or seek academic support. On top of these concerns, he worried that his mom might encounter immigration enforcement on her way to work or around town. Little things—like her not answering her phone or returning his calls quickly—would set him on edge. These added more mental health strains as he worried about being separated from his mom, the only close family member he had.

Aiden's educational experiences within a larger family context resonated with those of another student, Ruby Pedrosa, the eldest US citizen child of an undocumented single mother. Although Ruby and Aiden had differing immigration statuses and did not share the same individual constraints, they struggled with many similar family-related strains on their education. Ruby's mom worked as a seamstress and was paid by the piece, often not earning enough to cover all their living expenses. This chronic financial strain shaped Ruby's educational journey. She chose UC Riverside over UC Berkeley because living expenses would be more affordable and she could be closer to home, allowing her to check in on her mom over the weekends. She could not afford to get involved in campus activities and declined an invitation to join a sorority because of the fees. By her second quarter she was seriously considering leaving UC

Riverside for a more affordable community college. She found a job that helped with educational expenses, but if she switched to community college she could use her paycheck to help support her family. As Ruby put it, she became *desanimada*, disengaging from her academics and social life. Yet her friends stuck by her, providing emotional and sometimes financial support, and she stayed at UC Riverside and obtained her degree. Like Aiden, she wrestled with the threat of family separation posed by Donald Trump's first presidential administration, which coincided with her entire college career. She acknowledged, "I'm not the one that's going to get deported, but I know that someone close to my heart is."

Aiden's and Ruby's stories highlight how immigration laws and policies that threaten their families' well-being and stability seep into their college careers. Despite their different social positions—an undocumented student and a US citizen—their mothers' undocumented statuses created a shared sense of legal precarity and similarly compromised their educational trajectories. We conceptualize both Aiden and Ruby as *immigration-impacted students*, meaning that they are students whose trajectories are constrained by contemporary immigration policies that marginalize undocumented immigrants and individuals with precarious legal statuses. By thinking about students as immigration-impacted, we acknowledge the underlying family context that fosters similar experiences despite having differing individual social positions relative to the law.

Focusing on the case of Latino students attending the University of California system, we examine how immigration-impacted college students' educational experiences and social mobility are shaped not only by their own immigration status but also by their family members' undocumented immigration status. In Part I, we introduce *family legal vulnerability* as a novel framework and answer our first research question: How do immigration-impacted college students experience family legal vulnerability? It captures how students who are members of undocumented and mixed-status immigrant families collectively experience deportability, economic insecurity, and social exclusion. In Part II, we trace how family legal vulnerability cascades through the everyday lives of immigration-impacted students to address our second research question: How does family legal vulnerability shape students' mental health, academic success, and political engagement—and to what extent does it contribute to disparities? Part III centers policy implications by examining our final research question: How do immigration-impacted students draw on campus resources to alleviate the effects of family legal vulnerability—and what can universities do to improve student success?

Our survey of 1,645 college students with varying self and parental immigration statuses suggests that having undocumented parents results in similar experiences of family legal vulnerability regardless of one's own immigration status. We draw on 63 interviews with students who are undocumented immigrants and US citizens with undocumented parents to highlight the process through which this occurs. We show how the immigration policy context manifests as collective constraints on the family, wherein family members share in the material barriers and emotional turmoil produced by immigration policy. We identify collective constraints and trace how they spill over to create cascading consequences of family legal vulnerability. The resulting torrent of individual strains then compromise students' mental health, academic success, and political engagement. Our survey data reveals that family legal vulnerability contributes to significant disparities when we compare the outcomes of immigration-impacted students to their US citizen peers with lawfully present parents. Yet immigration-impacted students also demonstrate agency as they negotiate family legal vulnerability and seek out ways to bolster their individual and collective flourishing. Ultimately, we call on scholars, policymakers, and university administrators to account for family legal vulnerability when considering how immigration policies have undermined students' college experiences, and we identify actionable practices to advance greater equity and inclusion.

Immigrant Illegality and Mixed-Status Families

Theories of immigrant illegality have been used to conceptualize the sociopolitical positions of undocumented immigrants as well as those with liminal legal statuses.[1] This approach highlights that immigration laws and policies produce illegality and make it consequential. Specifically, a growing body of research has documented how laws and policies produce deportation threats, constrain employment, restrict spatial mobility and social participation, and offer few legalization opportunities. These constraints make immigration status a significant source of social stratification restricting undocumented and liminally legal immigrants' everyday activities, decision-making, and upward mobility.[2]

Much of this work documents the consequences of immigrant illegality and ensuing unequal incorporation outcomes experienced by undocumented individuals. To theorize this process, Cecilia Menjívar and Leisy Abrego define "legal violence" as "harmful effects of the law that can potentially obstruct and derail immigrants' paths of incorporation."[3] This lens "identifies harmful outcomes of the law in the lives of individuals" and labels these as violence to capture how such consequences are not simply exclusionary or marginalizing but violent and damaging.[4] Undocumented immigrants experience physical and psychological trauma during their journey due, in part, to US foreign and immigration policies.[5] Once in the United States, immigration enforcement practices make undocumented immigrants susceptible to deportation, leading them to develop persistent fears—sometimes realized, always harmful—of detention, deportation, and separation from family members.[6] The psychological violence associated with deportation threats can have consequences such as feelings of insecurity in public places and compromised social networks.[7] Many undocumented immigrants also encounter difficulties finding well-paid and stable jobs, limiting them to low-income, labor-intensive employment sectors and placing them at risk for workplace abuse.[8] State laws and policies may also block undocumented youths' access to higher education, limiting their ability to engage in this mobility pathway.[9] Undocumented immigrants also experience symbolic violence in the form of stigma and shame, often related to anticipatory or realized social exclusion because of their immigration status.[10] The accumulation of everyday incidents causes harm over the long term and results in limited incorporation opportunities and unequal outcomes for undocumented immigrants.

Seeking to demonstrate the far-reaching effects of immigrant illegality, scholars have turned attention to mixed-status families to show how the law also seeps into the experiences and life chances of US citizens with undocumented family members. Cassaundra Rodriguez refers to this as "family illegality" to describe how family members negotiate illegality in their everyday lives.[11] Most of this research has focused on how parents' immigration status constrains the lives of their minor US citizen children. Studies of young US citizen children of undocumented parents detail their delayed cognitive development, lower academic performance, and higher rates of adjustment and anxiety disorders relative to their peers who have lawfully present parents.[12] These inequalities extend into adulthood, as the older US citizen children of undocumented immigrants display worse educational and economic outcomes than their peers whose parents were born in the United States or whose formerly undocumented parents had adjusted their immigration status.[13] We focus on the transition to adulthood to examine how illegality emerges within families as children age into young adults, becoming more independent and simultaneously potentially able to contribute to the family's finances. Further, we establish that undocumented young adults in these families experience similar forms of family legal vulnerability when compared to their US citizen peers.

Building on this prior research, we take a multigenerational approach that takes the family into account and focuses on collective processes. We contend that inequities emerge for all members of undocumented and mixed-status families, regardless of one's own immigration status, because immigration laws and policies are felt and experienced as family units. Material constraints are shared among family members who are (inter)dependent upon one another. For example, undocumented immigrants' economic barriers translate into low incomes, unstable employment, and unfavorable schedules that constrain their contributions to family economic security. US citizen family members then share in this family economic insecurity. Minor children may have lower-quality child care and fewer educational and extracurricular opportunities.[14] US citizen family members who are old enough and eligible to work may feel pressure to financially contribute to the family or use their access to loans and/or credit cards to help maintain financial stability; this includes young adult children and romantic partners.[15] Having lawfully present extended family members in the household may also mitigate financial strains by increasing the number of people contributing financially—or it can create additional strains by increasing the number of household members who must be provided for.[16] Along these same lines, emotional strains are shared as all family members fear separation through deportation; this can lead them all to monitor and fear police interactions or isolate themselves from friends to protect their family's well-being.[17] Laura Enriquez previously developed the concept of *multigenerational punishment* to capture how the sanctions intended for a specific population spill over to harm individuals who are not targeted by a given law.[18] Specifically, strong social ties and daily interactions lead US citizen family members to witness how immigration laws constrain the lives and opportunities of their undocumented immigrant family members and also share in these punishments.[19] We apply this multigenerational understanding here to examine the everyday processes through which family members of multiple generations confront, experience, and navigate inequality as a collective.

Prior research has focused on examining the process through which individual immigrant illegality produces collective experiences of exclusion for US citizen family members. Building on this, we imagine a dialectical process whereby collective family experiences also condition consequential individual experiences. While we recognize the consequential nature of each family members' own immigration status, we focus our attention on the next phase of this process by asking: How are collective family experiences of legal vulnerability translated into consequential individual experiences and compromised outcomes? By focusing on how individual college students experience the family context, we turn attention to the family unit rather than the specific types of statuses occupied by individual family members. Situating individual college students within their undocumented and mixed-status family context, we unpack how collective experiences of illegality are made consequential for students' individual outcomes and future mobility.

To link the family context to student outcomes, we draw on socioecological approaches that recognize individuals as nested in multilevel ecological systems.[20] Uniquely, our study centers how the family is made meaningful at multiple levels within the ecological system. Most centrally, we recognize the family as a microsystem, an everyday social institution in which individual students are embedded and regularly interact with family members. By nesting students within their family microsystem, we seek to understand how a family's collective legal vulnerability shapes students' outcomes. Family remains relevant in the exosystem, or the external contexts and events that can indirectly affect an individual. In this case, family members traverse social spaces and experience legal vulnerability, bringing these experiences back home to affect the household, such as through low pay in the underground economy or experiences of discrimination. We also pay attention to the fact that the laws and societal values implicated by the macrosystem target undocumented and mixed-status families. Specifically, exclusionary policies aim to harm family units, such as through deportation practices that separate loved ones as a deliberate measure by the United States government to deter migrants.[21] Stigmatizing cultural narratives also extend beyond undocumented immigrants to criminalize mixed-status families with false assertions that they are "stealing" welfare benefits and starting families to birth "anchor babies" who will facilitate pathways to legalization.[22]

By addressing the impact of immigration policy, our multigenerational approach highlights the family as an important context for understanding individual student outcomes. By locating students within their families, we recognize that family members' lives are linked. This core principle of life-course theory centers the fact that people are embedded in social relationships, leading them to be interdependent upon one another.[23] Family scholars have documented the power of linked lives among family members as the misfortunes and opportunities of parents in turn structure the life chances of children. This concept recognizes that family members are connected to one another through the transmission of material, cultural, social, and emotional resources.[24]

Accordingly, our multigenerational approach allows us to establish how immigration laws are a deep-seated source of inequality within Latino immigrant families in particular.[25] Extensive research has documented that second-generation Latinos have lower educational attainment and poorer well-being outcomes compared to native-born whites and that exclusion persists well into the third generation.[26] However, most of this work does not fully account for contemporary experiences of legal violence that make individual and parental immigration status exceedingly consequential and may play a significant role in the trajectories of second-generation Latinos in particular. Latino immigrant families are disproportionately subjected to punitive immigration policies as half of Mexican and Central American immigrants in the United States are undocumented.[27] These immigrants live their lives and establish families in the United States, such that nearly 14.4 million people across the United States are members of mixed-status families[28] and a quarter of Latino children in the United States have at least one undocumented parent.[29]

Our study contextualizes these Latino children of immigrants within their families as they enter young adulthood and attend higher education institutions. This is a critical stage as they pursue higher education in hopes of securing a pathway to upward mobility for themselves and their families. We first establish shared family experiences of legal vulnerability through the eyes of the undocumented and US citizen children of undocumented immigrants. We then consider how the production, experience, and effects of family legal vulnerability shape their mental health, academic, and political outcomes. Ultimately, we argue that family legal vulnerability makes illegality a central source of inequality for undocumented young adults *and* US citizen children of undocumented immigrants.

Toward a Framework of Family Legal Vulnerability

Prior research has used theories of illegality to define the contours and consequences of immigration-related laws and policies for undocumented immigrants and their family members. Building on this work, we conceptualize legal vulnerability as a distinct step in the illegalization process. We define legal vulnerability as a social position in which there is risk of unequal experiences and outcomes because of exclusionary immigration laws and policies. It is the cause that gives way to the effect that is illegality. Similar to concepts like legal violence and multigenerational punishment, legal vulnerability highlights the role of the law in producing exclusionary consequences. Yet legal vulnerability allows us to take a step back to see the process through which individuals experience, interpret, and respond to the law, which gives rise to their unique experience of illegality.

Legal vulnerability allows us to account for an individual's agency to interpret the law and respond to it. According to Jorge Bustamante, immigrant vulnerability "lies in the realm of the relationship between individuals and the state, which might vary depending on the resources an individual has available to protect himself or herself."[30] In other words, personal agency yields unique experiences of illegality as individuals muster resources and legal knowledge to determine how they will negotiate immigration laws and policies. This impacts the scope of the consequences of illegality on individuals' everyday lives and overall incorporation. Thus, it is critical that we distinguish between legal vulnerability and the consequences of illegality. For example, Nicolas DeGenova previously distinguished between the lived experience of deportation and the risk of experiencing deportation. He conceptualized the later as deportability—a unique and consequential form of immigrant illegality—ultimately yielding a new way to understand the insidious effects of immigration policy.[31] Subsequent research has also shown that deportability can be felt and interpreted differently, leading some undocumented immigrants to isolate themselves while others fully engage in social life.[32] Thus, legal vulnerability allows us to distinguish between the risk for and actual experiences of exclusionary consequences at the hands of immigration laws and policies.

A range of immigration laws and policies are responsible for creating legal vulnerability. In prior work with our colleagues Sharon Velarde Pierce and Alein Haro, we conceptualized legal vulnerability as a multidimensional concept that includes the risks associated with undocumented immigration status, the threat of deportation or family separation, financial insecurity, discrimination, and social exclusion due to the immigration policy context.[33] This definition expands on the work of Kalina Brabeck and colleagues who have measured legal vulnerability as a combination of one's unauthorized legal status and history of interactions with the immigration enforcement system, specifically whether an individual or a family member had ever been detained or deported.[34]

We distinguish between individual and family legal vulnerability to clarify the intended level of analysis. *Individual legal vulnerability* refers to the risks experienced by individuals, whereas *family legal vulnerability* refers to the precarious position of the family as a collective unit. Family legal vulnerability nests individual experiences within the family unit by recognizing that families experience collective risk for exclusion due to immigration laws and policies. This term also builds on past research with families headed by same-sex couples, which has used the same concept to describe how the law produces an enduring and collective risk to all family members' well-being.[35]

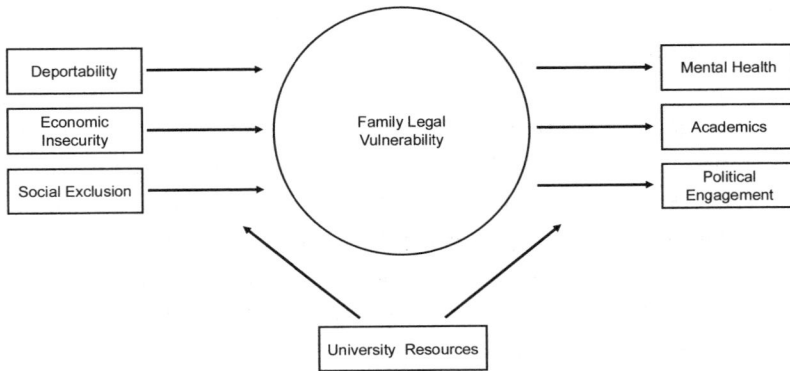

Figure 1.1. Theoretical framework for the present study.

Our study traces the process through which family legal vulnerability manifests and establishes the mechanisms that produce unequal student outcomes. Figure 1.1 depicts the theoretical framework for our study. We first envision deportability, economic insecurity, and social exclusion as the primary dimensions through which immigration laws and policies create experiences of family legal vulnerability. We then interrogate how family legal vulnerability impacts three key student outcomes: mental health, academic success, and political engagement. Finally, we investigate how university resources alleviate the effects of family legal vulnerability in students' lives. The following sections outline our theoretical framework.

Dimensions of Family Legal Vulnerability

We identify and focus on three primary dimensions of legal vulnerability: *deportability, economic insecurity,* and *social exclusion.* Each dimension, explained in the subsections below, is responsible for introducing a unique form of risk into the everyday lives and incorporation processes of undocumented immigrants and lawfully present members of mixed-status families. However, they are also mutually constitutive as they reinforce one another in their exclusionary effects.

Deportability

Deportability, defined as an individual's potential to experience deportation, is a prominent dimension of legal vulnerability.[36] At its core, being undocumented means that an individual can be expelled from the nation-state. Such deportations separate families across borders or simultaneously expel US citizens who accompany their deported family members. Both outcomes disrupt personal and familial economic and social mobility and well-being.[37] This threat has become increasingly salient over the lifetime of our participants as internal immigration enforcement practices have proliferated since the late 1990s. Agreements between local police departments and Immigration and Customs Enforcement (ICE) deputize local police officers to enforce immigration law by detaining immigrants for immigration officials. Other programs conduct immigration status checks in jails and prisons to identify individuals with deportation orders.[38] A growing awareness of deportation threats has contributed to rising concerns about deportation among Latino US citizens.[39]

We examine several manifestations of deportability throughout the book. Deportation concerns capture how frequently individuals think about someone's deportation. We consider potential concerns for one's own deportation and that of parents, siblings, and extended family members. We examine whether students have experienced the deportation of a family member to account for how witnessing and managing a deportation within one's family may affect one's material circumstances as well as symbolic understanding of deportation risks. We also consider threat to family more broadly using a survey scale that measures perceived threat to family due to restrictive immigration policy. It captures how frequently participants worried about the impact immigration policies have on them or their family, feared that they or a family member would be reported to immigration officials, and worried about family separation.

Economic Insecurity

Economic insecurity is a second dimension of legal vulnerability that encompasses a range of socioeconomic-related insecurities, including food insecurity, housing insecurity, and financial strain. For undocumented immigrants, a major source of economic insecurity is the inability to obtain a valid social security number. Without employment authorization, many seek self-employment, receive payment under the table, or use invalid social security numbers to complete hiring paperwork. Since 1996, E-Verify has allowed employers to check employment authorization via an online website, further restricting undocumented immigrants' access to employment.[40] The result is increased concentration in low-wage work. In 2012, approximately 62 percent of undocumented immigrants held service, construction, and production jobs, twice the share of US-born workers in these occupations.[41] Further, undocumented status increases the risk of low earnings and labor violations, including a higher likelihood of earning below minimum wage and experiencing wage theft.[42] DACA gives recipients the same access to formal employment as US citizens, but most have experienced delayed entry into the workforce and limited professional development due to lacking work authorization for some period of time as young adults.[43] Undocumented immigrants may also struggle to secure adequate housing, as landlords in more desirable neighborhoods and home loan agencies require a valid social security number.[44] These realities, coupled with low incomes, can subsequently limit undocumented immigrant-headed households from moving out of impoverished areas, further constraining upward mobility.[45]

We capture material experiences of economic insecurity by paying attention to food and housing insecurity. "Food insecurity" is defined by the US Department of Agriculture as reduced food intake as well as disrupted eating and reduced diet quality, variety, or desirability.[46] Housing insecurity similarly captures reduced safety or quality of housing, limited affordability and difficulty paying housing expenses, and the threat and/or loss of housing. We use measures of individual and family financial strain to capture more broadly students' and their families' difficulties making ends meet. These measures capture worries as well as actual experiences of financial difficulties.

Social Exclusion

Deportability and economic insecurity can set the stage for social exclusion. We define "social exclusion" as limited interpersonal exchanges or social interaction. Social exclusion can emerge as undocumented immigrants manage deportation risks by restricting spatial mobility, including restricting themselves to certain neighborhoods, staying close to home, and avoiding driving.[47] Indeed, one study found that undocumented immigrants who perceived local police as collaborating with immigration enforcement reported higher levels of social isolation than others, and this isolation was even more elevated among those who were parents.[48] Undocumented young adults also report retreating from their social lives—including putting off dating, marriage, and parenting—because of economic insecurity and concerns about being unable to provide for their families.[49] We pay attention to limited or constrained social interactions, such as not spending time with friends or avoiding certain locations or types of social activities. Social isolation is the ensuing result of these actions as individuals withdraw from activities, increasing the chances that they become more solitary as well as compromising existing relationships.

Anti-immigrant and racist-nativist interpersonal interactions and symbolic messaging can also increase social exclusion. Being perceived as an immigrant, as Latino, and/or as undocumented can raise the risk of facing racist-nativist discrimination.[50] These experiences reflect larger social threat narratives that portray undocumented immigrants and their US citizen family members as criminals and social burdens who steal resources, strain social services, and otherwise harm US citizens.[51] Both undocumented and US citizens report experiences of racist-nativist discrimination and vicariously experience the discriminatory experiences faced by undocumented family members.[52] Together material and symbolic experiences of real and anticipated discrimination can foster feelings of stigma and shame related to one's own or a family members' undocumented immigration status.[53]

Student Outcomes

We pay attention to how family legal vulnerability shapes and contributes to disparities in student mental health, academic success, and political engagement. These outcomes are areas in which colleges and universities have been shown to contribute to fostering student success. Further, they are linked to common incorporation outcomes, such as educational and political incorporation, that are traditionally used to measure immigrant integration and assimilation over generations.

Mental Health and Well-Being

Mental-health outcomes play a significant role in the lives of college students. Universities are reporting skyrocketing mental health rates among their student populations.[54] Prior research suggests that undocumented students and US citizen children with undocumented parents are at a higher risk for mental health issues as they express high rates of stress, anxiety, and depression.[55] Students' mental health not only poses concerns for well-being but may compromise academic outcomes. Thus, we pay attention to several forms of emotional distress, including qualitative discussions of chronic stress as well as quantitative assessments of depression and anxiety symptomatology.

Simultaneously, to advance a holistic understanding of immigration-impacted students' mental health, we explore their resilience and coping strategies.[56] We build on scholarship highlighting the resilience of undocumented students as they navigate higher education institutions not built to meet their needs.[57] Such research has identified the role of social support and individual coping strategies such as diversion, reframing, and normalizing in students' management of immigration-related stressors.[58] We consider such strategies practiced by undocumented students as well as their US citizen peers with undocumented parents to broaden this research. We also quantitatively measure positive well-being outcomes—namely, flourishing—to examine social and psychological prosperity through feelings of competence, self-acceptance, and optimism as well as thriving social relationships.[59] Such positive mental-health outcomes are widely recognized as critical resources for well-being and social and economic prosperity.[60]

Academic Engagement and Performance

Prior research suggests that undocumented students and US citizen children with undocumented parents have compromised academic performance outcomes.[61] As we conducted a cross-sectional study of students in the midst of their education, we address intermediary outcomes that have the potential to disrupt degree completion. Course failure can both stymie educational progress by extending time to degree and push students to shift their educational goals. Low grade point average (GPA), which we define as below a 2.5 on a 4.0 scale, can set the stage for academic probation and possible dismissal. In addition, at the University of California, most scholarships require at minimum a 2.5 GPA, which can push academically struggling, low-income students out of school by limiting their ability to cover educational costs. We also examine behavioral engagement, which captures participation in academic activities and efforts to complete academic tasks.[62] Positive academic engagement (i.e., attending class, studying, completing assignments, and engaging with peers and instructors) is associated with supporting positive academic outcomes (higher academic achievement) and preventing negative outcomes (dropping out).[63] In addition, we examine negative academic engagement including failing to complete an assignment or being unprepared for class.

Finally, participating in professional development opportunities can be a critical educational outcome for students. Internships, practicums, and field experiences are all considered high-impact educational practices that can foster increased student engagement and performance, especially among marginalized student populations.[64] In addition, research shows professional development opportunities such as internships are associated with postgraduation job attainment and early career success.[65] As such, professional development opportunities can ensure that students' time in college helps them capitalize on their degree and meet the desired professional goals that propelled them to college. Yet prior research suggests that lacking work authorization limits undocumented students' opportunities to engage in internships and career-related jobs.[66]

Political Engagement

We examine political engagement as a third outcome that is salient within the context of higher education because colleges and universities can be a training ground for such activity. College graduates are more likely to participate in civic and political life than those who do not have a degree.[67] Further, coursework—particularly coursework in the social sciences and humanities—in addition to participation in service learning and community-based projects can augment political knowledge; all are associated with higher rates of political engagement.[68] At the same time, the impact of immigration policy on families motivates immigration-impacted people to engage politically.[69] As a result, immigration-impacted college students are situated in a nexus of family, policy, and educational contexts that could spur their political engagement.

We explore a range of political engagement outcomes that are not conditional on immigration status. Although we spoke to US citizen students about voting, we do not assess this outcome quantitatively because many in our sample do not have this right. Instead, we examine actions like talking to others about voting or joining organizations to campaign and lobby for pro-immigrant candidates and policies. Finally, we examined more routine, everyday political behaviors that can be practiced beyond the timing of election cycles, including joining organizations to solve social problems as well as protest participation. Interviews also encompassed students' efforts to educate themselves about the policies and practices that would affect their families and sharing information online.

Alleviating Family Legal Vulnerability: The Power of Policies and Place

Government policy at every level affects the impact of legal vulnerability on undocumented immigrants and their families and the consequences of that vulnerability. Sociologists Tanya Golash-Boza and Zulema Valdez point to the important roles of policies and place in this process by theorizing "nested contexts of reception" to capture how federal, state, and local policies work together to shape undocumented immigrants' level of inclusion or exclusion.[70] Federal immigration policies can temper the effects of undocumented status by minimizing the salience of legal vulnerability in everyday life. For undocumented young adults who migrated to the United States at a young age, the Deferred Action for Childhood Arrivals program created a liminal legal status by providing temporary protection from deportation and access to employment authorization. For over a decade, DACA recipients reported decreased fears of deportation, greater economic security, improved education completion rates, increased access to professional development and career opportunities, and better mental health than their undocumented peers.[71] Yet state and local contexts affect the impact of DACA on recipients' legal vulnerability.[72] Further, the first Trump administration's rescission of DACA in 2017 and subsequent legal battle has muted the positive effects of this program.[73] Still, our study takes place in a relatively inclusionary state and institutional context, meaning it offers important lessons to learn from but is also a unique, best-case scenario.

State policies have established California as one of the most inclusive state contexts for undocumented immigrants.[74] In the 1990s California was known for anti-immigrant state policies and ballot measures that sought to deny undocumented immigrants and their family members' access to education and social services.[75] The early 2000s ushered in progressive policy shifts as activist groups successfully campaigned state lawmakers to pass Assembly Bill 540, which enabled undocumented youth to pursue higher education in the state's public university systems by granting them access to in-state tuition rates.[76] A decade later, in 2011, additional laws extended access to state and institutional financial aid to this same student group.[77] In subsequent years, laws continued to expand access to higher education by creating a state loan program for undocumented students and repeatedly expanding eligibility for in-state tuition to broaden access.[78] Concurrently, other measures were put in place to incorporate undocumented immigrant adults more broadly into the social fabric, providing them access to driver's licenses and reducing cooperation between police and immigration enforcement to reduce the threat of deportation in the state.[79] The state legislature passed additional bills to facilitate economic integration by enabling undocumented immigrants to obtain professional state licenses, promote well-being by providing access state healthcare benefits, and further restrict the federal deportation machine by limiting the state resources available to immigration agents.[80] The increasingly inclusionary nature of the California policy context reflects the success of many advocacy and activist immigrant organizations in lobbying for change and gives immigration-impacted students in the state a better foundation for success.

Situated within this unique state context, the University of California system has become a national leader in implementing policies and programs to address undocumented students' needs. While other institutions hosted projects and student organizations to support undocumented students, UC Berkeley was the first institution nationwide to establish an official program in 2012 dedicated to supporting undocumented students.[81] In 2013 the newly appointed UC president, Janet Napolitano, responded to student activist demands by committing $5 million to support the development of undocumented student resources across campuses.[82] A second wave of funding in the amount of $8.4 million was announced in 2016 and included allocations for loan programs and immigration legal services.[83] This funding facilitated concerted efforts across the ten UC campuses to develop institutionalized resources to advance equity and inclusion for undocumented students by providing academic, social-emotional, and financial support.[84] Further, the university established the UC Immigrant Legal Services Center to provide free, immigration-related legal representation for UC students and their immediate family members.[85] We investigate all these resources as potential sources of support that can help minimize the salience of family legal vulnerability on students' outcomes.

Working in tandem with inclusive state policies, UC institutional policies and programs have increased undocumented students' access to and success in higher education.[86] However, it is important to note that the UC student population represents the top 12.5 percent of California high school students.[87] Further, it is educating only 5 percent of California's undocumented college student population as an estimated 4,000 undocumented students were enrolled across its ten campuses around the time of this study.[88] California State University's twenty-three campuses, which are less selective and offer lower tuition rates, enrolled 15 percent, and the remaining 80 percent attended one of the state's community colleges.[89]

Place is a powerful determinant of family legal vulnerability because there is substantial variation in the extent to which state and institutional policies seek to include or exclude immigration-impacted communities.[90] Our study looks at the Golden State and the University of California as role models for other states and institutions looking to implement inclusive policies to alleviate legal vulnerability. However, this also means that we are documenting a best-case scenario. This group of immigration-impacted students is situated in a series of relatively inclusive nested contexts of reception. Specifically, the federal immigration policy context has cast this group of young adults as more deserving of relief than their undocumented parents, allowing about two-thirds of our participants to receive DACA protections before court injunctions prevented the processing of new applications. Meanwhile, the state policy context largely insulates them and their families from deportation threats and social exclusion. While the local policy context can vary, the UC system offers an inclusive institutional context and a plethora of resources and opportunities despite ongoing austerity measures. In other words, our participants are best poised to experience mobility through higher education than virtually any other undocumented student group.

Data and Methods

As educators and researchers on three University of California campuses, we have dedicated our careers to advancing equity and inclusion for undocumented and immigrant-origin communities. We come from families and communities whose ability to thrive has been constrained by exclusionary immigration policies. Our research has focused on documenting the inequalities they face and identifying pathways toward inclusion and justice. We have invested our time in mentoring immigration-impacted students, collaborating with on- and off-campus stakeholders, and advancing programs, policies, and practices that embrace equity. These shared experiences led Laura Enriquez to bring us together to establish the UC Collaborative to Promote Immigrant and Student Equity (UC PromISE) in 2019 with the intention of conducting cutting-edge, policy-relevant research that would allow us to identify and uplift best practices to promote immigrant and student equity.

This book draws on mixed-methods data collected through UC PromISE. First, we surveyed over 2,500 undergraduate students attending college on a UC campus who reported having immigrant parents. With the survey we aimed to assess the extent to which family legal vulnerability produces inequalities in the outcomes of undocumented students and US citizen students with undocumented parents when compared to US citizen students with lawfully present immigrant parents. We then conducted in-depth, follow-up interviews with sixty-three students experiencing family legal vulnerability: thirty-one undocumented students, and thirty-two US citizen students with undocumented parents. These interviews enabled us to trace the process through which family legal vulnerability produces inequalities among these student populations. Collectively, the survey and interview data enable us to detail inequities and the process through which they are produced, paving the way for us to identify points of intervention to advance equity, inclusion, and justice for immigration-impacted students.

The UC PromISE Survey

We administered our survey online from March to June 2020, with a total of 2,742 children of immigrants attending the University of California as undergraduate students. Soliciting detailed information from these implicitly vulnerable student populations was made possible through our connections to and trustworthy reputations among faculty, staff, and students across the UC campuses. We presented our project plans and solicited feedback from staff members at UC's Office of the President as well as at a meeting of UC undocumented student services professionals from across all campuses. Many of these staff members subsequently joined a community advisory board and provided feedback on the survey measures, recruitment strategies, and preliminary findings.

Participants were recruited at all nine UC undergraduate campuses.[91] Recruitment announcements were distributed widely, including emails and social media posts from each campus's undocumented student support services office, faculty teaching large general education courses and ethnic studies courses, departmental and university office newsletters, and undocumented student organizations. Our strong networks with staff and faculty helped ensure that students received recruitment information via trusted sources; we believe that this increased students' confidence in participating in the study. It seems likely that students also responded to our intentions to prioritize using the data to inform and foster institutional change.

Survey eligibility criteria included being over age eighteen, having at least one immigrant parent, and current enrollment. The survey took 25–35 minutes to complete and included questions about academic experiences, mental health, political engagement, the immigration policy context, the university context and resource use, and self and family demographics. Respondents received a $10 electronic gift card as compensation for their time. Appendix A includes a detailed description of the data collection process.

For the purposes of this book, we focus on Latina/o/x–identified students and restrict our sample to 548 undocumented immigrant students, 615 US citizen students with at least one undocumented parent, and 633 US citizen students with lawfully present parents, at least one of whom is an immigrant (n=1,796). We define undocumented status as having no permanent legal status, including those with DACA or another liminal legal status. Those with lawful presence include lawful permanent residents (LPRs) and US citizens, both naturalized and through birth. Undocumented students in our sample are 1.5-generation immigrants. The majority migrated as children under the age of five, and only 6.3 percent migrated at age eleven or older. Almost all had undocumented parents, with 95 percent reporting having a mother with no lawful status and 91.5 percent a father with no lawful status; approximately half had at least one undocumented sibling, and two-thirds had at least one undocumented extended family member. Of the US citizens with at least one undocumented parent, 81.4 percent reported having a mother with no lawful status, 84.6 percent a father with no lawful status. Three-quarters had at least one undocumented extended family member, and 17.6 percent had an undocumented sibling. US citizens with lawfully present parents were more likely to report having a US citizen parent, with 58.5 percent reporting a US citizen mother and 65.4 percent a US citizen father. Half had at least one undocumented extended family member, and 2.2 percent had an undocumented sibling.

Table I.1 provides a demographic breakdown of our study sample. Slightly more than three-quarters of participants were women. The vast majority were traditionally college-aged, with 75 percent being between ages 18 and 21. They come from all years in college, with 22.2 percent being first years, 18.2 percent second years, 28.7 percent third years, and 30.9 percent fourth years or higher. Slightly less than one in five

Table I.1. Demographic statistics of survey participants

	Undocumented Students (n=548)	U.S. Citizen Students with Undocumented Parents (n=615)	U.S. Citizen Students with Lawfully Present Parents (n=633)	Total (n=1,796)
	n (%)	n (%)	n (%)	n
Student's Immigration Status				
No lawful status	146 (26.6)	-	-	146 (8.1)
DACA	394 (71.9)	-	-	394 (21.9)
Temporary protected status (TPS)	1 (0.2)	-	-	1 (0.1)
Other: Pending asylum	1 (0.2)	-	-	1 (0.1)
Other: U-Visa	6 (1.1)	-	-	6 (0.3)
US citizen	-	615 (100)	633 (100)	1248 (69.5)
Gender				
Men	119 (21.7)	110 (17.9)	135 (21.4)	364 (20.3)
Women	417 (76.1)	497 (80.9)	481 (76.2)	1395 (77.8)
Alternative gender identification	12 (2.2)	7 (1.1)	15 (2.4)	34 (1.9)
Missing	0	1	2	3
Age				
18	59 (10.8)	93 (15.1)	94 (14.9)	246 (13.7)
19	76 (13.9)	142 (23.1)	105 (16.6)	323 (18.0)
20	128 (23.4)	141 (22.9)	136 (21.5)	405 (22.6)
21	118 (21.5)	124 (20.2)	144 (22.8)	386 (21.5)
22	92 (16.8)	81 (13.2)	84 (13.3)	257 (14.3)
23	24 (4.4)	16 (2.6)	28 (4.4)	68 (3.8)
24	10 (1.8)	7 (1.1)	11 (1.7)	28 (1.6)
25 and older	41 (7.5)	11 (1.8)	31 (4.9)	83 (4.6)
Missing				
Age of First Arrival				
0–5	381 (71.0)	-	-	-
6–10	122 (22.7)	-	-	-
11+	34 (6.3)	-	-	-
Missing	11	-	-	-
First-Generation College Student				
No	28 (5.2)	15 (2.5)	84 (13.3)	127 (7.1)
Yes	515 (94.8)	592 (97.5)	546 (86.7)	1653 (92.9)
Missing	5	8	3	16

(Continued)

Table I.1. Demographic statistics of survey participants (*Continued*)

	Undocumented Students (n=548)	U.S. Citizen Students with Undocumented Parents (n=615)	U.S. Citizen Students with Lawfully Present Parents (n=633)	Total (n=1,796)
	n (%)	n (%)	n (%)	n
Year in College				
1st	100 (18.3)	161 (26.2)	138 (21.8)	399 (22.2)
2nd	90 (16.4)	124 (20.2)	113 (17.9)	327 (18.2)
3rd	172 (31.4)	165 (26.9)	177 (28.0)	514 (28.7)
4th and higher	186 (33.9)	164 (26.7)	204 (32.3)	554 (30.9)
Missing	0	1	1	2
Transfer Student				
No	422 (77.3)	549 (89.3)	500 (79.1)	1471 (82.0)
Yes	124 (22.7)	66 (10.7)	132 (20.9)	322 (18.0)
Missing	2	0	1	3
Major				
Arts and humanities	86 (15.7)	81 (13.2)	85 (13.5)	252 (14.1)
Social science	220 (40.2)	279 (45.4)	299 (47.4)	798 (44.5)
STEM	161 (29.4)	159 (25.9)	165 (26.2)	485 (27.1)
Other and undeclared	81 (14.8)	95 (15.5)	82 (13.0)	258 (14.4)
Missing	0	1	2	3
Campus				
UC Berkeley	38 (6.9)	30 (4.9)	42 (6.6)	110 (6.1)
UC Davis	56 (10.2)	61 (9.9)	54 (8.5)	171 (9.5)
UC Irvine	115 (21.0)	114 (18.5)	69 (10.9)	298 (16.6)
UC Los Angeles	71 (13.0)	75 (12.2)	78 (12.3)	224 (12.5)
UC Merced	47 (8.6)	77 (12.5)	67 (10.6)	191 (10.6)
UC Riverside	96 (17.5)	113 (18.4)	131 (20.7)	340 (18.9)
UC Santa Barbara	54 (9.9)	62 (10.1)	53 (8.4)	169 (9.4)
UC Santa Cruz	50 (9.1)	59 (9.6)	99 (15.6)	208 (11.6)
UC San Diego	21 (3.8)	24 (3.9)	40 (6.3)	85 (4.7)
Mother's Immigration Status				
No lawful status	511 (95.5)	496 (81.4)	-	1007 (57.0)
DACA	1 (0.2)	2 (0.3)	-	3 (0.2)
TPS	4 (0.8)	15 (2.5)	-	19 (1.1)
Lawful permanent resident (LPR)	2 (0.4)	52 (8.5)	254 (40.8)	308 (17.4)
US citizen	0 (0.0)	35 (5.8)	364 (58.5)	399 (22.6)
Other	12 (2.2)	4 (0.7)	0 (0.0)	16 (0.9)
Does not live in the US	2 (0.4)	3 (0.5)	0 (0.0)	5 (0.3)

Deceased	3 (0.6)	2 (0.3)	4 (0.6)	9 (0.5)
Missing	13	6	11	30
Father's Immigration Status				
No lawful status	385 (91.5)	445 (84.6)	-	830 (55.9)
DACA	0 (0.0)	1 (0.2)	-	1 (0.1)
TPS	10 (2.4)	13 (2.5)	-	23 (1.6)
LPR	8 (1.9)	34 (6.5)	172 (32.0)	214 (14.4)
US citizen	4 (1.0)	22 (4.2)	351 (65.4)	377 (25.4)
Other	8 (1.9)	6 (1.1)	4 (0.7)	18 (1.2)
Does not live in the US	5 (1.2)	2 (0.4)	1 (0.2)	8 (0.5)
Deceased	1 (0.2)	3 (0.6)	9 (1.7)	13 (0.9)
Missing	127	89	96	312
Mother's Highest Level of Education				
6th grade or lower	191 (36.2)	255 (42.4)	174 (28.2)	620 (35.5)
Some middle or high school	149 (28.2)	193 (32.1)	143 (23.1)	485 (27.8)
High school diploma or equivalent	109 (20.6)	109 (18.1)	139 (22.5)	357 (20.4)
Some college	60 (11.4)	32 (5.3)	100 (16.2)	192 (11.0)
BA or higher	19 (3.6)	13 (2.2)	62 (10.0)	94 (5.4)
Missing	20	13	15	48
Father's Highest Level of Education				
6th grade or lower	159 (37.8)	222 (43.3)	163 (30.6)	544 (37.1)
Some middle or high school	124 (29.5)	177 (34.5)	132 (24.8)	433 (29.5)
High school diploma or equivalent	79 (18.8)	82 (16.0)	103 (19.3)	264 (18.0)
Some college	45 (10.7)	28 (5.5)	91 (17.1)	164 (11.2)
BA or higher	14 (3.3)	4 (0.8)	44 (8.3)	62 (4.2)
Missing	127	102	100	329
Mother's Employment				
Working for wages or salary	195 (36.8)	213 (34.9)	306 (49.4)	714 (40.6)
Self-Employed	96 (18.1)	109 (17.8)	71 (11.5)	276 (15.7)
Temporary/seasonal worker	33 (6.2)	41 (6.7)	37 (6.0)	111 (6.3)
Unemployed, looking for work	20 (3.8)	43 (7.0)	30 (4.8)	93 (5.3)
Not working	183 (34.5)	203 (33.2)	172 (27.7)	558 (31.7)
Deceased	3 (0.6)	2 (0.3)	4 (0.7)	9 (0.5)
Missing	18	4	13	35
Father's Employment				
Working for wages or salary	274 (65.6)	330 (63.7)	348 (65.1)	952 (64.7)
Self-Employed	95 (22.7)	120 (23.2)	84 (15.7)	299 (20.3)
Temporary/seasonal worker	28 (6.7)	42 (8.1)	29 (5.4)	99 (6.7)
Unemployed, looking for work	7 (1.7)	12 (2.3)	18 (3.4)	37 (2.5)

(Continued)

Table I.1. Demographic statistics of survey participants (*Continued*)

	Undocumented Students (n=548)	U.S. Citizen Students with Undocumented Parents (n=615)	U.S. Citizen Students with Lawfully Present Parents (n=633)	Total (n=1,796)
	n (%)	n (%)	n (%)	n
Not working	13 (3.1)	11 (2.1)	47 (8.8)	71 (4.8)
Deceased	1 (0.2)	3 (0.6)	9 (1.7)	13 (0.9)
Missing	130	97	98	325
Household Income				
$0–20,000	133 (25.3)	149 (25.0)	77 (12.8)	359 (20.9)
$20,001–$30,000	132 (25.1)	134 (22.5)	97 (16.2)	363 (21.1)
$30,001–$40,000	92 (17.5)	100 (16.8)	74 (12.3)	266 (15.5)
$40,001–$50,000	61 (11.6)	77 (12.9)	81 (13.5)	219 (12.7)
$50,001–$75,000	77 (14.7)	94 (15.8)	145 (24.2)	316 (18.4)
$75,001–$100,000	20 (3.8)	29 (4.9)	68 (11.3)	117 (6.8)
$100,001+	10 (1.9)	13 (2.2)	58 (9.7)	81 (4.7)
Missing	23	19	33	75
Has at Least One Undocumented Sibling				
No	247 (46.6)	487 (82.4)	588 (97.8)	1322 (76.8)
Yes	283 (53.4)	104 (17.6)	13 (2.2)	400 (23.2)
Missing	18	24	32	74
Has at Least One Undocumented Extended Family Member				
No	151 (30.3)	135 (24.3)	269 (46.1)	555 (33.9)
Yes	347 (69.7)	421 (75.7)	314 (53.9)	1082 (66.1)
Missing	50	59	50	159

transferred from a community college. Majors ranged from 44.5 percent in the social sciences, 27.1 percent in STEM (science, technology, engineering, and mathematics), 14.1 percent in arts and humanities, and 14.4 percent with other majors or who were undeclared. Respondents attended all nine UC campuses, with the most attending UC Riverside (18.9 percent) and UC Irvine (16.6 percent) and the least attending UC San Diego (4.7 percent) and UC Berkeley (6.1 percent). Among all three groups of students, the largest proportion of students reported that both parents had a sixth-grade education or lower; nearly two-thirds reported that their father worked. Among undocumented students and US citizens with undocumented parents, about a third reported that their mother worked; having a mother that worked was more common among US citizens with lawfully present parents. Undocumented students and US citizens with undocumented parents were more likely to come from low-income households, with a quarter reporting an annual household income under $20,000 and nearly two-thirds reporting a household income under $40,000; of US citizens with lawfully present parents, 12.8 percent reported a household income under $20,000 and 41.3 percent under $40,000.

We draw on our quantitative survey data to examine whether family legal vulnerability explains differences in these three student groups' mental health, academic, and political engagement outcomes or campus resource use. Specifically, we conducted a series of regressions to determine if family legal vulnerability contributed to disparities in immigration-impacted students' outcomes relative to their US citizen peers with lawfully present parents. We concentrated on three measures of family legal vulnerability: threat to family because of restrictive immigration policy; whether a family member experienced deportation; and family financial strain. Undocumented students and US citizens with undocumented parents reported similar levels of perceived threat to family and family financial strain. Their average scores indicate that they often worried about the threat immigration policies posed to their families and expected that their family would face financial strains more than once in a while in the next three months. Thirty percent of undocumented students and 43 percent of US citizens with undocumented parents reported having a family member who experienced deportation, with about twice as many reporting an extended family members' deportation as opposed to an immediate family member's deportation. US citizens with lawfully present parents reported lower levels of family legal vulnerability. Their average scores indicate that they worried about the threat immigration policies posed to their families at a frequency between rarely and sometimes, and they expected that their family would face financial strains less than once in a while in the next three months. However, the number who had a family member who had been deported was actually higher than that of undocumented students: 32 percent reported having a family member who experienced deportation; this generally referred to an extended family member. See Appendix B for a detailed description of all survey measures used in the book and descriptive statistics.

It is difficult to determine the degree to which our sample is representative of the immigration-impacted student population. We lack demographic information for UC's undocumented student population, and no data exists regarding the number and demographics of US citizen students with undocumented parents. It is possible that students who were more fearful of the consequences of disclosing their own and/or family members' immigration status were less likely to participate in the study, leading to the exclusion of the most vulnerable. Because recruitment was conducted through university channels, it is also possible that students who were less connected to university life were less likely to participate. Thus, our results likely underestimate the overall presence of perceived immigration threat as well as its effect on student outcomes.

UC PromISE Follow-Up Interviews

We recruited interviewees from a pool of eligible survey participants who consented to be contacted about future research opportunities; our eligibility criteria consisted of having identified as Latina/o/x in the survey and having been enrolled as a junior or higher at a University of California campus during the 2020–2021 academic year. Five trained research assistants and one faculty member conducted interviews from July to September 2021. All interviews were conducted over Zoom and lasted an average of 1.5 hours. Topics included experiences of individual and family legal vulnerability; academic, mental health, and political engagement outcomes; and experiences of campus resources and campus climate. Interviewees received a $40 electronic gift card as compensation for their time. Appendix A includes a detailed description of the data collection process.

Our interview participants are demographically similar to the larger survey sample. Among the thirty-one undocumented students, two-thirds were DACA recipients, and the remainder had no lawful status. All but one reported that they have at least one undocumented parent. Among the thirty-two US citizens, all had at least one undocumented parent, and only a handful had one lawfully present parent. Table I.2 provides additional demographic information for our interview sample.

Interviews were transcribed and uploaded to HyperResearch, a qualitative data management program. Each case was index-coded with

Table I.2. Demographic statistics of interview participants

	Undocumented Students (n=31)	U.S. Citizen Students with Undocumented Parents (n=32)	Total (n=63)
	n (%)	n (%)	n (%)
Student's Immigration Status			
No lawful status	10 (32.3)	-	10 (15.9)
DACA	21 (67.7)	-	21 (33.3)
US citizen	-	32 (100.0)	32 (50.8)
Gender			
Men	11 (35.5)	8 (25.0)	19 (30.2)
Women	20 (64.5)	23 (71.9)	43 (68.3)
Alternative gender identification	0	1 (3.1)	1 (1.6)
Age			
20	2 (6.5)	6 (18.8)	8 (12.7)
21	13 (41.9)	12 (37.5)	25 (39.7)
22	7 (22.6)	8 (25.0)	15 (23.8)
23	2 (6.5)	4 (12.5)	6 (9.5)
24	3 (9.7)	1 (3.1)	4 (6.3)
25 and older	4 (12.9)	1 (3.1)	5 (7.9)
First-Generation College Student			
Yes	25 (83.3)	26 (83.9)	51 (83.6)
No	5 (16.7)	5 (16.1)	10 (16.4)
Missing	1	1	2
Year in College			
3rd year	11 (35.5)	17 (53.1)	28 (44.4)
4th year and higher	20 (64.5)	15 (46.9)	35 (55.6)
Transfer Student			
Yes	9 (29.0)	4 (12.5)	13 (20.6)
No	22 (71.0)	28 (87.5)	50 (79.4)
Major			
Arts and humanities	4 (12.9)	3 (9.4)	7 (11.1)
Social science	10 (32.3)	21 (65.6)	31 (49.2)
STEM	11 (35.5)	4 (12.5)	15 (23.8)
Other	6 (19.4)	4 (12.5)	10 (15.9)

(Continued)

Table I.2. Demographic statistics of interview participants (*Continued*)

	Undocumented Students (n=31)	U.S. Citizen Students with Undocumented Parents (n=32)	Total (n=63)
	n (%)	n (%)	n (%)
Campus			
UC Berkeley	1 (3.2)	1 (3.1)	2 (3.2)
UC Davis	3 (9.7)	3 (9.4)	6 (9.5)
UC Irvine	7 (22.6)	11 (34.4)	18 (28.6)
UC Los Angeles	3 (9.7)	5 (15.6)	8 (12.7)
UC Merced	0 (0.0)	1 (3.1)	1 (1.6)
UC Riverside	12 (38.7)	6 (18.8)	18 (28.6)
UC Santa Barbara	0 (0.0)	2 (6.3)	2 (3.2)
UC Santa Cruz	4 (12.9)	3 (9.4)	7 (11.1)
UC San Diego	1 (3.2)	0 (0.0)	1 (1.6)
Mother's Immigration Status			
No lawful status	29 (90.6)	23 (71.9)	52 (82.5)
DACA	0 (0.0)	1 (3.1)	1 (1.6)
TPS	0 (0.0)	2 (6.3)	2 (3.2)
LPR	1 (3.1)	5 (15.6)	6 (9.5)
US citizen	0 (0.0)	1 (3.1)	1 (1.6)
Does not live in the US	1 (3.1)	0 (0.0)	1 (1.6)
Father's Immigration Status			
No lawful status	27 (87.1)	25 (78.1)	52 (82.5)
TPS	0 (0.0)	2 (6.3)	2 (3.2)
LPR	0 (0.0)	1 (3.1)	1 (1.6)
US citizen	0 (0.0)	2 (6.3)	2 (3.2)
No father reported	4 (12.9)	2 (6.3)	6 (9.5)
Mother's Highest Level of Education			
Less than high school diploma	16 (51.6)	20 (62.5)	36 (57.1)
High school diploma or equivalent	4 (12.9)	10 (31.3)	14 (22.2)
Some college	3 (9.7)	1 (3.1)	4(6.3)
N/A	4 (12.9)	0 (0.0)	4 (6.3)
Unknown	4 (12.9)	1 (3.1)	5 (7.9)
Father's Highest Level of Education			
Less than high school diploma	21 (67.7)	15 (46.9)	36 (57.1)
High school diploma or equivalent	6 (19.4)	6 (18.8)	12 (19.0)
Some college	2 (6.5)	4 (12.5)	6 (9.5)
N/A	0 (0.0)	3 (9.4)	3(4.8)
Unknown	2 (6.5)	4 (12.5)	6 (9.5)

demographic attributes and 10 index codes related to broad areas covered by the interview guide.[92] Analytic coding for each chapter focused on reviewing the interview content included under relevant index codes to develop a codebook that would capture the process through which family legal vulnerability was produced and/or impacted student outcomes. We then conducted comparisons across self/parental immigration status, revealing most often similarities between undocumented students and US citizens with undocumented parents; differences are noted where relevant. Because almost all interviewees had undocumented parents with no lawful status, in the text we report only parental immigration status when they occupy liminal or lawfully present immigration statuses.

Organization of the Book

This book is split into three parts that illuminate how family legal vulnerability is produced, impacts student outcomes, and can be alleviated by campus resources. Part I establishes and conceptualizes the power of family legal vulnerability. This introduction has defined the concept and positioned it in relation to recent scholarship of immigration illegality and mixed-status families. Next, chapter 1 draws on interview data to trace the process that produces family legal vulnerability. Specifically, we examine how family legal vulnerability is produced and experienced in the everyday lives of immigration-impacted students. We trace how immigration laws and policies enter the family sphere through undocumented family members, including students' parents. We show how these individual strains manifest as collective constraints as family members share in the material barriers and emotional turmoil brought out by deportation threats, lack of access to lawful employment and fair wages, and anti-immigrant sentiment. Further, the family context sets the stage for cascading consequences as family legal vulnerability prompts individual students to respond, yielding new individual strains as they attempt to manage collective constraints.

Part II continues to trace the cascading consequences of family legal vulnerability to show how they impact a range of student outcomes and create inequalities among the children of immigrants. Chapter 2 focuses on students' mental health and well-being. We illustrate how immigration-impacted students experience family legal vulnerability as a chronic or long-term stressor. Undocumented students and US citizens with undocumented parents experience their parents' deportability and family economic insecurity long-term, often starting in childhood. These stressors are woven into the fabric of their day-to-day lives as they worry and feel sad and anxious due to the threat to their families. We highlight students' resilience as they actively care for their well-being by leaning on their social networks and employing multiple coping strategies. Chapter 3 examines academic performance and engagement. We show how family legal vulnerability is never far from students' minds, permeating their educational experiences with consequent effects on their educational incorporation. We demonstrate how students' rumination on parental safety, and their attempts to manage family economic insecurity, can disrupt attention to academics, adversely affecting educational success. We underscore students' agency as they seek to address family legal vulnerability through educational success and commitment to pursuing professional development opportunities. Chapter 4 explores political and civic engagement. We establish that students develop political consciousness based on experiences with immigration policy in their own lives. They often hone their political skills in college alongside other students. Concerns about deportation threats for themselves or their family members often constrain their participation in public-facing forms of political engagement, but they find other ways to influence policy, including campaigning for candidates, sharing political information, and, for US citizens, voting. These actions help immigration-impacted students develop and assert a political voice and advocate for their families and communities. Survey analysis at the end of each chapter reveals that both undocumented students and US citizens with undocumented parents often have disparate mental health, educational, and political engagement outcomes when compared to US citizen students with lawfully present parents. Frequently our measures of family legal vulnerability explain these differences.

Part III turns attention to the university campus to examine how educational institutions can help alleviate the effects of family legal vulnerability in students' lives. In chapter 5 we show that the resources provided by the University of California system help students ease some of the collective strains associated with family legal vulnerability, particularly financial strain but to some extent deportability and threats of family separation as well. Additional support services disrupt the cascading consequences for students' academic, mental health, and political engagement outcomes. Often the most innovative resources that directly addressed legal vulnerability were created and offered by undocumented and immigration-impacted student services. In line with our commitment to informing policy and practice, we offer explicit recommendations for how campuses can strengthen the institutional support available to lessen the initial and cascading effects of family legal vulnerability on student success in order to work toward greater equity.

1

"We Are All in This Together"

Collective Constraints and Cascading Consequences

"We're all so united, and everything that happens to them affects me."
—Diana Mora

Diana is the eldest daughter of two undocumented immigrants. Reflecting on how immigration policy affects her as a natural-born US citizen, Diana quickly pointed to her family's linked lives. In her early twenties and about to graduate from college, she was focused on trying to get her career started quickly so she could "help balance out everything" by paying some of the bills. Her father was the primary breadwinner in their family and had spent most of his life working in restaurants, "just stuck in a cycle and can't get out of it" because his immigration status limited the jobs he could apply to. Growing up, this meant that Diana and her family lived in rented rooms, never even a whole apartment of their own, and at one point had to live in a shed in her aunt's backyard. The food stamps she and her two younger siblings received provided some food security, and their living situation improved as she and her sister got older and were able to work to supplement the family income. Her family's collective experience of financial precarity meant that she worried about controlling her spending and "really putting thought into it" before she bought anything. She asked her mom permission to buy things with her own money because "I feel like my money isn't really my money. I feel like it's all of our money."

In addition to their financial struggles, Diana worried about her parents' deportation risk. She explained that their deportation had "been one of my greatest fears since I was a child. I've always had that in the back of my mind." The first Trump administration's anti-immigrant rhetoric and exclusionary immigration policymaking amplified her fears. Diana remembered how the 2016 election infused alarm into her family and community, how a friend whose parents are also undocumented said "they could literally take [our] parents away from [us]." She knew that if her parents were deported she would be heading the family and caring for her middle school–age brother.

Hemmed in by such fears, Diana struggled to make sense of the reality that she could do things her parents could not: "Honestly it kills me because I feel sometimes like my parents are in this bird cage and they're just stuck there. And it sucks because I can do other things they can't. I can travel, but there's always that guilt that they can't do the same things and it's just a lot. It makes me really sad when I think about it that way." Traveling for the first time to visit her parent's hometown was exciting, but doing so also filled her with guilt and sadness. Meeting family members in Mexico for the first time in her late teens, Diana was a living link for her parents, showing them their pueblo via video chat, as if "giving them a little piece through me." Diana took on increasing emotional and financial responsibilities, using her citizenship status to try to make her family more stable because "we are all in this together at the end of the day and we do want to help each other."

Diana's story exposes the production of family legal vulnerability. In some instances, such as with family financial insecurity, Diana experiences her parents' legal vulnerability as a *collective constraint* when the strains associated with one family members' undocumented immigration status affects all family members as they are subjected to shared material and emotional consequences. In other instances, *cascading consequences* emerge as one family member's legal vulnerability prompts another to respond, thereby yielding new strains. For Diana, this emerged as family responsibilities and guilt as she tried to manage the legal uncertainty that her parents faced while negotiating her privileged position as a US citizen. Through these processes, immigration laws and policy play out in the family sphere.

Drawing on interviews with immigration-impacted students, this chapter examines how the individual legal vulnerability of any one family member is translated into experiences of family legal vulnerability. Family members share in the material barriers and emotional turmoil brought about by deportation threats, lack of access to lawful employment and fair wages, and anti-immigrant sentiment. The ever-shifting and unpredictable immigration policy context exacerbates these strains and compromises students' ability to envision their own and their families' collective future. Family legal vulnerability also encroaches on individual family members' everyday lives as they attempt to manage collective strains, producing cascading consequences as immigration-impacted students attempt to preserve their family's well-being. Collectively, family-level manifestations of exclusionary immigration policies create family legal vulnerability, thereby perpetuating educational, economic, and social harm.

Collective Constraints Shared Within Families

When talking about their own or family members' immigration status, undocumented students and US citizen students with undocumented parents used collectivizing language, linking their own lives to their family members. Alonzo Ramirez, an undocumented student without lawful immigration status, shared his vision for the future:

> I guess it's wishful thinking, but anything that would get me excited about the future is my family being financially stable and having figured out this whole immigration status thing and not having to worry about deportation or anything like that. . . . I hope that one day that all gets sorted out and we're just able to be here without having to worry about all these things.

Alonzo highlighted his family's experience of deportation threats, financial strain, and general uncertainty and worry, not his own immigration status or personal constraints. Like Alonzo, we focus on the family unit to examine how individual legal vulnerability is translated into a lived experience of family legal vulnerability.

We define *collective constraints* as the material and emotional consequences shared among all family members due to the individual legal vulnerability associated with one or more family member's undocumented immigration status. This builds on prior research that has documented the multigenerational punishment of young US citizen children of undocumented immigrants whose dependent status forces them to witness and share in the punishments produced by immigration policies.[1] Here, we assert that this shared suffering exists for both undocumented and US citizen children of undocumented parents and persists as they grow into young adulthood. Three collective constraints emerged in interviews: *the threat of family separation, economic insecurity,* and *social exclusion.*

Deportability and Concerns About Family Separation

Sociologist Joanna Dreby has conceptualized the burden of deportation and immigration enforcement policies on children as a deportation pyramid; a few people (those existing at the top of the pyramid) directly experience the most severe impacts, such as themselves being deported or suffering nuclear family separation; other consequences are felt much more broadly, including fearing family separation or conflating being an immigrant with having undocumented status.[2] Indeed, scholars use the concept of *deportability* to characterize the threat of potential deportation and to capture its effects in everyday life.[3] Immigration-impacted students wrestling with this dimension of family legal vulnerability may become concerned with a range of specific outcomes, including deportation, detention, or family separation.

When asked about how deportability tended to occupy their thoughts, both undocumented and US citizen participants focused most on family separation:

> AIDEN CHACÓN (DACA recipient): I think it's just the thought of separation for me, but there's no huge triggers. It's just the thought of just losing the only person that I've been with my whole life.
> ALONZO RAMIREZ (No lawful immigration status): Mostly family separation. We're all very close to each other and if any one of us got deported or was detained, it would be pretty difficult.

While undocumented participants acknowledged their own risk, they focused most on their parents' risk of deportation when discussing their fears. Amanda Tobar, a US citizen with immigrant parents, emphasized that even as an adult her parents' deportability frightened her:

Family separation, that's the worst thing. I think someone from the out-side would think that, "Oh, it wouldn't be as bad if your family was de-ported" because my siblings and I are in our twenties, [and my youngest] brother's about to graduate [high school] in a year. So you would think we're pretty well off, but we're not. We are not ready. I'm not ready to be separated from my parents. I'm still living with them. I still need their constant support financially. I don't have a stable job myself. And then, once I graduate [college], I might not be able to find one. So it's not just money concerns about family separation, also that support that we need, just having them near.

Fueled by a nuanced understanding of deportation threats, immigration-impacted students primarily understood the everyday individual risk of deportability as a collective constraint of threatened family separation.

Our survey data also revealed a near universal fear of parents' deport-ability among students with undocumented parents. Undocumented students and US citizens with undocumented parents reported thinking about their parent's or guardian's deportation with similar frequency. Figure 1.1 displays these frequencies, showing that nearly all participants thought about their parent(s)/guardian(s)' deportation, and over half did so once per week or more.

Monitoring the deportation threats around them, immigration-impacted students learned early on that such risks materialize through interactions with police officers and immigration enforcement officials. Awareness of this threat was often informed by early childhood mes-sages and deportation experiences within their extended families:

BIANCA MERCADO (DACA recipient): I grew up hearing about
    uncles who were going to or from work, who would be stopped and
    deported just like that. And after you hear that sort of similar story
    for so long, it kind of gets ingrained in your head, like, "Okay, if I
    drive, then I'm going to get deported."
EDWIN GORDILLO (No lawful immigration status): In our household,
    we grew up associating the cops with immigration. And then when
    I was 15, one of my uncles got pulled over for a DUI and then
    he got put into jail. After jail, he got deported. So then that secured
    the way I grew up thinking that any type of association with

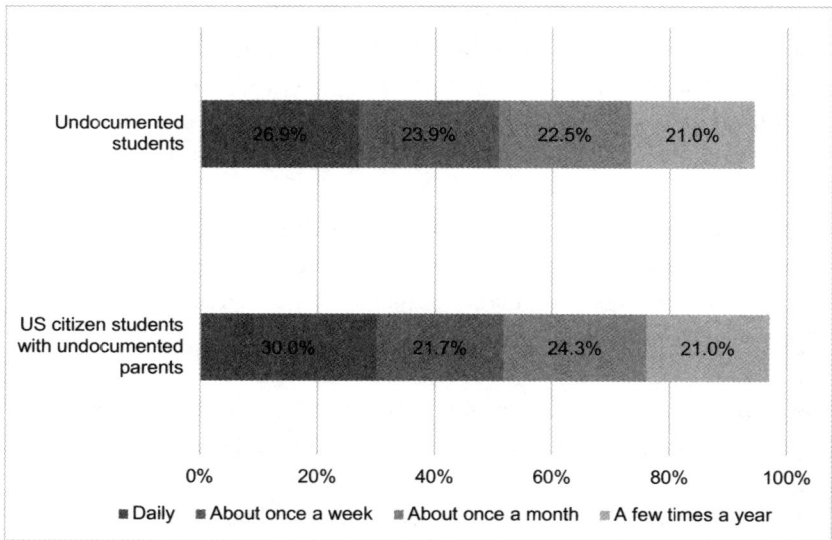

Figure 1.1. Frequency survey participants thought about parent(s)/guardian(s) deportation.

the cops would equal immediate deportation. So when I was younger, I would see a cop, and then especially because I didn't have any license or DACA or any of that, I would be scared to even encounter a cop or even ask them for help.

RUBEN HUERTA-DIAZ (US citizen with undocumented parents): That sense of fear that my parents had when we were younger. . . . It was kind of like, no sense in going out if you don't have to. Being extra careful around police officers, around authority, just being aware of your surroundings and being extra careful about your actions. You don't want to be in any legal trouble to provoke anything.

Often, these early messages translated into a blanket fear of police and immigration enforcement.

As participants became attuned to immigration enforcement practices, they began to link the risk of encountering deportation threats to specific spaces where their parents spend time. Julia Soto, a US citizen with undocumented parents, shared that she thinks about deportation "all the time. All the time, my mom is working in the fields. I just think it's so easy for ICE to be wandering around and just stop at the fields and just get everybody." Similarly, Sabrina Soriano Trejo, a DACA recipient, said: "It's not that [my parents are] less careful [than me]. It's just, my mom doesn't know how to drive. So she's always walking around everywhere, taking the bus. So that's my biggest worry that she's going to get stuck somewhere where something's happening and she can't get out." In most cases, participants perceived their parents to be frequently negotiating spaces—workplaces, physical locations, public spaces—that put them at risk of interacting with immigration enforcement officials, whether directly or indirectly through police. This contrasts sharply with the experiences of undocumented young adults, both with and without DACA protections, who are more likely to feel insulated from deportation threats in the protective spatial and social locations they occupy.[4]

Participants' perceptions of parental deportation risk directly translated into worries and anxiety at times when they knew their parents were in spaces they perceived as risky. Ava Cornejo, a US citizen with undocumented parents, explained that she worried a lot for her father, who was undocumented and drove a truck for work. Aware of increased border patrol presence in San Diego near the United States–Mexico border, her dad "was terrified to go drive out there. He would have to do it because at that point he didn't have another job waiting," she said. When Donald Trump first assumed office in 2017, his administration threatened to increase internal immigration enforcement activities.[5] These highly visible threats fueled deeper fears among Ava and her family members: "We couldn't go to sleep. He never had an *horario* [schedule] when he would come back. So sometimes he came back like at two in the morning, three in the morning. And he couldn't really use his phone, because he doesn't like using it at all when he's driving. So you're just kind of worried. There's so many things that could have gone wrong. So we were definitely worried about him." These fears extended to others when reports of local immigration enforcement efforts would circulate among their social networks: "A lot of the times, it was where my aunts and uncles, [or] my mom, would work."

Participants' perceptions of deportability translated into perceived threats to family due to restrictive immigration policy. We asked survey participants three questions to assess the frequency of these feelings:

"Do you fear that a family member will be reported to immigration offi-cials?", "Do you worry about family separation due to deportation?", and "Do you worry about the impact immigration policies have on you or your family?" They could respond never, rarely, sometimes, often, or al-ways, resulting in a score that ranged from three—indicating a response of "never" to all the questions—to fifteen if they responded "always" to each. Undocumented students had a mean of 12.47 on the scale, and US citizens with undocumented parents a mean of 12.34, indicating that, on average, both groups responded "often" to all items. In contrast, US citi-zen students with lawfully present parents had a mean of 7.87, indicating that, on average, they responded "rarely" to two items and "sometimes" to a third. These results affirm that immigration-impacted students de-velop similar perceptions of immigration-related threat to their family's stability.

In line with Dreby's description of the deportation pyramid, most participants had not been separated from a close family member through deportation. Eleven percent of our survey participants and a handful of our interview participants reported that one of their im-mediate family members had been deported. Among interviewees, the separation following a deportation was brief, as the deported parent clandestinely reentered the United States after a short time. The excep-tion was Carolina Aguilar, a US citizen. At the time of the interview, she had been separated from her undocumented mother for six years. This was devastating for Carolina and her two younger half-brothers; they all were split up and sent to live separately with their respective fathers. Carolina's father lived on the West Coast, which took her away from extended family as well as her siblings, all of whom remained in the Midwest. She felt the pain of the physical distance from her mother, made worse because her mother did not have reliable wi-fi where she lived following her deportation. A plethora of research has established that deportation and family separations like Carolina's shatter family members' lives.[6] In particular, young adults report that parental depor-tation disrupts their educational journey, as they have difficulty concen-trating on their academics and often take on competing responsibilities such as supplementing the family's income and caring for younger siblings.[7] Thus, the low rates of parental deportation and family sepa-ration we identify among our participants likely reflect our sampling strategy: People who have suffered the kind of devastation that Carolina experienced are rare in college, especially at academically competitive four-year institutions like UC system schools.

Employment Authorization and Economic Insecurity

Edwin Gordillo, an undocumented student without lawful immigration status, reflected on the ways in which immigration laws affect him and his family: "It highly impacts [us] . . . because if there was a law where it allowed us to be able to get some sort of benefits from the jobs we do and from the work we do, we could then maybe have a little bit more cushion and we wouldn't have to work twice as hard." Participants felt it was clear that their family's economic insecurity related to members' undocumented status rather than other factors. They recognized the structural nature of this constraint; as Edwin aptly pointed out "you need a work authorization, or any of that, to be able to get a legit job." Restricting undocumented immigrants' access to work authorization effectively constrains access to formal employment and fair wages, leading to increased collective economic insecurity within undocumented and mixed-status families.

Participants were familiar with the details of their parents' experiences being limited to low-wage and precarious employment:

> ROCIO CARRILLO GUERRA (DACA recipient): Not being able to . . . have a job or have a well-paying job because we don't have a social security [number]. I think that has always been an issue because I've known for the longest time like my dad has always had to work, either get paid cash or like get a fake social or something. So that's always been I guess more of a burden on the financial and stability in my life and our lives.

> BENJAMIN PONCE (US citizen with an undocumented parent): Because of my dad's [undocumented] immigrant status, he doesn't have a social security [number]. . . . He is limited in what roles he can work in because of that situation and that oftentimes limits him to lower paying, low wage, very labor-intensive positions. . . . It's not that he's not prepared for higher roles or high paying wages. It's just that he is limited in what jobs

he can actually apply for without fear of consequences because of his immigration status.

Both Rocio and Benjamin highlighted how their undocumented fathers lacked a valid social security number, limiting their pay and constraining their family's financial stability. Other students mentioned limited occupational mobility, as a lack of work authorization prevented promotion to better paying managerial positions and prompted undocumented individuals to hold on to the same job for fear of being unable to secure another.

Deportability compounded undocumented parents' economic exclusion. Reflecting on their undocumented parents' precarity, participants recalled how deportation threats made them vulnerable to wage theft:

BELÉN MESA (DACA recipient): I think it's happened maybe twice this entire ten to fifteen years, that [my dad's] been working in construction where he goes and does a job, and he won't get paid for it because they know he's undocumented. . . . That's just really, really messed up. It's abusive, and he can't really do anything about it because having to report that is going to be difficult. He'd just rather not. There's also that fear of talking to the police for anything.

EDWIN GORDILLO (No lawful immigration status): When there's people who are uncooperative . . . it's best to disengage and just walk away in this scenario. . . . With my mom, the client starts harassing her, "Oh, I'm not going to pay you to do a bad job, whatever," then we just have to take the loss and move on. That's better than engaging.

VALENTINA SALAZAR (US citizen with undocumented parents): My dad fixes cars. Somebody didn't want to pay him. . . . [My dad] was all like, "You have to pay me or I'm going to have to get the police involved." But the person refused and threatened him. Then he mentioned, "Oh your status." Then [my dad], didn't end up saying anything about it.

Threatened with the intervention of police and fearing immigration authorities, those without work authorization have little recourse when they experience wage theft, especially in cash-based payment transactions. Limiting movement to prevent police encounters can also have employment impacts. Isaiah Avalos, a US citizen with undocumented parents, shared how "my dad can't work in certain places or go as far as he would like. Only because he worries that, maybe by going into a certain area, like let's say a construction job in Orange County [a historically conservative and white area of Southern California], maybe there might be immigration officers there where they can get him and that would be awful for him."

Given that families function as important economic units, undocumented parents' limited employment options and low incomes resulted in collective economic insecurity for their families. Cynthia Cardenas, a US citizen with undocumented parents, noted that immigration policies constrained her family financially and deprived her of "the right to grow up financially secure." Many participants' families struggled to make ends meet, especially during their childhood, as the family's primary economic providers were their undocumented parents. Alonzo Ramirez, an undocumented student without lawful immigration status, recalled that his family had to move frequently:

> Because rent was getting more and more expensive and it was hard to pay the bills, and so we moved quite a bit. We've been on food stamps for as long as I can remember, because that's always been hard to keep up with as well. There's been multiple times where we've been short on electricity bills and internet bills and stuff like that. That's something I've had to deal with for a while.[8]

Aimee Bañuelos, a US citizen with undocumented parents, recalled her family having similar worries:

> Those worries of not having enough to pay for the water bill, the light bill, even rent or things that probably aren't necessarily required or necessities, like for example having cable or having wi-fi internet at home. Having to take away some of those things just to be able to make ends meet.

Families' chronic financial instability was managed by lowering expenses, often compromising housing quality as rent consumed a large part of the household income. Amanda Tobar Vargas, a US citizen with undocumented parents, described her living situation: "We live in a crappy apartment. We've lived in apartments all our lives. . . . This is our third apartment, and it's terrible. We don't like living here. We're all cramped. The walls are super thin; we can hear everything from our other neighbors, so it's not the best experience." Others recalled derelict landlords who refused to repair broken fixtures. In light of their undocumented parents' persistent economic barriers, many undocumented and US citizen participants faced similar financial challenges during childhood and adolescence.

Our survey affirmed that immigration-impacted students continued to contend with family financial strain while enrolled in college. Specifically, participants rated the frequency of two items: "Thinking about your family's current economic situation, indicate how often you expect that your family will face the following circumstances in the next three months: (1) Your family will experience bad times such as poor housing or not having enough food and (2) Your family will have to do without the basic things that your family needs." Participants responded using a scale including almost never or never, once in a while, sometimes, a lot of the time, and almost always or always, resulting in a cumulative score ranging from 0 to 8 where higher scores indicate greater hardship. Undocumented students scored a mean of 2.51 and US citizens with undocumented parents a mean of 2.40, the equivalent of responding "sometimes" to one question and "a lot of the time" to the other. US citizens with lawfully present parents scored a mean of 1.58, indicating that immigration-impacted students have a higher risk of family economic insecurity compared to their more legally protected peers.

Precarious financial balancing acts allowed most families to meet their basic needs most of the time, but students shared stories of severe shared financial strain when this delicate balance failed. Bianca Mercado, a DACA recipient, remembered a time when her family reached a milestone of financial stability, which proved fleeting: "My dad was working at a warehouse, and he was making really, really good money. And [my parents] bought a house, they got a house, and it was a really nice house in a really nice part of town. I remember liking that place. I felt safe for once and it was nice. It was pretty." But then there was a sudden change:

From one day to another, my dad was out of a job, and he wasn't making any more money. He wasn't earning anything. And so my mom got a job, but her income wasn't enough to keep the house. And so they lost it. They lost the house and that made my dad really depressed to the point where he didn't want to get out of bed, he didn't want to do anything.

The experience of losing the house created a spiral in which Bianca's father was unable to work due to his failing mental health.

For Madeline Salinas's family, the sudden change was because of a physical injury:

When my dad broke his leg . . . my mom was working at Target and my dad was not working. We didn't have a lot of money. So I remember at the time we would go to food banks, and we would get tortillas, frijoles, a lot of canned stuff, not delicious things. So we would eat a lot of pan with frijoles and queso [bread with beans and cheese] on top, just as dinner.

Madeline, a US citizen, and her brother remembered the pan with frijoles and queso fondly: "Me and my older brother were like, 'When are you going to make that again?' And my mom was like. 'Pendejos we were poor! Why do you want all of that?'" The family's nutritional compromises had clearly been a strain for her mother. Edwin Gordillo, an undocumented student without lawful immigration status, described instead his awareness that his family was at risk:

Sometimes they can't take the breaks they need because if they do, they won't make enough money to pay off the bills. And so if they don't pay off the bills, then that's where we'll run into the problems where, oh, well, if you miss a month of rent, well then that's it, you no longer have a roof. If you no longer have a roof, then you no longer have a place where you can secure your food.

As Bianca's and Madeline's experiences and Edwin's concern reflect, individual economic setbacks experienced by one of their parents due to precarious and often labor-intensive employment resulted in collective insecurity, regardless of students' own immigration status.

In some instances, a family member's legal vulnerability prevented US citizens from availing themselves of resources that could help close financial gaps. Whereas undocumented immigrants are barred from accessing many public services, including supplemental nutrition assistance, US citizens with undocumented parents are eligible for such aid.[9] Yet undocumented parents must negotiate whether or not they are willing to engage with such government programs on their children's behalf or avoid them to protect themselves and their families from immigration officials.[10] Shortly before our interviews, the first Trump administration increased the stakes vastly. There is a provision in US immigration law that allows officials to deny permanent residency or citizenship to an individual they believe will become a "public charge"—a cost to society. Regulations had exempted the use of health, nutrition, and housing support programs to make such a determination, but Donald Trump's administration proposed to reverse that exception.[11] Isaiah Avalos and Ruby Pedrosa, US citizens with undocumented parents, both gave up their food stamps because of this proposal. Isaiah had tried to argue with his family that, since it was his name on the account, they would be protected, but he said they "insisted, 'Don't renew it. Don't renew it. Just as a precaution.'" In Ruby's case it was she who initiated the discussion about giving up the benefit. While neither family knows whether its undocumented members will ever have a path to citizenship, jeopardizing that theoretical possibility was unthinkable.

Being aware of their undocumented parents' economic precarity manifested in students' own lives as substantial worry. Rubén Huerta-Diaz, a US citizen with undocumented parents, referenced persistent fear that his father would lose his job. Questions swirled in his head: "The documents [my dad uses], they're falsified. How long are they going to hold up? How long is this employer going to cover it up? And is there ever a chance that one day they would decide they don't want anything to do with immigrants anymore?" Similarly, Lucia Ortega, a DACA recipient, recounted the economic stress she felt around DACA's threatened rescission: "I was scared that if I wasn't going to be able to renew, I wouldn't be able to work which [meant] I wouldn't be able to bring an income for myself and my family and for a car and things like that. It makes you spiral a little." For students with undocumented parents, a doctor's appointment or news accounts about federal immigration policy could set off a wave of economic worries as they traced the ripples of lost income through their family's ability to secure their economic well-being.

Even when not confronted with direct threats to financial stability, participants recognized how undocumented family members' employment situations could be harmful to their collective emotional well-being. Fernando Medina, a US citizen with undocumented parents, fretted about the pressure his father faces to keep food on their table, even if "for a while it was just rice and beans." The need to support the family creates "this pressure on [Fernando's father] to go out and find a job, any job. He's done everything. And it always puts us on edge of how much that everything takes a toll on his body. Because some jobs have overworked him harder than others and the pay is no comparison."

Others worried about the unjust employment situations their family members tolerated because of their lack of access to employment authorization. Arely Barajas, an undocumented student without lawful immigration status, recounted that her undocumented father has been in the same job for ages, where he experiences routine mistreatment from supervisors and nonexistent breaks. At one point, he had to take time off for his mental health. "It's obviously very stressful for him," Arely said. She said that her father's exploitative employment situation "causes stress on the whole family" as they worry about his emotional well-being and their collective economic future.

Racist-Nativism and Social Exclusion

Participants identified racist-nativist social exclusion as a third collective constraint that was shared among family members. "Racist-nativism" in the United States is defined as a "form of racism that has historically targeted Latinx communities that is based upon real or perceived immigrant status that in turn, assigns a foreign identity that justifies subordinating practices and policies."[12] Gabriel Ballón, a DACA recipient, linked racialized stereotypes to his experiences of discrimination, suggesting that immigration-related discrimination transpires regardless of one's immigration status: "I think I have faced discrimination because I'm Mexican or Latino. . . . But not because of my immigration status because it's like I don't really tell them [my status], right? But I think sometimes they assume. . . . White people don't even know if you have papers or

not. So they just like discriminate [against] you based on how you look."
Similarly, Samantha Arroyo, a US citizen with an undocumented parent,
explained the link between nativism and racism:

> There's a lot of immigrants that aren't Mexican, but because they're white,
> they're not targeted as much; they're not asked for if they're legally here be-
> cause they have blue eyes or green eyes. But because we're Mexican, even
> if we're legally here, I mean, even if we're born in the [United States], they
> still question whether we're legal or not. And so I think that's the thing
> that's the most frustrating because they really only target people by their
> color instead of actually by their legal status.

Both undocumented and US citizen survey participants reported similar rates of experiencing immigration-related discrimination, including
being treated unfairly at a restaurant or store, feeling ignored when seeking help, or being taken advantage of at work; their average score on this
eleven-item scale was equivalent to responding "sometimes" on most
items. When describing discriminatory experiences, most interview
participants recounted witnessing racist-nativism through their parents'
interpersonal experiences and being exposed to anti-immigrant narratives circulated through media and public policies. These racist-nativist
threats to parental and family well-being were experienced collectively
so that immigration-impacted students internalized feelings of social
exclusion.

In most cases, interview participants reported direct experiences
of immigration-related discrimination when they were in the presence of
their undocumented parents. Paloma Montoya, a US citizen with undocumented parents, described a horrible experience her mother had:
She "accidently spoke Spanish" at a government office and "this lady, she
got so angry, and she started yelling at my mom and telling her, 'No, you
can't speak Spanish in here, speak English.'" Paloma also talked about
more subtle experiences, such as when she and her parents travel outside
of their neighborhood to go to specialty grocery stores. "We obviously
stand out a lot because Trader Joe's are only in neighborhoods with white
populations." She said, "I can't help but notice the way people look at us.
I can't help to notice the way the cashiers treat us. It's not in your face
like they're being racist or anything, but I guess you can say it, like it's a

microaggression where they even avoid eye contact. . . . Or the way they kind of look at the way my mom is paying with . . . an EBT card." Paloma explained how she internalizes such incidents: "I think it's just situations like that that make it really difficult to even feel comfortable in spaces like that." Such interactions have enduring effects on students' feelings of belonging when they enter public spaces with their parents or on their own.

Immigration-impacted students also reported that people assume they are undocumented when they are with their parents, and they experience discrimination as a result. Camila Rios Echeverria, a US citizen with undocumented parents, recalled an interaction with a woman who worked in the office where Camila was helping her mom clean. Then a high school student, Camila was wearing a UCLA t-shirt, and the woman asked her if she wanted to go to UCLA:

> I didn't want to brag that I already got admitted. So I was just like, "Yeah, hopefully." And then the lady was like, "Oh, that's a really good school. I mean, you should also apply to [community college] because you never know. And UCLA is really expensive too. So you also have to think about that." And I got really mad because she was only telling me this because she saw me as the cleaning lady's daughter, "what [are] you doing thinking about going to UCLA."

Camila linked these comments to negative popular rhetoric about immigrants, undocumented people, and Latinos, which then informed the discrimination she experienced in this and similar instances when in the company of her undocumented mother.

Similarly, Mateo Olivares Galvan, a DACA recipient, said that when he accompanies his undocumented father to work in demolition and other landscaping work, people assume he is a recent immigrant. He said: "Because of my age and I guess the way I look . . . a lot of the times these people that my dad would work with would think that I didn't speak English, they would say, 'Oh, is that your son that just came from Mexico.'" In these cases, social context informed immigration-impacted students' experiences of immigration related discrimination. When accompanying their undocumented parents to work, participants were assumed to be undocumented due to the social context and subject to anti-immigrant sentiment.

Witnessing their undocumented parents' experiences of racist-nativist discrimination was painful, and participants often internalized these attacks. Bianca Mercado, a DACA recipient, recalled an instance when she was about ten years old and witnessed discrimination aimed at her undocumented father:

> My dad works nights . . . as a janitor. . . . And part of his cleaning involves power washing the floor [and] there was a white man there who was yelling at my dad, telling him that he shouldn't be spraying chemicals on the earth, and that we're the reason why climate change is happening and we're ruining the earth. Just yelling at my dad. And I got really angry, and my dad just said, "Don't say anything, just ignore him."

Bianca recognized the precarious position that forced her father to put up with such treatment: "By choosing not to engage, he's probably saving himself from getting deported." Maricela Paredes, a US citizen with an undocumented parent, explained why she takes such incidents to heart: "I'm still standing next to the person whom I love and who gets disrespected." Our prior research indicates that such experiences of witnessing discrimination against their parents are risk factors for depression and anxiety for undocumented students and US citizen students with undocumented parents.[13]

Immigration-impacted students also felt personally implicated in the collective threat of generalized anti-immigrant, racist attacks on the Latino immigrant community. Coming of age during an increasingly anti-immigrant policy context, participants were exposed to exclusionary laws and explicit anti-immigrant sentiment from powerful political leaders. Santos Castro, a US citizen with an undocumented parent, recalled that he and his family felt threatened by the development of anti-immigrant policies, even when they did not directly affect them. DACA's rescission as well as Arizona's SB 1070, which allowed the state's law enforcement officials to request proof of immigration status beginning in 2010, both had an impact even though they were not directly affected by these policy changes. He described his understanding of and reaction to SB 1070:

> They will stop individuals like Mexicans. They're profiling. So that's a toll on me because I myself am brown and just knowing that the

law enforcement could stop anyone who looks brown like me and be like, "Oh, hey, show me your papers." That took a toll on me, because I might have my papers, but . . . these are my people. These are my cousins. And that took a toll on me. Like, "What the fuck? Where's the justice in this country?" We talk about freedom, we talk about liberation, but really, it's just a racist country that still holds power to control people.

Similarly, Isaiah Avalos, a US citizen with undocumented parents, explained that he experienced Donald Trump's racist-nativist rhetoric as an attack on himself:

The bond with my family, . . . it's like a hit on one of us is a hit on all of us. So for example, with the Trump administration speaking terrible things of undocumented people. The very first day of his [first] campaign [when Trump said,] "They're bringing drugs, . . . they're criminals, they're rapists and some I assume are good people." That was a direct hit on them. But I took it personally because since they're my parents, it's like you're also attacking me.

Aiden Chacón, a DACA recipient, also traced a rise in anti-immigrant sentiment to Trump's first presidential campaign. He remembered visiting his college campus after being accepted and that "the morning of [his visit], some students had . . . put on our library wall, with chalk, they wrote 'Go back to your country. Build the wall.' . . . I felt very uncomfortable being there." Other participants recalled confronting anti-immigrant sentiment through media coverage and their alarm at the societal shift toward more widespread acceptance of anti-immigrant sentiment. Regardless of its source, these collective threats yielded collective social exclusion.

In sum, deportation threats, lack of access to lawful employment and fair wages, and anti-immigrant sentiment work together to produce family legal vulnerability. These mechanisms turn the individual strains of undocumented family members into collective constraints as family members share in material barriers and emotional turmoil. Specifically, immigration-impacted students share experiences of threatened family separation, economic insecurity, and social exclusion.

Shifting Policies and the Uncertainty of Living with Family Legal Vulnerability

For many college students, the future seems uncertain. But for immigration-impacted students, family legal vulnerability deepens this sense as they contend with an ever-shifting and unpredictable immigration policy context. Cynthia Cardenas, a US citizen with undocumented parents, recounted anxious feelings about what lay ahead:

> CYNTHIA: It's just sometimes the future's very, it seems like a really insecure place to think about. It does make me a little anxious.
> INTERVIEWER: Do you find yourself thinking less about the future? How do you cope with that?
> CYNTHIA: I guess we don't make future, long-term plans because we kind of don't know what's ahead.

Cynthia attributed these feelings to "the uncertainty of not knowing if one day ICE is going to pop out at my family's house," while others linked such threats to the broader political context that advanced exclusionary policy shifts. Because immigration-related laws and policies change frequently and unpredictably, the legal landscape can feel unreliable. Sociologist Alexis Silver conceptualized this political reality as tectonic incorporation to capture how local, state, and federal laws and policies can shift with little warning (and potentially in opposite directions), leaving undocumented immigrants needing to continually assess and adjust their plans in response to new policy landscapes.[14] In line with her work, we find that feelings of uncertainty characterize the dimensions of family legal vulnerability discussed so far—deportability, economic insecurity, discrimination—making it difficult for students like Cynthia to envision their own and their family's collective future. Thus, the unpredictability of the immigration policy context exacerbates feelings of family legal vulnerability.

Participants expressed feeling little control over their future, noting the reality that public officials hold the key to legal integration. Rocio Carrillo Guerra, a DACA recipient, explained: "The uncertainty is already crazy for everyone. Not just undocu-folks. Life is uncertain as it is, but for us, it's having to wait on someone else to make a decision on our sadness. That's just the uncertainty." At the time of our interviews, participants were focused on the threat posed to their family's security by the first Trump administration's anti-immigrant agenda. Most of our participants were in high school and/or their first years of college during this time. Camila Rios Echeverria, a US citizen with undocumented parents, recalled how his first campaign and election affected her:

> I think [my feelings of vulnerability] increased a lot when Trump came into office. Just because we all know how he felt about undocumented immigrants, the way he talked about a lot of our community members, whether documented or undocumented. I remember it was a general sense in our house whenever we would see the news, we would always think about, oh my God, what if he gets elected? What's going to happen? And I really did think that if he got elected, my parents were definitely going to be deported.

Taking in anti-immigrant rhetoric and proposed policies, Camila felt an increasing sense of doom about her family's ability to remain secure.

The unpredictable and volatile policy context fueled fears that family legal vulnerability could suddenly derail their collective well-being and future. Camila recalled heightened feelings of uncertainty under the first Trump administration: "I was a lot more fearful than I had been before because I thought, this time, police officers were looking for undocumented immigrants. If they [my parents] got pulled over, it wasn't [like] they *might* ask you for your papers. It was like, they *will*." For many, the political uncertainty of this time period centered on explicit threats of family separation. According to Sabrina Soriano Trejo, a DACA recipient, these feelings of uncertainty persisted under Joe Biden's administration:

> In the split of a moment, anything could change. It could be that Biden all of a sudden hates everyone and decides to deport every single person. Or they stop accepting DACA and then I ended up losing my work permit. . . . It could be that my parents get deported, and I have to leave my master's program and have to find ways to get money, to pay for a lawyer, to help them through their situation. There's just so many things that could change in an instant that could just change my future completely.

Like Camila, Sabrina shared concerns about family legal vulnerability and the potential deportation of her parents. As a DACA recipient, she also expressed heightened feelings of uncertainty about how losing these protections would alter their lives.[15] Notably, Sabrina's concerns about losing DACA did not merely revolve around herself; there were also implications for her family.

Feelings of uncertainty were also experienced collectively as family members worried about immigration-impacted students' future as a result of the immigration policy context. Sylvia Molina Santoyo, a DACA recipient, explained that she and her family monitored the news for information about the "government's policies [because] they're changing all the time. New presidents are coming in. . . . It's just chaotic. We try to keep up just to become aware. We don't like surprises." She felt like her own status affected her undocumented family members: "My grandparents and my mother, they all knew I wanted to succeed in life, but they just maybe worried about my future given my status." These worries were tied to "what's been going on lately with the President, both Trump and Biden. . . . Policies are constantly changing. Of course, they worry but they try not to worry so much to the point where they make me maybe fall into depression or just get anxiety."

Absorbing these feelings of uncertainty, immigration-impacted students found it difficult to plan for the future. Arely Barajas, an undocumented student without lawful immigration status, remarked: "I think the biggest thing with being undocumented is just how much uncertainty there is about everything. So I think whenever I plan, I always have to acknowledge the uncertainty that exists. I have to acknowledge that a lot of things can change. . . . [You're] planning [the future] with a grain of salt because you never know what can happen." Similarly, Diana Mora, a US citizen with undocumented parents, reflected on how she has a hard time planning for the future because she must also consider how she will be "growing along with my parents beside me. How are they going to evolve in this time period? And how is the law also going to evolve? How is that going to impact us?" Like most participants, Diana recognized that immigration laws and policies, and the politicians who pass them, are linked directly to their ability to plan for a stable future in the United States. Arely's and Diana's statements mirror prior research findings that undocumented students struggle to visualize their future and must wrestle with the potential ways in which legal uncertainty may compromise their ability to realize their goals.[16] Although Diana is not undocumented, her citizenship status does not protect her from the strains affecting undocumented people.

A lifetime of limited progress and political setbacks made it difficult to hold out hope for positive immigration reform. Nicole Robles, an undocumented student without lawful immigration status, felt that "it's very unlikely there will be any changes." She reflected on the US presidents of her lifetime:

> Obama was a great president and he supported undocumented individuals. But he was one of the people that deported the most undocumented folks, more than Trump. . . . I feel like if we have a Democrat or a Republican, regardless, undocumented folks face the same amount of oppression and discrimination. . . . Now that I have seen with three presidents, just how policies and things are, it's kind of like you're aware of the situation.

Bouncing back and forth between pessimism and optimism, Nicole concluded: "We still need to have that hope," but to protect herself she also said she took care that "you don't have your hopes up." While many wished for comprehensive immigration reform, gesturing to the 1986 amnesty policy of President Ronald Reagan, this was well before most participants had been born. With little indication that real change was on the horizon, uncertainty reigned.

Cascading Consequences for Immigration-Impacted Students

Faced with the weighty collective constraints of family legal vulnerability, immigration-impacted students must learn to navigate them as they go about their day. During this process, family legal vulnerability yields cascading consequences. We define *cascading consequences* as the emergent repercussions of family legal vulnerability in the everyday lives of individual family members. Cascading consequences are the channels through which family legal vulnerability inserts itself into individual family members' everyday lives. Here, we discuss two strains that emerge for immigration-impacted students as they attempt to manage collective constraints and protect their family's collective well-being: family responsibilities and strained social relationships.

Shouldering Family Responsibilities

Cognizant of their family's legal vulnerability, participants often began shouldering family responsibilities as they entered young adulthood. Rubén Huerta-Diaz, a US citizen with undocumented parents, reflected on how his collective orientation yields a sense of family responsibility:

> We're very family oriented. I always have to think about my family, and my trajectory and how that includes my family. I think one of the common goals that you'll hear is, I want to have a house, or I want to buy a house for my parents. And all that stuff is not possible if they're deported, if they're not physically here, if you're separated. And it makes things more complicated, and you have to keep in mind how you can advance, but at the same time, not leave anybody behind. . . . Like my parents, I can't leave them behind.

Like many participants, Rubén wanted to protect his family's future. He hoped to stave off deportation threats and secure their well-being by providing economic security and by petitioning to adjust his parents' status. His dreams translated into day-to-day responsibilities as he moved toward making this a reality. Many participants similarly responded to family legal vulnerability by taking on family responsibilities to promote collective well-being. Such actions yielded cascading consequences as students sought to contribute to the household income, petition to adjust their parents' immigration status, and prepare for increased responsibilities in the event of family separation.

BOOSTING THE HOUSEHOLD INCOME

Many immigration-impacted students said they worked to counteract their family's economic insecurity. Gabriel Ballón, a DACA recipient, noted that, despite stagnated opportunities for his parents, his family has enjoyed an improved economic situation "because now both my brother and I work. We're able to help a little bit more. So in that case, it has become a little bit more easier now, right? Now we have a little bit more money and our quality of life has improved, and it keeps improving. Because now both of my parents don't bear that burden of taking care of us." US citizen participants noted similar improvements as they also aged into young adulthood and contributed to the family income. Diana Mora explained that this happened gradually as her mom started helping out "by selling other things," her sister started working, and Diana began "earning money at university." As a result, she felt the family was "better off than we were a few years ago where we couldn't support ourselves on our own." Many low-income college students similarly strive to manage financial constraints and pressures with negative consequences for their education, but for immigration-impacted students family legal vulnerability is at the heart of their stressors.[17] As anthropologist Heide Castañeda has documented, many immigration-impacted youth enter the labor market early to be able to purchase desired items that their parents could not afford.[18]

Participants often felt family financial strains as pressure to work to supplement household income. Violeta Perez, a DACA recipient, recalled feeling "a little bit of pressure of like, 'Okay, you have to start contributing. You have to help out.'" This pressure increased as her family set their sights on moving from their cramped apartment to a house with more space. She recognized that their ability to achieve this household goal is dependent on her being able to "contribute a lot more." In their studies of US citizen youth and young adults whose parents are undocumented, anthropologist Christina Getrich and sociologist Cassaundra Rodriguez identified similar pressures as young people sought to offset the financial difficulties endured by their undocumented parents who have limited job prospects.[19] Our findings indicate that undocumented students felt the same way. Further, all immigration-impacted students felt torn at times as they desired to help support their family's immediate financial needs but also pursue their own aspirations.

Students often sought to minimize the costs they placed on their parents' earnings. Bianca Mercado, a DACA recipient, shared that she did not receive much financial support from her parents: "My tuition, my financial aid. I was working, I was paying my own groceries. I was paying my own rent, doing all those things and my parents never helped me, but I felt I never asked for them to help me." She attributed her commitment to covering her own college expenses to growing up "knowing that there was no money available. Whenever I would ask for new shoes, I was told, we don't have money right now. I knew what our financial situation was like, and this is why I didn't ask for them to really help me." Edwin Gordillo, an undocumented student without lawful immigration status, faced food insecurity but did not turn to his family for help. He said matter-of-factly: "I know my folks didn't have the budget to be able to support me like that, so I didn't want to be a burden on them." He sought out support from his university's food pantry instead.

Making financial decisions in light of their undocumented parents' limited economic resources, immigration-impacted students confronted individual economic insecurity as they sought to pursue college careers in a university system that assumes parental financial support. Julia Soto, a US citizen with undocumented parents, explained that she tried to wean herself off her parents' financial support in her second year "because to me it was like, I'm living 15 minutes away so why am I going to ask you for money when I can be living at home? I had my reasons, and it was difficult, there was sometimes where there wasn't enough money for food or there wasn't enough money to buy certain items, for example, pads or tampons." Some students hid their financial struggles from their family. Xochitl Amador, a US citizen with undocumented parents, shared how "I don't want my parents to find out that I'm struggling [with money] . . . because then they're gonna feel obligated to help me out." Not having their help caused her stress, but, she said, "They're barely able to help themselves out. I didn't want to put them in that situation." Given the financial roles they had stepped into within their families, participants' financial worries extended into the future as they anticipated needing to take on additional financial responsibilities as their parents aged. Julia Soto, a US citizen, mentioned this as one of the ways her parents' undocumented status impacts her family: "Not having those papers prevents them from also having that retirement fund or having the social security [payments]. So that's also a worry of mine. [For my parents,] when you retire, you're not going to get anything, you're not going to get any of that. And because you can't retire . . . you constantly have to be working." This hypothetical knowledge came to the fore as her mom struggled to continue her job as a farmworker:

Her body is just not holding up the way it used to. And even my dad, now as they're getting older, I start to notice more of how they start walking, how it hurts to just get up and get inside of the car so it's just little things that I notice and to me, it's like, as you get older, how is that going to be? How are you going to be able to make that work?

As emerging young adults, immigration-impacted students like Julia anticipated increased family financial strain as parents aged and faced the risk of injury, reduced incomes, and possibly job loss. Such expectations fostered feelings of collective worry as students anticipated that they would face increased financial responsibilities down the road.

PETITIONING FOR PARENTS' IMMIGRATION RELIEF

A cascading consequence unique to US citizen family members is their sense of responsibility to adjust their parents' undocumented status to eliminate family legal vulnerability at its source. When reflecting on how her status as a US citizen affects her undocumented family members, Amaya Martinez was quick to remark that "it gives us hope. Because hopefully I'll be able to get my mom her green card and her papers and her work permit." Like many US citizen participants, Amaya was aware that US immigration policies center family-based immigration petitions. Indeed, such petitions made up 58 percent of all new permanent residents in 2022.[20] Particularly relevant to this group of young adults is a pathway that allows for US citizen children to petition for their parents once reaching age 21.[21] This pathway is complicated by laws that require many applicants to leave the country to process their application and risk a 10-year ban on their return; thus, the potential to adjust one's status through a family-based petition is determined by their mode of entry, prior adjustment petitions, and other features of their migration experiences.

In line with past research, many of our US citizen participants were at or approaching this milestone age with hope and concern.[22] They were facing cascading responsibilities and emotional burdens but also a possibility of finally having relief from the fear of family separation. Ava Cornejo shared how she felt privileged as a US citizen because this pathway was open to her. It had also offered her family hope over her lifetime: "Since I was born, it's like, 'Oh, faltan veinte años [twenty years to go],' or like 'faltan diez años [ten years to go].' So it's like, now [I'm twenty] it is getting closer, so it does hit a little different." In preparation for this momentous opportunity, a few years prior her family had tried to meet with a legal representative but had been scammed out of $10,000. Ava shared in her parents' demoralization from this experience, saying how "I can't help but feel at fault." As the eldest child who speaks English, gets good grades, and is receiving a college education, she felt like she should have been savvy enough to spot fraud. In many cases, this sense of responsibility created a deeply shared sense of uncertainty as young adult children tried to lead their family through the complicated web of immigration law with few tools to actually understand the process.

Participants who were in the midst of the petition process found themselves taking on additional family responsibilities as they were entrusted with guiding their family through this critical opportunity. Camila Rios Echevarria was navigating this demanding process when we interviewed her. Hoping to avoid any problems, she found a lawyer and paid $3,000 for services to submit her mother's case. She had to dip into a fund she had originally intended to use to pay for books and other school materials, but she felt it was worth the sense of security. Camila also took on additional labor, "double-checking the lawyers' work and word-by-word explaining [the paperwork] to her [mom]" and translating all the official immigration letters that were sent to their home. These responsibilities contributed to a sense of anxiety and hope as she negotiated the process with her parents.

As US citizen children stepped into these responsibilities, some encountered complicated legal realities that could delay or prevent the successful petitioning of their parents. The financial precarity caused by their family's legal vulnerability constrained US citizen students' ability to do so. Ava Cornejo worried about whether her family's financial woes would compromise her ability to petition for them:

> We're not really equipped with resources or friends that really know how to handle a situation like that. . . . Just like trying to find out how is everyone going to pay for the immigration lawyer and the paperwork and the background check and all of that. . . . If they offer payment plans or stuff,

because [my parents] do need the [legal] residency at the end of the day. Like it will pay off, but it's just too much, too soon to pay upfront. So it is just that financial worry.

Fernanda Nava was ready to petition for her undocumented mother but needed a fiscal sponsor for the application because she did not earn enough annually to be able to apply on her own. With limited social networks, neither Fernanda nor her mom had been able to find a US citizen who was in a strong enough financial position and willing to cosponsor the application. This left Fernanda with a "nagging thought that . . . I could be doing more." At the same time, Fernanda and her dad had visited multiple immigration lawyers: "They've all told him that his case is a little bit more complicated because of things that happened when he was young and stuff." All of them had turned down the case, leaving her and her family to realize that her dad may forever remain undocumented.

ANTICIPATING FAMILY SEPARATION
Confronting the collective threat of family separation, immigration-impacted students anticipated that a parents' deportation would have cascading consequences for their own emotional and material well-being. Imagining what would happen if someone in their family was deported, participants expected to bear a heavy burden:

FERNANDO MEDINA (US citizen with undocumented parents): I think it's definitely going to be hard. If we lose my father, then it's going to be a financial burden that falls on me. If we lose my mother, then it's going to be an emotional burden that gets put on me. . . . We have had conversations about like, what would happen if she's gone? Or what would happen if my dad's gone? It's a very heavy burden because they, like we all agree, that I would be the one to take care of my little brother.

PILAR BAUTISTA (DACA recipient): I think if my dad were to be deported, that would be difficult for all of us because he's the breadwinner, so we would all have to get a job to provide for everybody else. And it will be hard for my sister and I because we both go to school, so we would have more responsibilities taking care of, not only paying for our school, but also providing for our family. . . . If my mom were to get deported, I feel we'd probably go and have an emotional breakdown because she's who supports us emotionally.

Participants conceptualized the individual deportation threats their parents faced as collective risks. Pointing to gendered family roles, Fernando and Pilar anticipated financial burdens if their fathers were deported and emotional strains if they lost their mothers. Students reveal that their parents' deportability gave way to haunting fears that their family's social fabric would tear, yielding shifting family roles and emphasizing the development of distinct consequences for themselves.

Students anticipated that family separation would have cascading economic consequences. Ruby Pedrosa, a US citizen with an undocumented single mother, spoke about the immediate financial needs: "If my mom ever gets deported . . . then I would just have to drop everything and just work, work, work to bring her back." Others anticipated having to financially support families in the longer term. Marcos Villaseñor, a DACA recipient, expanded on this:

My parents are still a strong [financial] support [for me]. So if one day something happens, I may still be able to go to college, but at the same time, I probably won't be able to [continue my degree]. Because, I'll have to start working. And working a 40-hour job and going full time for your college is very difficult. And then, I've thought about this multiple times. My career is just, it's hard on its own. And what I would see myself doing is maybe shifting to shorter term education. Because, going through engineering school, if something like that were to happen, I would have to start working full time. I'll transfer all my classes to a community college, and I'll get an AA [associate's] degree in some sort of electrical technician career or some sort of manufacturing. There's still a lot of well-paying jobs in those areas. And the work that I would have put in wouldn't go to waste either. So things like that would definitely be my backup plan. If all of a sudden, I have to take the lead.

Marcos was unique among participants in that he had developed a detailed plan for how he would shift his educational and employment goals to step into new financial responsibilities. However, most participants anticipated increased financial responsibilities, as their parents' deportation would lower the household earnings and create new costs.

Students also predicted the evolution of their caretaking responsibilities, as they would have to step into the vacuum left by their parents' deportation. Luz Campos, a US citizen with undocumented parents, said: "Sometimes my mom even brings it up. She'll be like, oh, you know, you're gonna have to take care of your brothers and you're gonna have to do everything if we ever get deported or anything." Similarly, Edgar Lopez Linares, an undocumented student without lawful immigration status whose aunt was his legal guardian, explained that, if she "is removed from the country because of her undocumented status, I have to take an approach of being the caregiver for my little cousins, like emotionally, because my uncle is the one who provides financial support, but I'm going to be the one who's going to be like, 'Hey, how's school going?'" This level of detail suggests students' preoccupation with this risk.

When undocumented students imagined their own deportation, they highlighted the cascading consequences for themselves and their families. Edgar worried about helping his family from abroad:

It's not just about myself, about my future. . . . I take into consideration how much [more] I could help both families when in the States, than in Mexico. There's a big difference. Yes, I will be fine if I get deported, because I'm pretty sure I'm going to get a job in Mexico, but I will not be helping my family as much as I want to.

Some, like J. D. Armenta, a DACA recipient, highlighted their limited centrality to their families: "I feel like I'd feel better if I was the one that got deported. Someone like my mom, there's a lot more people that rely on her emotionally." Others focused on how their absence would leave holes in their family structure:

ADRIAN VILLAGOMEZ (DACA recipient): I think about my family, just because as the oldest of three brothers, I tend to help out my family a lot. And I feel that if I wasn't here, I don't know what would happen to my parents, if they would be able to make it without me.

BIANCA MERCADO (DACA recipient): My younger brothers do look up to me. . . . They rely on me again to provide food, just help them. And if I'm not there, then I don't think they would be seeking out more opportunities for themselves.

As young adults, participants assumed critical roles within their families and worried substantially about how their absence would affect those that depend on them.

Strained Relationships and Social Exclusion

Family legal vulnerability also manifested as a strain on everyday social interactions, prompting cascading consequences in the form of deepening feelings of social exclusion and isolation. Both undocumented students and US citizens with undocumented parents remarked that it could be difficult to explain to peers how they and their families differed from families that are not managing immigration-related threats. For example, Emilia Negrete Romero, an undocumented student without lawful immigration status, shared that her and her family members' undocumented status restricted their social networks: "'Cuz we feel like we have to do things very differently than others, explaining why or how we do things. [When] we interact with them [we can get] into arguments, or like get tired of explaining stuff." Similarly, Ignacio Padilla Cortes, a US citizen with undocumented parents, explained that his "majority white" peers did not understand his experiences: "It was just really hard to find other people who could understand what you're dealing with. Like they did not understand that you're not just living for yourself. You're taking care of friends and family back home who are undocumented and are in a vulnerable spot because of their immigration status." As they struggled to navigate family legal vulnerability, participants' social relationships were compromised, caught up as cascading consequences in their attempts to protect their family's well-being.

Secrecy around immigration status had interfered with some students' ability to build and maintain social relationships. Madeline Salinas, a US citizen with an undocumented father, remembered her anxiety growing up when talking to peers and "the topic of immigration would come up." She recalled: "That was always really awkward because I never knew what to say. And it sort of felt like I was keeping something hidden because my parents would say, 'You can't tell anybody that we're not here legally.' [My mother] was like, 'You don't know.' Like, '*Uno nunca sabe* [You never know].'" Protecting their secret compromised her relationships with peers:

> It would just make me feel I didn't belong, or I was also living this double life. I also didn't ever really invite anyone to my house just because I was really worried that they would know where I live. I guess it's just a sense of, oh my God, what if I have a fight with this white girl and she is mad at me and calls immigration. Things like that just really freaked me out.

Despite recognizing and coming to terms with the shame she internalized growing up, Madeline continued to feel the need to protect her family's safety. She shared that she was currently hiding their status from her boyfriend.

Structural barriers related to family legal vulnerability, such as being low-income, also strain relationships by limiting time spent with friends. Cognizant of their family's tenuous financial situation, students in mixed-status families reflected on their tight budgets when making plans. Aimee Bañuelos, a US citizen, explained that her parents' undocumented status and ensuing financial challenges had affected her socially in college: "I think sometimes, especially my first two years of college, I didn't have a lot of money left over to go out with friends, even out to eat. I had a certain budget that I had in mind. . . . It wasn't always so easy to say yes to people when they wanted to go out to eat or things like that." Arely Barajas, an undocumented student without lawful immigration status, similarly remarked that her finances prevented her from socializing with friends, recounting that she did not attend a trip for her friend's twenty-first birthday because of the mounting costs associated with paying for an Airbnb, presents, and activity costs: "A lot of times, too, I'll just lie about the situation. I never say, 'Oh, it's about money.' It was at the start of the summer, and I was just like, 'Oh no, I'm okay.'" She said that she referenced concerns about COVID-19 infection, which remained a severe risk at the time, instead: "[That was] true in part, but it's also like everybody was vaccinated. . . . And the honest reason is because

I didn't feel like I could pay for the trip." In addition to being left out of activities, making excuses and hiding truths can compromise one's ability to maintain fulfilling friendships. Indeed, anthropologist Christina Getrich documented that immigration-impacted youth who are aware of these constraints may alter their plans to be inclusive of the vulnerabilities their undocumented friends face, but youth had nonetheless faced challenges.[23]

Financial burdens could also seed discord between friends. Fernanda Nava, a US citizen with undocumented parents, recalled difficulties with her roommates over shared groceries: "I was splitting them with my roommates because, for the most part, we got a lot of the same stuff, so we figured we'd just buy kind of a group thing. And then, we split it kind of evenly. But even when we split it evenly, I was like, 'This is kind of a lie.' There's four of us and I'm like, we can go through groceries pretty quickly." Stress mounted as her roommates continued to shop at expensive specialty markets nearby, compared to the low-cost alternatives Fernanda was used to back home. She knew that her parents' low income meant that she would need to pay for her groceries on her own, while her roommates were "pretty well off" and "their parents pay for their groceries." Fernanda longed to ask to split the costs differently but never did because "I don't want to be that person." But she recognized that "it just kind of created this weird thing" between her and her roommates. Such instances compromised relationships as participants struggled to navigate their own and their family's financial constraints, especially in light of their more affluent peers. Notably, low-income students with lawfully present parents also struggle to socialize and forge connections due to limited disposable income.[24] Uniquely, our participants tied the cascading consequences of their socioeconomic status directly to their family's legal vulnerability and parents' inability to access formal, well-paid employment.

Apart from financial concerns, the consciousness that they cannot leave the country further divided participants from their peers. Pilar Bautista, a DACA recipient, explained that invitations abroad can be awkward:

I have friends who are US citizens, and it's kind of hard to be like—Oh, I can't do this because I'm not legal. Oh, I can't go on trips, or I can't get out of the country because of that. . . . It comes up . . . when I'm hanging out with friends who don't know about my status and then they make comments like, "Oh, you should come visit me in Europe," or "Oh, let's go to Japan." I'm like, "Oh I can't." And then I have to explain my status to them.

Ignacio Padilla Cortes, a US citizen with undocumented parents, mentioned that his friends' families had travelled internationally during summer break. While financial reasons were a major reason that Ignacio's family, in his words, "didn't do anything" because his parents "just worked all summer," he was also conscious that his friends' parents had the international mobility his parents lacked. "I felt a sense of shame there," he said, reflecting on conversations about their trips. Both Pilar and Ignacio must navigate personal and family members' limited capacity to engage in travel, particularly international travel. Whether they chose to confront this difference directly, like Pilar, by explaining their status to friends, or sidestepping it, like Ignacio, these experiences made them feel different from their peers.

As with Ignacio, even US citizen participants who could leave the country were conscious of the fact that their parents could not. Fernanda Nava explained that she feels left out when her friends talk about family vacations:

It can be something as simple as like, my friends are talking about how their families go on vacation. Right? I'm just like, I could probably never go on a family vacation. I know that's probably super dumb and it's probably a super privileged thing, but it's— I don't know. I feel like it's something quintessentially American, right? Like the middle-class thing. . . . Hearing people talk about all the places that they've traveled to, right? With their families and stuff. And just thinking about how I probably will never get to experience that and all of the trips that I have to take, will probably have to be by myself or with other people that I know, whether that be my friends or even my sister or something like that.

For Madeline Salinas, her own travel as a US citizen created feelings of guilt because her undocumented father cannot join her:

I've always really wanted to travel. And when I went abroad, my family was just pretty sad that they couldn't go visit me. And it just felt really bad not having them there. And at this time my mom was already a [lawful] resident so she could travel, but I remember it was sort of a huge issue that my dad couldn't come. So in the end, nobody ended up coming because they were just like, my dad would feel really bad if we all just went without him.

Madeline's ability to visit Mexico was a particular source of strain:

And I do travel to Mexico a lot, really me and my siblings. And I think it's just really hard on my dad to see that we can go to his home, and he can't go home. . . . I just felt really guilty. I think we all do any time we talk about traveling anywhere. I always say, "I want to go here, and I want to go there." And then sometimes my dad's just like, "Yeah, me too." I shouldn't have brought it up.

Research by Emir Estrada and Alissa Ruth document similar feelings among DACA recipients who have traveled to their country of origin with Advance Parole, a unique permission to travel abroad they applied for from US immigration authorities.[25] Thus the travel limitations that accompany family legal vulnerability can complicate US citizens' relationships with their undocumented parents.

In sum, cascading consequences are the pathways through which family legal vulnerability inserts itself into individual family members' everyday lives. As members of undocumented and mixed-status families, immigration-impacted students seek to help insulate their families from the worst effects of family legal vulnerability. These actions initiate cascading consequences as students take on emerging responsibilities and worries during this process; these set the stage for other compromised outcomes.

Conclusion

Widening our lens to focus on the family, we show how individual experiences of immigration laws and policies are nested within the larger family context. Individual legal vulnerability has family-level consequences because it is experienced as a collective constraint; family members share in the material and emotional consequences of exclusionary immigration policies. Further, the family context sets the stage for cascading consequences within students' own lives as they seek to navigate and protect their families from the collective constraints associated with family legal vulnerability.

Together, collective constraints and cascading consequences translate immigration laws and policies into a lived experience of family legal vulnerability. *Collective constraints* capture how individual legal vulnerability becomes collective family harm, while *cascading consequences* characterize the next step in the pathway wherein family legal vulnerability shapes individual family members' everyday lives. Building on prior research that focused mostly on US citizen children in mixed-status families, we show that undocumented and US citizen students with undocumented parents share similar experiences of these processes. This prompts us to conceptualize them jointly as immigration-impacted students. Part II continues to explore the cascading consequences of family legal vulnerability as it ripples through immigration-impacted students' everyday lives by straining their mental health, compromising their academics, and curtailing their political engagement.

The Cascading Consequences of Family Legal Vulnerability

2

"It Begins to Take Its Toll"

Mental Health and Well-Being

"When I was younger, I do remember that people would say that immigration trucks and vans would hide behind the Walmart we have here, where the truck loading zone is. I don't know why, but I still wonder, 'Are those actually loading trucks, or are the immigration trucks there?' It may be silly, but it's always my thing. Literally, eyes can be anywhere."
—Julia Soto

In the early 2000s, a teen mother migrated to the United States from Mexico with her young son in tow; both became undocumented. Shortly after arriving, she started working in the agricultural fields of Central California, where she met the man she would marry. Their daughter, Julia, was the first one in her family born in the United States, and two younger siblings eventually followed. Her father "was lucky enough to get hired into a company in town," but her mother remained in the fields working a physically demanding job with low wages. Although her parents were active members of their community and settled into a pattern of working and providing for their family, they continued to face structural inequities such as low-wage employment and risk of deportation due to their immigration status. Though Julia is a US citizen, she spent her childhood looking out for and avoiding immigration enforcement to protect her family. As she has gotten older, she recognizes it is unlikely that the trucks behind a big-box store are coming to haul immigrants away, but she cannot completely ignore the possibility. She characterized this constant alertness as making her childhood a "stressful experience." Coupled with worry for her undocumented parents was the added pressure of being unable to help. Even as she watched for threats she acknowledged, "I just feel like I can't really do much. I literally can't really do much."

Such pervasive stressors were the cascading consequences of family legal vulnerability, and they affected Julia's mental health.

Concern for her parents took an emotional toll on Julia as she experienced intrusive thoughts. When asked about the extent to which she worries about parental deportation, she responded: "All the time." Thoughts about her mom's deportability came up unexpectedly, frequently amplifying her anxiety. Her father's use of a false social security number also concerned her. What might happen to him if he tried to get a new one? "What if somebody is already there keeping track of who's buying one?" Julia's worries about this intensified her experience of family legal vulnerability. Stress manifested physically for Julia. As she described, it affects her speech patterns:

> When I'm very stressed . . . I can't even process my speech correctly. It's like my words trip over each other, I don't know, the words just don't come out. And it's a huge indicator because I also know that other people notice it as well, like my coworkers, my mom even has caught onto it, [asking] like, "What are you stressed about?"

Julia sought help from professionals and at one point was on medication for anxiety and depression. Still, she found it difficult to talk about threats to her family. "Talking about them doesn't even help because to me it's like, people will see it as you're being paranoid, but it's not paranoia. It can literally happen." She often felt powerless but also recognized her parents' strength, concluding: "I just think, 'okay, they've managed to do this for over 20 years, so I hope that they'll be okay.'" She coped by trying to "not think about it. Just trying to stay positive, trying to hope that immigration reform is coming . . . just keeping positive thoughts."

In this chapter, we turn attention to one cascading consequence of family legal vulnerability: the pernicious effects on emotional health and well-being. Drawing on interviews, we illustrate how these students experience family legal vulnerability as a chronic stressor, regardless of their own immigration status. Both undocumented students and US citizen students with undocumented parents share similar long-term stressors as they confront the threat of deportation and economic insecurity that have imperiled their families since childhood. Chronic stressors can become emotionally debilitating as students experience trauma responses such as intrusive thoughts and hypervigilance that persist over time. Yet they also identify ways to cope with stressors, shifting their thinking or turning to their social support systems to promote well-being. Such positive mental health behaviors may lessen the harmful impact of family legal vulnerability. Our quantitative survey analysis assesses the impact of these stressors and reveals that immigration-impacted students experience similar rates of emotional distress as their US-born peers who have lawfully present parents; however, their distress is explained by immigration-related threats to their family's stability. Overall, we demonstrate that family legal vulnerability strains immigration-impacted students' psychological well-being, exposing them to chronic stressors that increase their risk of poor mental-health outcomes. At the same time, factors associated with positive mental health, such as flourishing, coping, and leaning on others for social support, may provide a countervailing response to immigration-related stressors that diminishes their impact.

Growing Up with Undocumented Parents: Enduring Chronic Stressors

As students reflected on the impact of immigration policies on their family and themselves, both undocumented and US citizen students with undocumented parents shared poignant examples of how parents' deportability and economic insecurity shaped their emotional well-being. For instance, Isaiah Avalos, a US citizen with undocumented parents, characterized persistent thoughts about his undocumented parents' safety as "thinking and overthinking." He admitted that, at times, he and his parents could "dramatize a situation" to the point that they created "their own little deportation scare." He offered an example of reading a book for English class that detailed a story of grief and loss regarding a father's death. That afternoon, he was unable to shake the feeling that his dad might have been "deported somehow." Ultimately his dad was okay, and he chalked up the feelings he had to "the circumstances, the context that I'd set." He recognized that these experiences were associated with family legal vulnerability, which generated cascading consequences that affected his mental health:

I feel immigration policies have definitely had that detrimental impact on my emotional and mental health. Because there's always that worry, right, that builds up as a result of thinking, "Will my parents be deported, or will they eventually be legal? How will we get past these hurdles?" That's where it begins to take its toll on emotional and mental health.

For Isaiah, pervasive worry and fear for his parents' safety harmed his emotional well-being. And Isaiah is not alone. Research has established that exposure to long-term or chronic stressors places people at risk for mental health disorders, including depression and anxiety.[1] For immigration-impacted students, parents' deportability and economic insecurity function as chronic stressors, giving way to cascading consequences of family legal vulnerability.

The Prolonged Threat of Family Separation and Parental Deportability

Immigration-impacted students recounted how they had wrestled with persistent concerns about their parents' deportability since early adolescence and, for some, their whole lives. Early messages meant to reassure children about their family's safety simultaneously contributed to the proliferation of stressors as they sought to make sense of the very real threats to family. Rocio Carrillo Guerra, a DACA recipient, explained that these fears were prevalent when she was younger: "When I was smaller, I think I was scared of the police, police cars. I would always see them, and I would think, Oh my God, they're going to take my parents." Like Rocio, many participants recounted chronic fears of family separation as children. As young adults, such fears sometimes forced their way into students' consciousness with little warning. Rocio explained that the "fear in the back of my mind" could be "triggered" "when I hear another undocumented friend talking about their parents and their deportation stories." Sudden glimpses of police in young adulthood continued to remind her of the threat of deportation, as did "hearing about ICE raids or checkpoints." Laura Enriquez and Daniel Millán conceptualize moments like these as situational triggers, defined as "specific situations that prompt real or perceived risks of interacting with immigration enforcement."[2] It is the prevalence of situational triggers that determines how frequently latent deportation concerns surface to force undocumented immigrants and their US citizen family members to confront fears of deportation and the possibility of family separation. In these moments, chronic stressors can feel acute, as situational triggers heighten stress levels and often lead to intense emotional reactions including fear, worry, and anger. For example, Violeta Perez, a DACA recipient, tearfully recounted a time when she received a text from her sister notifying her that her parents had been pulled over: "She told me the cops had pulled them over—they were just at a regular checkpoint—but I think my whole body went into panic at that moment. It was just a really scary time, but everything ended up being okay. It was just at that moment, and not being able to be close to home, that kind of freaked me out." As Violeta explained, her feeling of powerlessness was extreme. Such moments bring chronic stressors to the surface and contribute to the strain of family legal vulnerability. For Violeta this meant feeling emotional distress whenever she recalled this moment, which happened each time thoughts of deportation popped into her head.

The cascading consequences of chronic stressors, such as deportability concerns and fear of family separation, compromised students' mental health over the years. Camila Rios Echeverria, a US citizen student with undocumented parents, elaborated on the impact that such stressors had on her mental health:

> Just the fact that I have to think about my family's well-being and there's nothing I–I feel guilty, I feel sad, I feel worried. And I think that's something that's impacted my health or my mental well-being, having to constantly worry about their safety. And then, also just the fact that if something were to happen, I'm limited in how I can help. So that's just always been a worry of mine throughout, from elementary school to my undergraduate career.

Camila's chronic concern for her parents was compounded by feelings of helplessness as she recognized that, if her parents were to be detained, she would have limited options to secure their release. She recalled that when she was a child her family moved around a lot because they would move anytime police knocked on the door. She recalled "those obnoxious, loud knocks" when police would ask for her parents by name and her terrified mom would cry. It was then that her perception of "if we're home, we're safe" shifted; she realized "it can happen whenever, wherever." Such feelings of sadness and worry continued to harm her mental health in college, as she admitted she had "a harder time concentrating" on schoolwork due to ongoing concerns. She concluded that her parents' immigration status "causes most of my anxiety or my worries about the future."

Sociologist Martha Morales Hernandez documented how chronic stressors contribute to an emotional distress process; she conceptualizes this process as a rollercoaster whereby the uncertain sociolegal context tosses around undocumented students and can plunge them into downward spirals when they are unable to control the onslaught of negative thoughts like those study participants described.[3] The cost for most respondents was high and included compromising their enjoyment of and engagement with the college experience.

The Persistent Risk of Economic Insecurity

Persistent, lifelong economic insecurity manifested as a chronic stressor with detrimental consequences, much as deportability did. Students typically became aware of economic hardships early in their lives through experiences of financial strain and housing instability. Diana Mora stated: "I just remember it being very stressful . . . even though I was a child and I wasn't supposed to know about it." A lifetime of financial precarity manifested as distress tied to everyday spending. At the time of her interview, Diana's family had more stability; her father, while still undocumented, earned more than he had before, her mother was working, and she and her sister had jobs that contributed to household finances. This greater stability reduced her stress but did not eliminate it. For example, she still monitored her spending closely. "There's always worries. Am I spending too much? What do I have to allocate for the rent here or for food or things we need?" Like Diana, many participants endured economic hardship as children; these memories bolstered chronic stress as they worried that such troubles might resurface.

Chronic financial stressors sometimes triggered emotional distress when such feelings went unchecked. Students were all too aware that their parents' precarious status limited their labor market opportunities and earnings capacity. Fernanda Nava, a US citizen student with undocumented parents, described how her father had been displaced from his job multiple times over the years, frequently because employers began to use E-Verify to confirm employees' work authorization and he was unable to produce a valid social security card. Chronic financial instability haunted her family and her own peace of mind, as she acknowledged that uncertainty was "the biggest thing" that "impacts mental health just because there's always anxiety around that." Amaya Martinez, a US citizen student and the only child in a single-parent home, expressed frustration that she was not able to "be there" for her mother financially, though she held down a part-time job while attending college to help pay the bills. She characterized her mother's precarious immigration status and unstable employment as a shared stressor; "finding work is something that *we've* struggled with":

> That's something that's always in the back of my mind. It's definitely always a scary thing to think about, and . . . just seeing [my mother] struggle to get work, especially without papers so she does a lot of work under the [table]. She does housecleaning but that's just on her own without anything, so that's definitely where I think about it a lot. Because I even hear her being like, "Oh, if I had papers, it would be so much easier for me to get a job cleaning a hospital or an office," versus her just struggling to find a job.

Amaya concluded that thinking about her mother's financial situation was "triggering" and sent her "into a negative headspace." At the same time, trying to offset the "burden" of economic insecurity with a part-time job also affected her mental health, as she struggled with sadness and frustration at falling short, unable "to do better in helping economically." She concluded that she "internalized" such feelings and kept them from her mom to protect her from "being even more worried if she sees me being sad or upset."

Intrusive Thoughts and Hypervigilance: Trauma Responses to Chronic Stress

Parental deportability and economic insecurity represent chronic stressors that emerged in childhood, persisted through adolescence, and were reconfigured in young adulthood as immigration-impacted students realized the full implications of family legal vulnerability. For many, these chronic stressors precipitated feelings of deep psychological distress and trauma. "Trauma" is defined here as the "personal experience of an event that involves actual or threatened death or serious injury . . . or learning about unexpected or violent death, serious harm, or threat of death or injury experienced by a family member or other close associate."[4] Lisa Lopez Levers and Debra Hyatt-Burkhart make the case that undocumented immigrants, including undocumented and US citizen children of undocumented parents, are at a heightened risk of experiencing trauma or severe stress related to processes of migration, settlement, and postmigration living conditions. In part, this is due to an increasingly restrictive immigration policy context, which has expanded possibilities of deportation.[5] Children of undocumented immigrants, in particular, "are put at risk for psychological trauma, abandonment, and distress" because of their own personal experiences or vicariously as a result of witnessing parents' distress.[6] These researchers also emphasize that, in studying trauma among undocumented immigrants and their families, it is important to avoid pathologizing immigrants or the migration process; instead, they underscore the potential for severe stress and trauma that emerges from the sociopolitical context.[7] For some students, the cascading effects of family legal vulnerability condition significant stress and trauma-related distress as students recounted trauma responses such as intrusive thoughts and hypervigilance that persist over time.

Intrusive thoughts are unwanted and unbidden thoughts that are so upsetting that they interrupt the flow of task-related thoughts.[8] Intrusive thoughts, images, or memories often occur after a traumatic event or—as was more common among our participants—in people with chronic stress. For students in this study, such thoughts were often associated with immigration-related concerns for their parents. For Camila Rios Echeverria, for example, intrusive thoughts emerged in the form of "what if?" scenarios where she questioned her parents' safety and considered what their response would be in case of an actual threat, such as her parents' detention. She explained:

> My parents have been undocumented for my entire life, and it's always impacted how I am in school. Like being in class sometimes and not even realizing I was thinking about, "I wonder what my mom's doing right now. Is she driving? Is she okay?" So I think that's definitely impacted me, just my ability to be as focused as I can be. And it's not to say that every single day [that] I'm in class my mind is thinking about something else, but it happens pretty frequently. I think about my family and what they're doing, if they're safe.

These types of intrusive thoughts served as a frequent reminder of family separation and deportation threats to their families and took away from focusing on other aspects of their lives; in Camila's case, she found her attention being pulled away from school. Camila also reported intrusive thoughts that originated from concerns about her family's economic insecurity. She stated: "I think about my family . . . also financially, just wondering if my parents are going to be able to pay the bills because a big part of that is their immigration status, the type of job they're able to do." Unlike the thoughts that emerged in response to situational triggers, intrusive thoughts were unprompted by external threats. They took an especially taxing emotional toll on students because they often did not have a solution to the what-if scenarios they imagined.

Hypervigilance is "a state of abnormally heightened alertness, particularly to threatening or potentially dangerous stimuli."[9] Research on mixed-status families commonly identifies hypervigilance as a response among children and youth who fear family separation or the deportation of a parent.[10] Our participants' experiences suggest that hypervigilance continues into young adulthood as students report openly assessing threats of detention and deportation around them. Julia Soto, introduced at the opening of this chapter, experienced hypervigilance as she worried about her mom getting swept up in an immigration raid while she worked in the fields or the possibility that someone monitoring false social security cards would discover her dad's immigration status. Gabriela Ortiz, a US citizen student with undocumented parents, experienced nightmares about her parents being deported, which she described as "a world without them." She also detailed her hypervigilant reaction to hearing a knock at the door late at night following a stint of local immigration raids:

> Whenever people would knock on the door, like at night. Not that it happened frequently. But just people asking for money for, say, donations because somebody died or whatever. . . . My heart would stop for a quick second. Like, oh, God no. That time period just really, really affected me.

Gabriela experienced every knock on the door as a threat to her family—she imagined ICE raiding her home—and her emotional reaction was fear and even panic. "My parents would have to reassure me that nothing's going to happen," she said. This constant state of alertness, much like Julia's concerns about trucks behind a Walmart store, was common. Like Gabriela, immigration-impacted students frequently assessed the threat that an unexpected knock at the door or a delivery truck pulling up might bring, often perceiving such banal and commonplace occurrences as menacing.

Hypervigilance was also prevalent as students described their family's economic insecurity. Aiden Chacón and his mother are both undocumented and have always been on top of their finances. They both work, have savings, and even "back up savings." Despite his financial vigilance, however, Aiden worried about his family's economic security. While he recognized that a two-person household is "not really that expensive," they still "limit their spending to essentials. And that's kind of how we've always been living, with buying the essentials." His mother sent remittances to his grandmother and sister who live in Mexico, "paying for their expenses, too." He explained how "that's another expense that she needs to also take into account every month." Aiden characterized their lives as "always being in survival mode." His "survival mode" included prioritizing school-related costs in spending while also experiencing nagging worries about the future and what would happen if his mother was unable to work. "She's very productive, and she has a plan for everything. But I still worry a lot about finances . . . it'd be really hard [if she] stopped working," he said. He admitted that he worries about his mom losing her job because "it's already tough being a student and working." He declined to answer a question about how much he worried, stating simply: "I can't say . . . I don't know how to answer that." Later in the interview, he admitted "I feel that I over-worry sometimes in the nights." For Aiden, unbidden thoughts about financial ruin reinforce hypervigilance around spending, taking a toll on his mental health.

These examples illustrate how students' chronic stress can manifest into more severe symptomatology such as intrusive thoughts and hypervigilance. These trauma symptoms have long-term implications as depression and anxiety are common outcomes.[11] Not all students reported experiencing such symptoms, however. This is likely the result of both differing levels of underlying trauma due to family legal vulnerability and varying access to coping resources. To be sure, many immigration-impacted students mentioned positive mental health markers, such as robust coping strategies and learning to lean on sources of social support to effectively counter immigration-related stressors.[12] Positive mental health behaviors provided a countervailing response to stressors associated with family legal vulnerability for those students who could develop them, but in all cases such vulnerability put their well-being at risk.

Fostering Well-Being: Internal and External Sources of Strength

Contending with chronic stressors and trauma responses, immigration-impacted students sought to promote personal well-being and mitigate the cascading consequences of family legal vulnerability on their own mental health. Stress process theory establishes that both coping strategies and social support can buffer the effects of stressors, thereby protecting one's psychological well-being.[13] Indeed we found that immigration-impacted students drew on both to manage chronic stressors associated with family legal vulnerability.

Coping Strategies

Coping is defined here as "cognitive and behavioral efforts to manage specific external or internal demands" that a person finds "taxing" or "exceeding [their] resources."[14] Coping strategies cannot eliminate family legal vulnerability; rather they help students regulate their own responses to such chronic stressors. We found that immigration-impacted students commonly engaged in what health disparities scholars call "shift-and-persist coping" to buffer the effects of family legal vulnerability. That is, students *shift* by cognitively reappraising and accepting uncontrollable life stressors and *persist* by finding meaning in life and holding positive beliefs or aspirations for their future.[15] Previous research suggests that most people, by engaging in shift-and-persist coping, can minimize the impact of uncontrollable stressors, such as poverty, on physical and mental health.[16] In line with this work, we find that students recognized the constraints posed by family legal vulnerability, accepted their limited ability to assert control over situations, refocused their energy on things they could control, and understood their family's experience as the driving force needed to achieve their goals.

Immigration-impacted students recognized their inability to control the immigration policy context and sought to shift their attention away from associated stressors. When considering the threat of parental deportation, Benjamin Ponce, a US citizen with an undocumented parent, described that, in order to manage the stress, he shifted his focus away from problems that "can't . . . be fixed":

> It's more of trying to forget it and get it off your mind, rather than doing anything toward fixing the problem because again, sometimes it feels like you can't. You just have to deal with the reality that it [deportation] happens to some [people], and we hope it doesn't happen to us. And it's more of just trying not to focus on it. [Instead] focus on the daily activities that we're doing, going to work, going to school, managing the household. We try not to think about it.

Likewise, Mateo Olivares Galvan, a DACA recipient, explained that he fully understood how his family members' precarious status affected them. Instead of being mired in hopelessness or anxiety for the future, he opted to focus on what he could control, which was how to live his life to the fullest:

> I definitely think about [the barriers my family faces]. I know they're real and I know that it could happen, but I don't think it affects me because

I live with this philosophy of like, "I'll be here today. I might not be here tomorrow, so I'm going to do whatever I have to do today." I live everyday as if it's my last. . . . If I can spend time with my family today and as long as I'm able to see them, that's what matters more to me than anything else.

Mateo coped by shifting his focus to being present and cherishing time with his family.

Students developed strategies to refocus their attention, including positive counter-framing. For instance, Violeta Perez, a DACA recipient, explained how she avoided entering a "negative mindset" after experiencing a situational trigger:

I think every time I'm in a situation where there's a checkpoint or anything like that, or anytime I see a police officer. It's just kind of in the back of my mind always, it's just there. I'm like, "Okay, we're doing nothing wrong. Nothing should happen." . . . I think it just puts me in a negative mindset, and I focus on a lot of the what ifs—"What if this happened? What would we do?" But I try not to go there a lot just because if I go down that route it would never end. I just try to tell myself, "There's a lot of things that are out of my control. I can't really do anything about them."

Like some of her peers, Violeta practiced self-reassurance in which she reminded herself that she has not done anything wrong, thereby reinforcing the idea that she will be safe. In these moments, students exerted agency as they sought to navigate threats and reduce the impact of acute and chronic stressors.

Other participants shared examples of being extra cautious in an effort to shift their attention away from family legal vulnerability and reduce its negative impact. Ava Cornejo, a US citizen with undocumented parents, explained how her parents' cautiousness provides her with the reassurance she needs to feel they are safe:

I feel like [in the past] I let [the fear of family separation] consume me. . . . But then, I remember, thankfully, my parents have always been very, very, very cautious. They've never tried to do anything outside of their boundaries. They've always been very safe. So I feel like that really gives me a security blanket to know that the possibility of things coming out wrong could be a little less. Because they are trying their best every day, like they really do. So I feel that helps me calm down.

Marcos Villaseñor, a DACA recipient, also focuses on personal measures to cope. He takes extra precautions to safeguard a future opportunity to adjust his immigration status to preserve the possibility of a better life for himself and family: "I pretty much just try to be as much of a good citizen as I can. And that can be as minuscule as not [running] a stop sign." He said he tries to be "perfect or good" and stay out of trouble. "Any little thing, you just want to be better safe than sorry," he said. Thus he exercised both real and perceived agency and control over an unknowable future that threatens himself and his family. It is through these actions that hypervigilance extends beyond a trauma response to function as a way to adapt to stress.[17]

In addition to shifting their attention away from threats posed by family legal vulnerability, students reframed their own struggles as they empathized with the challenges and dangers their parents have faced. Many students sought to highlight their parents' persistence in the context of restrictive immigration policy and a highly stratified labor market, which functioned as a source of motivation and determination. Aimee Bañuelos, a US citizen student with undocumented parents, recognized the multitude of challenges her parents encountered as undocumented immigrants, which motivated her:

> I definitely feel motivated, just because both of them, since they are un-documented, they came here to the United States at an early age. Back in their country, they didn't really— I think my dad didn't even finish high school and my mom didn't either. So I think just seeing all the struggles that they've been through and the many risks that they've taken coming to this country and even still being here—I can see how hardworking they are. So that's served as my motivation to one day repay [them] for every-thing that they've done for me and my younger sister.

Acknowledging their ability to overcome such hardships encouraged Aimee: "They're able to push through all these different obstacles and at the end of the day . . . provide for us." She was grateful for their strength and determined to "repay" her parents for "all the sacrifices and risks that they've taken."

In much the same way, Carolina Aguilar, a US citizen whose mother was deported and then came into the care of undocumented guardians, noted how far her family members have come since leaving Mexico. "I feel like seeing their hard work motivates me to work even harder, because I want to make them proud. And I want to show them that their hard work wasn't in vain." Parents' resilience during migration and settlement and in the face of anti-immigrant sentiment, unfair labor practices, threats of deportation, and financial insecurity inspired students to keep going. Family histories of legal vulnerability served as a catalyst for immigration-impacted students to find their purpose and drive.

Social Support

Family and friends are a critical source of strength for students in undocumented and mixed-status families as they provide psychological support and material resources.[18] Social support enhances well-being by strengthening conceptions of self,[19] decreasing feelings of isolation,[20] and facilitating stress management.[21] For immigration-impacted students, social support helps buffer the effects of immigration stressors related to family legal vulnerability.[22] Members of their social networks frequently provided emotional sustenance, signaling care and sympathy while also offering a comforting presence.[23] Along these lines, we found that social support served to protect students' emotional well-being.

Reflecting on social support systems, immigration-impacted students revealed diversity in the composition of their social networks, which included family members, friends, and peers. Carolina shared how "I feel like I have a pretty good support system" of extended family members and friends. Carolina expressed the emotional support provided by her family that kept her optimistic about the future:

> My family's pretty supportive. I feel they're always pushing [me] to do more than I think that I can do. They push me to think about things in a positive way, when I'm being negative. That's a big thing. I'm not a very big optimist; I would label myself as a pessimist, and they forced me to

switch the way that I think and look at the positive side. They teach me that focusing on the positive, it's what's going to help make me feel better, and not feel hopeless.

In addition to her family, Carolina described her college friends, now her roommates, as a "second family," who share and navigate similar immigration stressors:

> We're pretty close. I complain to them, they complain to me. We have fun together. I feel like they've become my second family. That has helped my mental health a lot. Because whenever I feel overwhelmed, I can just talk to them. I feel like they understand because we're all in a similar situation.

Connections like those Carolina described provided the stability and reassurance participants needed to counter the stressors in their lives.

Research on mixed-status families with young children shows that parents frequently console their children to convey they are safe.[24] We found that parents continued to provide this reassurance into young adulthood. Amaya Martinez, a US citizen with an undocumented single mother, explained that she and her mother have an open line of communication when it comes to discussing restrictive immigration policies. Both freely share and express concerns with one another—for example, after reading a newspaper article or watching a news program that triggers worries about deportability and family separation:

> I will try to talk to my mom about [immigration policy on the news] and then she'll just reassure me that everything's going to be fine and that if, God forbid, it's meant for her to be deported, then that's just how life is. That's just how destiny is; but the times that I am open to her about it, she just tries to act like an emotional support for me.

For Clara Dominguez, an undocumented student without lawful immigration status, family provided the stability and strength that she needed to thrive in the face of legal vulnerability. "I have the support of my family," she said.

Like I said, if anything happened to me or will happen to me, my mom is the one who will respond to me—in a way that, if for some reason I get deported, my mom is the one who is willing to help me, so mentally they help me.

The interactions Amaya and Clara described can be understood as emotionally sustaining behaviors that can reduce distress by "confirming the individual's sense of truly mattering to other people, sustaining [their] sense of self-worth, and bolstering the belief that [they] indeed [belong] to and [are] accepted within a network of caring others."[25]

Several students also indicated that having ties with friends who were undocumented or had undocumented parents was critical. They characterized these relationships as "special bonds" because they felt understood and could fully empathize with one another. When asked about coping strategies, Lucia Ortega, a DACA recipient, described how talking with "like-minded" individuals about deportability concerns is validating as she does not feel alone in her experiences:

If it's too much, I will talk about it with friends who understand. My two best friends, one of them is undocumented herself and the other one, her mom's undocumented. So I guess talking with like-minded individuals who understand how serious it is, how stressful it could get [is my coping mechanism]. We relate to each other. It makes you feel more relieved that you're not the only one having the stress or anxiety over it.

Lucia's interactions with friends allowed her to process and understand her feelings and her response to the threat of deportability and family separation as both familiar and common under such circumstances. Such conversations helped her feel understood rather than making her feel like she was overreacting or "paranoid."

Rocio Carillo Guerra, a DACA recipient, similarly described the emotional relief that her undocumented friends provided her: "My friend group that I'm so grateful that I have, they're all undocufolks, too." Her friends helped her navigate feelings of anxiety. They vented their frustrations and concerns in a group chat in which they "send each other memes and uplifting quotes." Her undocumented circle of friends reminded her that she was "not in this alone." Their support uplifted her spirits. "I'm like, You know what? We'll be fine. We graduated, we made it. We'll be fine. So that helps me." Like Rocio, many participants found that friends who were undocumented or members of mixed-status families were well positioned to provide emotional support because of their shared lived experience. Indeed, research suggests that significant others with similar experiences can provide a "wider range of effective help."[26] Such conversations encouraged students to work toward their goals and feel validated in their experiences. Such access to social support from family and friends, coupled with their own efforts to implement various shift-and-resist coping strategies, helped immigration-impacted students alleviate the cascading effects of family legal vulnerability.

Implications for Mental Health Outcomes: Comparing Immigration-Impacted Students to Peers

Thus far we have traced how immigration-impacted students experience the cascading effects of family legal vulnerability as a chronic stressor that can escalate to more severe trauma symptoms. We turn now to our quantitative survey data to determine if these experiences contribute to unequal outcomes. Specifically, we compare the current mental health of undocumented students and US citizen students with undocumented parents to US citizen students with lawfully present parents. Regression analyses consider to what extent these two groups of immigration-impacted students differ from their peers and whether family legal vulnerability explains disparities in students' well-being. While participants did not address specific mental health conditions in their interviews, the stressors they describe are known to play a major role in determining one's mental health, leading us to examine three outcomes: *depression, anxiety,* and *flourishing.* Appendix C provides full details on the regression models.

Depression and Anxiety

A recent US study on mental health among young adults in college found that over 40 percent of college students reported having some symptoms of depression, with one in three experiencing significant

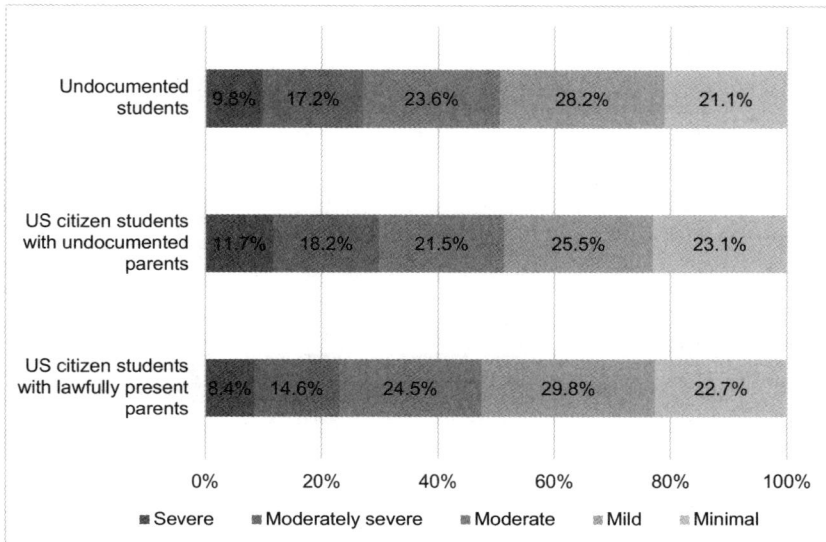

Figure 2.1. Depression scores of survey respondents by self and parental immigration status.

symptoms.[27] In this general population of college students, those at greater risk include low-income, students of color, and students who are family caregivers, all being characteristics common among survey participants. In line with these national trends, our survey revealed high rates of depression in all three groups: undocumented students, US citizens with undocumented parents, and US citizens with lawfully present parents. Moderately severe and severe depression symptoms—categories that capture the clinically significant cutoff point for depression— affected immigration-impacted students at slightly higher rates than US citizen students with lawfully present parents. Specifically, 23 percent of citizen students with lawfully present parents reported clinically significant symptoms, in contrast to 27 percent of undocumented students and 30 percent of US citizen students with undocumented parents (see figure 2.1). Anxiety rates were higher and showed a similar pattern: 41 percent of US citizen students with lawfully present parents reported moderate or severe anxiety, in contrast to 45 percent of both undocumented students and US citizen students with undocumented parents (see figure 2.2).

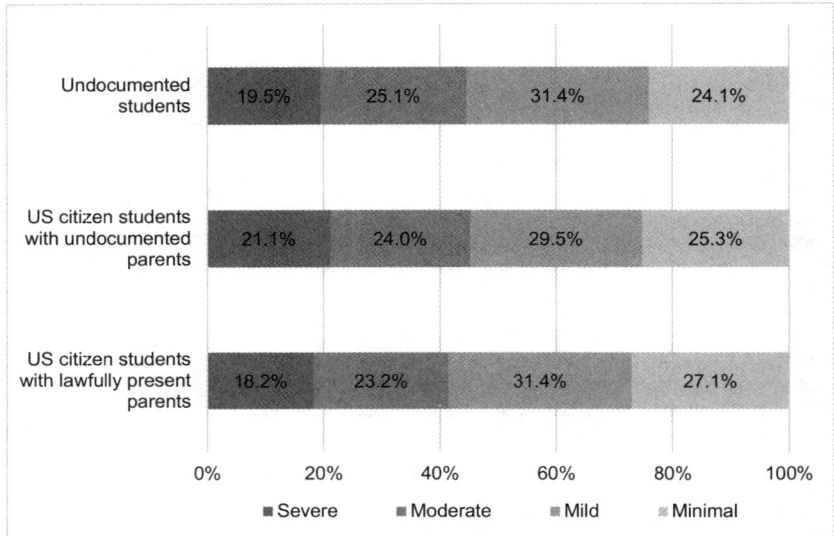

Figure 2.2. Anxiety scores of survey respondents by self and parental immigration status.

Yet our regression analyses revealed that all three student groups, after we controlled for demographic characteristics, reported statistically similar levels of depression and anxiety symptoms. This is indicated in Figures 2.3 and 2.4, which graph the mean score of each outcome after controlling for demographic characteristics (i.e., at baseline). Neither undocumented students nor US citizen students with undocumented parents had statistically significant differences in depression or anxiety scores when compared to US citizen students with lawfully present parents. Given national statistics, this may reflect elevated mental health challenges among college students generally. It may be that all three groups of students have similar symptomatology but that this is due to different sources of emotional strain.

We considered this explanation by taking a closer look at family legal vulnerability as a mechanism that may drive group differences. Specifically, we examined whether group differences for each outcome changed as we accounted for three dimensions of family legal vulnerability: *immigration-related threat to family*, *having a family member who had been deported*, and *family financial strain*. This sequential modeling approach allowed us to see whether and how unique conditions associated with family legal vulnerability shape immigration-impacted students' mental health profiles relative to peers who do not experience these same stressors. Figures 2.3 and 2.4 graph the mean score of each outcome when controlling for each dimension of family legal vulnerability. Comparing each model to baseline allows us to determine whether each dimension of family legal vulnerability contributes to mental health disparities.

We find that perceived threat to one's family due to the exclusionary immigration policy context is an important driver of depression and anxiety among immigration-impacted students. In broad terms, this measure captures the threat of deportation alongside a range of inter-related policy threats by assessing how frequently participants worried about the impact immigration policies have on them or their families, feared that they or a family member would be reported to immigration officials, and worried about family separation. Once we accounted for this perceived threat, we saw lower depression and anxiety scores among undocumented students and US citizens with undocumented parents.

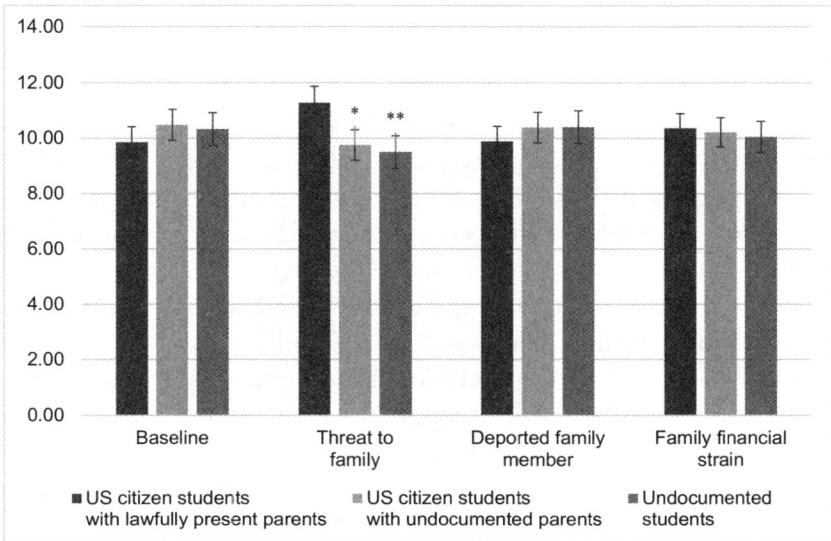

Figure 2.3. Predicted mean depression scores when controlling for family legal vulnerability.
NOTE: Statistically significant differences from the reference group are indicated by ** when p<.01 and * when p<.05.

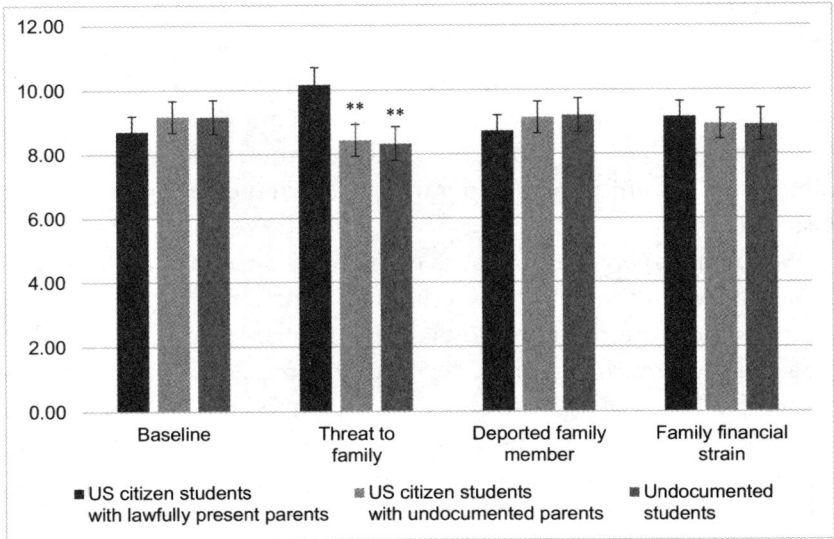

Figure 2.4. Predicted mean anxiety scores when controlling for family legal vulnerability.
NOTE: Statistically significant differences from the reference group are indicated by ** when p<.01.

That is, if immigration-impacted students did not experience the burden of immigration policy threat, they would have lower levels of depression and anxiety symptoms compared to their US-born peers with lawfully present parents. These findings underscore the substantial weight of deportability and threats of family separation on the emotional health and well-being described by students in the interviews.

Controlling for whether or not a student had an immediate or extended family member who was deported did not substantially alter immigration-impacted students' depression and anxiety scores. Our interviews suggest that such may be the case because this group of students is most likely reporting the deportation of an extended family member or the past separation from an immediate family member who subsequently reentered the United States. In nuanced ways, these findings complicate extensive research that has established the severely detrimental impact of deportation on family members.[28] Rather than refute this evidence, our work suggests that responses to deportation are complex; those that responded with reentry or that involve a distant family member may be less likely to have lasting, substantial effects on young people's mental health, especially when compared to the profound impact of threatening long-term separation from immediate family members.

Analysis of family financial strain reveals that, when holding it constant, undocumented students and US citizen students with undocumented parents experienced lower levels of depression and anxiety than US citizen students with lawfully present parents. However, the differences among these groups were more modest and not statistically significant. Thus, in contrast to the marked findings for perceived threat to family, it appears that family financial strain is not as salient in explaining group differences in depression or anxiety.

Flourishing

To consider the potential for positive mental health and resilience, we also examined the extent to which survey participants experienced flourishing, a form of social and psychological prosperity that includes feelings of self-respect, optimism, purpose, and living a meaningful life.[29] Figure 2.5 displays the mean scores across the three student groups; these scores were consistent with the average reported in many other samples of college students.[30] Notably, undocumented students reported higher levels of flourishing on average when compared to their US citizen peers regardless of parents' status. The left-most set of bars in Figure 2.6 compares the mean flourishing scores of these three student groups at baseline. It reveals that undocumented students continue to score about 1.5 points higher on the flourishing scale on average than both groups of US citizen students after controlling for demographic characteristics. Research by Amy Hsin and Holly Reed suggests that this may be because undocumented students are hyper-selected relative to their peers.[31] Drawing on administrative data from a large public university, they establish that undocumented students enter college with higher high-school GPAs than their peers because sociolegal factors disproportionately push otherwise eligible undocumented students off the college attendance track.[32] Further, our qualitative analysis suggests that undocumented students' high level of flourishing may be rooted in effective coping strategies—that is, a capacity to call upon a

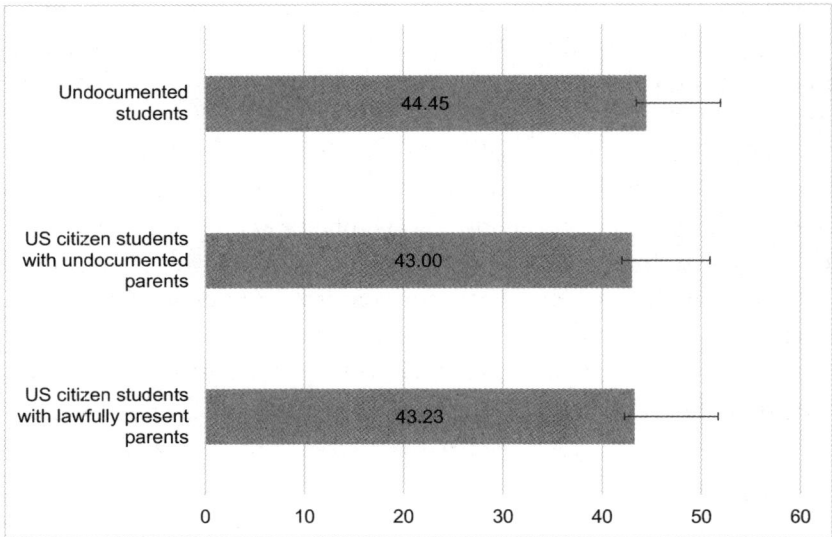

Figure 2.5. Mean flourishing scores of survey respondents by self and parental immigration status.

strong social support network and access to specific resources. Their ability to do so may enable them to better withstand stressors associated with family legal vulnerability. Thus, undocumented students' higher levels of flourishing likely reflect their resilience in light of the tremendous hurdles their own immigration status has required them to overcome to enroll in and persist at the academically selective University of California.

We also explored the relationship between flourishing and family legal vulnerability. Our findings show that, once we account for perceived threat to family, immigration-impacted students—and undocumented students in particular—exhibit higher flourishing scores than US citizen students with lawfully present parents (see figure 2.6). Family financial strain had a similar effect; more specifically, relieving the burden of family financial strain would allow immigration-impacted students' flourishing to increase, with undocumented students showing marked improvement. While accounting for these two dimensions of family legal vulnerability appear to increase the chances of flourishing among US citizens with undocumented parents, it is not to a statistically significant level that would differentiate them from their US-born peers with lawfully present parents. Finally, as with depression and anxiety, flourishing patterns across the three groups did not change once we accounted for past family experiences with deportation.

Taken together, our quantitative analysis reveals the important role that family legal vulnerability plays in the mental health patterns of immigration-impacted students. Although all three student groups reported high levels of depression and anxiety, immigration-related threat to family is a stressor that compromises immigration-impacted students' mental health in a distinctive way. Further, undocumented students' flourishing is dampened when threat to family, and to a lesser extent family financial strain, are considered. These findings suggest that undocumented students and US citizen students with undocumented parents would enjoy greater flourishing than their counterparts with lawfully present parents in the absence of family legal vulnerability. These findings likely reflect the hyperselectivity of the immigration-impacted student population as well as their resilience and engagement in effective coping strategies.

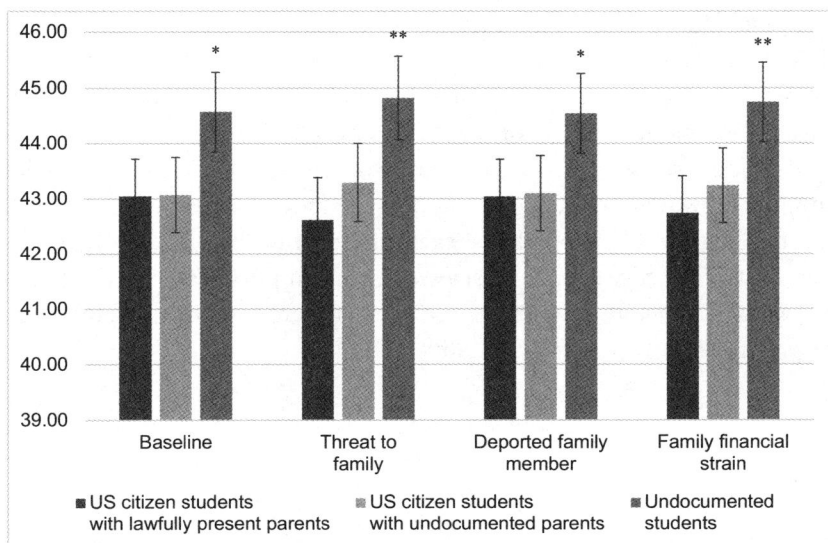

Figure 2.6. Predicted mean flourishing scores when controlling for family legal vulnerability.
NOTE: Statistically significant differences from the reference group are indicated by ** when p<.01 and * when p<.05.

Conclusion

This chapter provides an account of how cascading consequences of family legal vulnerability shape students' mental health and well-being. Our interviews with immigration-impacted students revealed strong similarities between undocumented students and US citizen students with undocumented parents. This further supports our conceptualization of these two groups of students as immigration-impacted; having undocumented parents leads both groups of students to experience, understand, and respond to family legal vulnerability in similar ways regardless of their own immigration status. Both contend with chronic immigration stress as family legal vulnerability manifests in childhood and continues into adulthood. In some cases, these experiences condition trauma responses, and some students describe intrusive thoughts and hypervigilance in their day-to-day lives.

The quantitative analyses demonstrate that immigration-impacted students experience similar rates of emotional distress as their US-born peers who have lawfully present parents; however, their distress is at least partially explained by immigration-related threats to their family's stability. At the same time, students address these chronic stressors with positive, protective mental health behaviors and strategies that ease the cascading effects of legal vulnerability on their psychological well-being—namely, through coping strategies and supportive social support networks. Indeed, undocumented students express high rates of flourishing, rates that would be even higher if not for family legal vulnerability. The coexistence of stressors and support systems highlights the ways in which immigration-impacted students are influenced by and respond to family legal vulnerability.

"I Push Away from School"

Academic Engagement and Performance

"Just recently, . . . I helped pay my grandma's funeral expenses and my mom's medical bills. And that took a toll on me during finals week, in my last quarter. . . . And I felt like I was going to fail this one class. I don't even know if I did—I haven't looked up the grades."
—Penelope Mejía

College was a struggle for Penelope Mejía not only because of the challenges associated with being an undocumented student but also because of her role in the family as the "careful" and "responsible" one when it came to money. Because she did not have employment authorization, Penelope's income and savings came from her work as a nanny, a job she held throughout college and past graduation when we interviewed her. Family financial emergencies of one kind or another fell onto her shoulders throughout her time in college—her mother's medical bills, her brother's rent, her spouse's loans, her grandmother's funeral expenses. She dipped into her meager savings on a semiregular basis to cover such family emergencies, whereas her brother did not make enough to give and her sister (who made more than she did) spent what she had. As the "sister bank" keeping the family afloat, she felt the need to make work her top priority, over and above her academics.

Penelope always tried to make it to class but sometimes was late or had to skip it altogether. She explained that she had a "love/hate relationship with class time," which took her away from family and work responsibilities. At the same time, she "wished the classes were longer" so she could continue to learn and engage academically. She wanted to participate in class discussions but acknowledged that, most of the

time, "I was just either too early or too late and I had to go to work."
Ultimately, prioritizing work over school resulted in a lack of preparation and failing grades. She said: "I remember one time crying to my
English professor because I was working and I didn't know how to be
a good student and I was going to fail the class, and I did fail the class."
Not surprisingly, Penelope had little time for extracurricular activities
or professional development opportunities. She had once tried working
at a campus-sponsored internship program but quit when the project
manager grew angry at her for delaying the completion of a project due
to work and family responsibilities. Although she would have liked to
connect with other students, it was difficult. She opted to "lay low" and
often left right after class for work or due to sheer "exhaustion."

Penelope's undocumented status also caused hardships in school,
such as feeling "discouraged" and "losing time" when seeking relevant
financial aid and scholarship information. She struggled to find an "undocumented student–friendly" placement to satisfy her major's required
field study program. That said, she felt her role as the sole provider for
family financial emergencies was a main source of strain that took a toll
on her academics.

In this chapter, we examine the college experiences and academic
outcomes of immigration-impacted students like Penelope. Prior research on young children with undocumented immigrant parents has
demonstrated how family financial strain and deportation threats—
two of the three *collective constraints* that we discuss in chapter
1—prompt delayed cognitive development, compromised peer relationships, and lowered academic performance.[1] Here, we trace how
such concerns persist into college, thereby demonstrating how the
cascading consequences of family legal vulnerability permeate all levels of education. Drawing on interviews, we trace how family legal
vulnerability shapes immigration-impacted students' decisions about
where to attend college and how it affects their lives once on campus.
Our quantitative survey analysis reveals that immigration-impacted
students report poorer academic performance and more academic disengagement than their US citizen peers who have lawfully present parents. However, we also find that undocumented students express more
positive academic engagement than their US citizen peers regardless

of parents' status. Overall, much as Penelope experienced, family legal vulnerability strains immigration-impacted students' academic engagement and performance by making them choose between school and competing responsibilities.

College Choice: Affordability and Proximity to Family

For most undocumented students and US citizen students with undocumented parents, family financial strain and deportation threats informed decisions about which colleges to apply to and attend. In discussing these decisions, students emphasized that they had prioritized two characteristics influenced by these dimensions of family legal vulnerability: financial affordability and remaining close to home. These factors were important for both individual and collective reasons.

Immigration-impacted students knew their parents would not have the financial resources to contribute much to cover their educational costs or to support their individual living expenses. Most wanted to help their children, but strained family finances made it difficult. Gael Yepez Correa put it this way: "To them, it was always like, 'Well, you can't really go to college unless you can pay for it or afford it yourself.'"

As a result, students took it upon themselves to avoid placing financial burdens on their parents when making college decisions. For most this meant choosing campuses close to family regardless of college prestige, rankings, or specialized programs, factors that typically influence the college choice of more traditional students.[2] Benjamin Ponce, a US citizen with an undocumented parent, expressed a strong desire to stay close to home to continue to fulfill his family responsibilities. As he explained:

> I limited the campuses I applied to because I didn't want to be far from family. I felt obligated to stay and help them financially and socially and support them in any way that I could. To me, I was like: Okay, well, I'll go to community college instead of a four-year college. Stay at home and commute to classes and then from there transfer to university and just maintain my residence at home, rather than applying to a four-

year institution and having that typical college experience of going to a dorm.

By making this choice, Benjamin could continue his efforts to support his family's financial security while also "living rent-free" at home. He acknowledged that these forms of family legal vulnerability constrained his college decision-making process: "I had to kind of limit my educational opportunities near enough to the household so that I could still stay and help financially." He landed on his final choice "because of my parents' situation." Other participants emphasized how attending college nearby would also let them continue to provide social and emotional support for family members, including caring for and aiding younger siblings.

Still others, like Lucia Ortega, a DACA recipient, explained that being nearby was vital because she wanted to be able to show up quickly in the event of an emergency, such as a parental deportation or illness: "I chose [this campus] as my school because I'm undocumented, I'm so close to my family here. If anything happens, I'll be right here." Research suggests that low-income students consider the financial and social costs associated with moving away from family to attend college.[3] Immigration-impacted students' college decisions are similarly shaped by their commitment to helping maintain their family's stability and well-being.

Adrian Villagomez, an undocumented student, was an exception, but his selection process still suggests the impact of family legal vulnerability. He was attending a campus much farther from home than he had originally planned, but financial aid had been determinative. As he explained:

At the beginning [of my college search] I was trying to stay local, because I was thinking, no way I'm going to go that far away. I was thinking, no, stay local so that I don't have to worry about rent or more food. And I'll be closer to my family. That was the goal. [Our shared undocumented status] was the main determining factor of having that mindset. . . . I ended up going to school far away, but only because I knew that there was going to be financial assistance regardless of our immigration status.

For students like Adrian, sufficient financial aid packages are critical to mitigating the limitations posed by family financial strain on immigration-impacted students' college choice.

Family legal vulnerability also meant that students avoided certain campuses because their location or distance increased the risk of deportation when traveling between home and campus. For example, most specifically avoided UC San Diego, a campus located approximately 30 miles from the United States–Mexico border, well within the 100-mile border zone that is subject to heightened immigration enforcement. Students referenced the high visibility of Border Patrol agents and checkpoints in San Diego and on the freeways leading out of San Diego as a reason to avoid it.[4] UC San Diego had been at the top of Fernando Medina's college list. However, he elected to attend another campus after his undocumented mother pointed out these concerns. Despite Fernando being a US citizen, he worried that his parents would have been unable to visit him. As he said, "it was way too close to the border." He conceded that, in his excitement about college, he had originally failed to consider how his parents' undocumented status would affect his final choice. He admitted that it came as "a shock" to absorb the geographic restrictions that his parents' legal vulnerability placed on what he had imagined to be his unencumbered decision to make.

Rocio Carrillo Guerra, a DACA recipient, decided against UC San Diego because of her parents' deportability, although it was originally her first choice. She recalled:

I went to go check out UCSD on the overnight trip that they had. They got a bus and they let us apply, and they took a couple of us, and they let us stay over there for one night to check out the campus and get the vibe. So that was nice, and I was able to see, but unfortunately, I was like, "Okay, I can't go here because there's a checkpoint. How are my parents going to drive me over here?" That was all in my head as I was touring the campus: How am I going to go back home? How are they going to come to my graduation? What if something happens? And so that was a huge turnoff for me to go to UCSD and I didn't really talk to anyone about it. I think I just, people would ask me, "Oh, I thought you were really excited about UCSD." And I would just be like, "Oh, no, I didn't click with the campus." I would use another excuse, but that was predominantly why I didn't choose it.

As a DACA recipient, Rocio had some concern about her own legal vulnerability at UCSD, but her parents' legal vulnerability was determinative.

While family legal vulnerability played an important role in college choice, many undocumented students simultaneously took their individual legal vulnerability into account. As an undocumented, first-generation college student with no lawful status, Arely Barajas's own legal vulnerability became more prominent. Like other immigration-impacted students, she wanted to "save money and stay local," "so if I ever need to go home, I could, to be with my family." But she also highlighted the sense of safety she felt in her majority-Latino community in Southern California:

> I think, considering that I am undocumented, and I don't have DACA or anything, that definitely made me not even consider the schools that were in NorCal, or I mean—I didn't apply out of state—but it made me not consider anything that was more than a two-hour drive [away from home].

Arely initially planned that, like almost half of Latino high school graduates in California,[5] she would attend community college to enable proximity to family and college affordability. Yet one of her teachers convinced her that UC Irvine, a forty-five-minute drive from her hometown, was "very much worth it . . . [and] still very close to home." Arely noted that this one teacher took a special interest in helping her with this decision because she was undocumented. "That [played] a big role, because that teacher wouldn't have had the initial conversation with me had I not been undocumented," she said. Nevertheless, the factors that influenced her decision—financial strain and immigration policy threat—manifested as both individual and family legal vulnerability, which intertwined to shape her decision-making.

These examples reveal that college choice is made with family legal vulnerability in mind, as students weigh familial safety and security against their own personal preferences and ambitions. Though students' own undocumented status mattered, family legal vulnerability affected all immigration-impacted students' college choice in similar and salient ways.

Academic Distractions: Mental Health In and Out of the Classroom

Once immigration-impacted students arrive on campus, family financial strain and deportability concerns continue to shape their academic engagement. Our past research with Karina Chavarria and Monica Cornejo found that most undocumented students experience immigration-related academic distractions due to both their own and family members' immigration statuses. Such distractions are consequential because students who reported more frequent distractions were more likely to report negative academic engagement behaviors.[6] Extending this work, we find that undocumented students and US citizens with undocumented parents experience immigration-related distractions that stem from the chronic stressors and trauma responses discussed in chapter 2. These family legal vulnerability stressors prompt intrusive thoughts and hypervigilance, leading to cascading consequences for students' attention and academic engagement.

Intrusive or unwanted and upsetting thoughts disrupt immigration-impacted students' focus both in and out of the classroom. As US citizens, Amaya Martinez and Ava Cornejo did not worry about being deported or experiencing other forms of legal violence, such as being detained by ICE or questioned about their legal status during a routine traffic stop. Nevertheless, Amaya expressed a near constant fear that her undocumented single mother could be deported at any time. She admitted that such pervasive thoughts affected her focus and concentration when studying. She wondered where her mother was and whether she was safe. She imagined the worst-case scenario of family separation. She recalled: "It's what I think about the most versus when I should be thinking about studying or when I'm trying to study, that [the thought] arises and puts me in a bad headspace." Ava also reported that the fear of her parents being deported distracted her from studying. She said:

> It does get in the way of your studying and always that constant fear of that thought . . . it just comes like, oh, what could happen with my parents? What would happen to my parents? Like, are they even going to be able to—when I'm 21, will they still be here? Is there a time thing? Will

they get deported still? We're so close to the finish line . . . [but] we're not there yet. Anything can go wrong. I think it's just like the anxiety and the fear mostly.

Ava's use of "we"—"we're so close to the finish line"—underscores the perception that her life is linked to her parents. She suggests that her college career is a collective goal that is shared across generations.[7] But the anxiety and fear associated with family separation made it difficult for her to study and achieve that goal. Likewise, Isaiah Avalos said that frequently his thoughts during class often drifted toward "thinking, Hopefully when I get home my parents will be there. Or even thinking, When I get out late from school, hopefully my dad will be there waiting for me, to take me home." He was fully aware of the threat that they might have been detained by immigration enforcement.

Immigration-impacted students also shared that class assignments and interactions with peers about immigration issues could compromise their attention and academic engagement, especially when conversations included expressions of support for anti-immigrant policies and sentiment. Amanda Tobar Vargas, a US citizen student with undocumented parents, described how she avoided thinking about immigration issues as much as possible so that she could instead focus on schoolwork. Yet sometimes her coursework addressed restrictive US immigration policies. She shared how "sometimes the immigration laws intertwine and combine with academics . . . and they want us to write about those laws, so it's hard to avoid. . . . I get reminded once again [of my family's vulnerability] but I try not to let [it] affect me too much." Amanda's narrative illustrates how immigration-impacted students' academic interests may be informed by their circumstances, encouraging them to take immigration-related courses that then require them to face their family legal vulnerability. Such classwork could be triggering, prompting negative effects for their academic engagement and performance.

While distractions could be chronic, some participants referenced acute instances in response to specific, immediate threats. For example, Maricela Paredes, a US citizen with an undocumented father, said that her academic performance dropped during a period of intense Border

Patrol actions in her hometown. The increased threat of family separation and the danger of detention fostered within her a sense of hypervigilance due to "the added stress of the raids that were going on," which caused her to "push away from school." Her grades "dropped a little" during that period. She explained that, in addition to the stress of knowing about the raids, she was bothered because her mom would "visibly not be feeling okay or be too scared." At such times Maricela "wouldn't go anywhere" and might miss class or work to stay home and comfort her mom.

The stressors associated with family legal vulnerability piled atop the existing academic stressors of college, pushing immigration-impacted students to question their academic pursuits. Carolina Aguilar, a US citizen student, described feeling a kind of survivor's guilt because her loved ones face the threat of deportation and she does not; her mother was deported, and Carolina worries a good deal about her undocumented aunt and uncle, to whom she is close. She explained:

> Whenever I would hear about [the struggles of my aunt and uncle] . . . when it does slip out, or when I could see it, it makes me feel stressed. I'm sitting at a computer all day, while they're stressing about [their deportability]. And their issues seem huge. And I'm just here. . . . Sometimes in class, sitting in nice air conditioning. I don't know, I start comparing situations, and I just feel stressed, and I feel hopeless, and I feel like I'm not doing anything.

Reckoning with guilty feelings made Carolina unsure if she should stay in school, and she was aware that her anxiety was making it difficult to get the most out of that privilege: "And academically, I think it just adds more stress. Because school's already stressful. And the emotional stress of knowing what they're going through makes it worse." Other immigration-impacted students also expressed this form of survivor's guilt—the distress of comparing their situation to those of their more legally vulnerable family members. The stress of family legal vulnerability intertwined with such feelings and, combined with general academic stressors, prompting students to question the purpose of their educational pursuits.

Taken as a whole, our findings indicate that family legal vulnerability conditions a chronic stress response among immigration-impacted students and sometimes an even more elevated trauma response. These stressors have cascading consequences not only for immigration-impacted students' mental health and well-being (see chapter 2) but also for their academic engagement. These cognitive disruptions and academic distractions can be thought of as downstream consequences that dampen students' ability to focus on their academics and stay engaged in their education.

Paying for College: Unpacking Family Financial Strain

Money is a persistent barrier for low-income students' college success. Sociologist Sara Goldrick-Rab followed 3,000 young adults who entered public colleges and universities in Wisconsin in 2008 with the support of federal financial aid; she found that half left without a degree and less than 20 percent finished within five years.[8] This is because students from low-income backgrounds struggle to stretch their financial resources to cover tuition, school materials, and living expenses while also straining to effectively balance work and academics.[9] We found that immigration-impacted students' efforts to pay for college are similarly constrained because of the low incomes that characterize most undocumented and mixed-status households, with consequently similar effects for their college experiences and academic outcomes.

Chapter 1 introduced the concept of *cascading consequences*, as immigration-impacted students helped their families manage chronic financial strain by seeking out employment when they became old enough to work. Their efforts helped address family financial strain in two ways. First, they contributed wages to the household income, helping to move their families away from chronic insecurity. Second, they limited the financial demands they personally placed on parents' limited incomes; this means they either worked to cover their own expenses or went without. These two management strategies foreshadow the cascading consequences of family financial strain on students' college careers. Specifically, family financial strain compromised students' academics as they sought to maintain enrollment, invest time in their academic success, and afford educational materials.

Securing Financial Aid to Maintain Enrollment

Attending college and maintaining continuous enrollment creates an additional family financial burden that often rests almost exclusively on the shoulders of immigration-impacted students themselves. Unlike the average parent in the United States who covers roughly half the cost of college for children through income, savings, and loans,[10] immigration-impacted students cannot always rely on parents for financial support or help navigating the complex financial aid process. Although traditional college students are expected to be dependents who are financially supported by parents, the immigration-impacted students we spoke to were largely responsible for funding their own college expenses. Bianca Mercado, a twenty-two-year-old fourth-year student attending UC Riverside, captured this when she said: "It was me being on top of everything, my tuition, my financial aid. . . . I never asked [for my parents' help]. And I feel like that stems from growing up knowing our financial situation, that there was no money available."

Californian undocumented students like Bianca qualify for in-state tuition rates and state and institutional financial aid due to their long-term residency and prior education within California. At the University of California they receive financial aid packages equivalent to their US citizen peers, although they must complete additional paperwork such as filing an out-of-state tuition waiver and completing a California Dream Act application. While US citizen students with undocumented parents are eligible for federal financial aid, they also must figure out how to report their parents' lack of a social security number and complicated employment and tax histories on the Free Application for Federal Student Aid (FAFSA). Immigration-impacted students must successfully navigate these processes to secure necessary financial aid, without which they would have no other choice but to temporarily stop attending or permanently drop out.[11]

In rare cases, financial aid was generous enough to cover most if not all college- and living-related expenses. Belinda Avila, a 21-year-old student with DACA, experienced this. She confessed:

> I still don't know how to apply for the loans [laughs]. But that's just because I've never had to apply for loans. Because the financial aid covered

everything. They even gave me extra money. So it was just really good.
I'm really happy with that. I'm not in debt.

For most students, however, financial aid awards were not sufficient to
cover the total cost of college. Many had to cobble together funding for
tuition, fees, books, and living expenses from several different sources,
which often varied from one year to the next.[12] Camila Rios Echeverria,
a 21-year-old US citizen, relied on multiple sources of funding that were
provided by the university and a corporate-sponsored scholarship. She
explained:

> I'm a financial aid recipient, so I feel like that covers a lot of my expenses,
> like tuition, books, housing, all of that. I also have work-study, so I do
> part-time jobs at school. So I cover college expenses through a combina-
> tion of financial aid, work-study, and also scholarships. I was able to get a
> lot of small scholarships my senior year in high school and then, I got one
> big scholarship that I still use until this day. And they guarantee twenty-
> thousand dollars for your entire undergraduate education and that was
> a big part of being able to pay for school because whatever financial aid
> didn't cover, that scholarship did cover. So thankfully, to this day, I've
> been able to pay for school through financial aid and scholarships.

Though Belinda's and Camila's financial aid experiences were relatively
pain-free, for others the financial aid was inadequate, requiring time and
attention to figure out how to pay for college so as to maintain continuous enrollment. In less inclusionary state contexts where state financial
aid and/or in-state tuition waivers are not available, undocumented students struggle even more to cover the costs associated with pursuing
higher education.

Given the critical importance of financial aid awards, immigration-
impacted students found the application and verification process extremely stressful. Both undocumented students and US citizens with
undocumented parents lamented the difficulties associated with providing parents' income and tax information on required forms. Lucia
Ortega, a DACA recipient, expressed her dismay at not only having to
fill out the California Dream Act application the first time, which was

"already pretty stressful," but also being one of the unfortunate few who were audited to verify the information provided:

> We got selected for random verification and we had to send all this extra information. I know that they do that with FAFSA students as well but usually around the people I know, it's mostly lower income people and a lot of times it's people who are doing the [California] Dream Act [application]. I just find it unfair because financial aid is already stressful plus all the documents [I needed to collect and submit] to confirm it.

For Lucia and other undocumented students, the anxiety associated with the responsibility of securing financial aid was a unique "extra struggle," one they often felt they were navigating alone.

If parents or siblings were able to assist financially, students might enlist their help to close the financial aid gap. These families had sufficient material resources to include college and living expenses as part of the overall household economy, even as students acknowledged that doing so resulted in a significant drain on their collective family resources. Julia Soto, a US citizen student with undocumented parents, explained the process this way:

> I think I was very fortunate because I was able to get the Pell Grant. I qualified for a lot of the financial aid that was offered through FAFSA. So my first year, my tuition was paid for, but the dorms were not covered. My parents would give, I think they started giving about $900 a month for my rent, which was on top of their [$1,200/month] rent.

Though Julia was grateful that her parents were able to cover on-campus housing, she was mindful that the dorms were almost as expensive as her parents' rent.

Zoe Duenas Urias, a DACA recipient with undocumented parents, relied on her father and eldest brother to help with housing costs:

> I lived my first three years at the dorms and I think last year it was $17,000 give or take. And the school gave me, I think $10,000 or $11,000 in grants. And then the rest I paid, well my dad and my brother would pay. I wasn't

scared of not being able to pay because I knew if push came to shove, I do have three brothers and my dad that would come in and pay, but it's still always that, you don't want to ask for money. Especially for my second brother, for him, I don't ask for money.

Zoe explained that her oldest brother earned an engineering degree from another UC campus, so he was both supportive of her attending college and able to "really help me financially." She said that her family is "all very helpful toward each other," but she preferred not to ask for money from her second oldest brother, who was less stable financially. That said, she planned to help her younger sister through college. She concluded: "That's something that my parents always told us: 'If you're doing better off than one of your siblings, try to help them.'"

Juggling Work and School with Limited Time

With families in precarious financial situations, immigration-impacted students often worked to make money to cover expenses. Their employment commitments became a drain on the time they had available to invest in their academic success. Adrian stated: "When my family situation was bad financially, I had to spend more time working than studying. So there'll be times I'll miss a lecture or two just because things were bad." As students faced mounting individual and family expenses, they struggled to balance academics with attempts to earn more money. Juggling work and school almost always had negative effects on students' academic engagement by limiting the time they had to invest in their own academic success.

Cascading consequences associated with working negatively shaped students' academic performance as well, and this was especially true for those students whose financial needs were greatest. In moments of extreme financial duress, students often had no other choice but to prioritize work over academics. Maribel Aranda, a DACA recipient and fifth-year business major, spoke wistfully about the missed opportunity to excel academically because of work. She wondered: "Maybe I could have performed better [if] I didn't have to worry about working, but I guess we'll never know." She connected her modest academic performance to immigration policy because her financial aid was only enough "to just stay" in college rather than what she needed to flourish.

Benjamin Ponce, a US citizen, was clear-eyed about the toll that working throughout his undergraduate years took on his academic performance and time to earn a degree:

> I'd be very exhausted when I had to shift to college mode whether that be doing homework super late at night after work or trying to complete homework on the weekends after a shift. There were times that working and getting my own income on the side to cover my expenses during my college years affected my GPA.

For students like Benjamin, working compromised their study time and ability to complete assignments. He concluded that working to cover his educational expenses was a "burden" that "affected my grades for sure." It also shaped the courses he could fit into his work schedule, impacting his ability to complete his degree in the expected four years. He added:

> [Working] did affect which classes I could take because if they weren't at night or at certain times throughout the day, I wasn't able to take them because I couldn't take time off of work to take those classes. Working and trying to cover my own expenses during college did affect how fast I progressed through college and also my performance. There were some semesters I was like, "Man, this is not a good semester." And then there was other semesters where I could only take one or two classes because I had to work and there weren't any classes offered that semester that were fitting with my work schedule.

For many immigration-impacted students, the costs of college fell disproportionately on them, and they struggled to pay for their college careers while also engaging in them.

Moreover, family financial strain motivated some students to live at home to save money. These students cut costs associated with rent and food, but the trade-off with academics can be steep. Living at home, they confront greater pressure and responsibilities, including taking care of siblings, engaging in activities to protect or advocate for undocumented parents, and helping around the house. Mateo Olivares Galvan, a DACA recipient, lived in the dorms his first year in college but then decided to move back home, roughly forty-five minutes from campus, to save money. His calculations failed to account for increased family responsibilities:

> Now that I live back home my family responsibilities definitely increased, but some of those responsibilities are like, help taking my mom to the hospital or taking my mom to get her medication or to the grocery store when my dad comes late or taking my little brother to these school programs. And sometimes that takes away . . . even in summer school, that could take a toll on my schooling because I have these assignments, but I know I also want to be there for my family.

These responsibilities took a toll on Mateo's grades. After he moved home, he was placed on academic probation. While he was able to recover, he said—referring to his time in college—that he struggled with imposter syndrome and "always sort of had this financial and career burden that hasn't allowed me to always focus fully on my academics." Like Mateo, Santiago Zaragoza Zamora, a US citizen with undocumented parents, also made the decision to leave the dorms for home to save money. He recalled: "My first year I would say it was extremely tough just because I lived in the dorms the first year. So there was that added expense. So I ended up taking out, I think, three loans." Unfortunately, moving home necessitated commuting by bus at 5 a.m. to avoid the exorbitant parking fees; this ultimately affected his academic performance and engagement. He explained:

> I did start commuting and I tried to work full time in that first quarter, so it was really hard to balance it. Emotionally I was drained because, you know, going back and forth from school in my second year. Also with that, it's the stress of trying to help out my parents. And then I guess, mentally, as well it was draining, sometimes there were nights where I had to stay up all night just to study before tests because I didn't feel prepared. So there's those struggles.

At one point, he missed a "heavily graded" exam when his bus was late, "so, I mean, I had to drop the class soon after." For students like Mateo and Santiago, the difficult decision to save money by moving home often resulted in unintended consequences like commuting or increased family responsibilities that affected their academic performance.

Students who lived on or near campus but attended college close to home also felt a responsibility to relieve their parents' burdens by taking on family responsibilities. They also found themselves expending time that might otherwise have gone to studying. Ava Cornejo, a US citizen student, said:

> I do still feel that pressure to come back almost every weekend to just see what's going on. If not, my mom would call like, "Hey can you come help your sister with her homework?" and "Oh, she's struggling." It's like, you do have your time that you dedicate to studying [at home]. But at the same time, it's like you hear your mom cooking and you want to help her. Like you hear your dad doing something and you just kind of want to help him or help my sister.

Ultimately, the responsibilities she felt toward her family negatively affected her GPA: "I did not pass my classes last semester because things at home were really tough."

Notably, family responsibilities could easily span distance through technology. Mateo recalled pressure to help his younger sister in school:

> I did have to help out my little sister with the homework a lot. . . . She would send me pictures of her homework and stuff. But that's kind of been ongoing. And I felt like I kind of expected that. But it's pretty tough when you're in class and your sister's like bugging you, like, "I need to turn this in tomorrow."

These examples illuminate how students' efforts to protect their time were compromised when family responsibilities took precedence and academics suffered.

Prioritizing Family Financial Support Over Educational Materials

Though some families might support students with modest financial contributions, for most the collective financial situation did not make this possible. Many students avoided asking for help altogether because they knew their families could not provide this material support. Indeed, some students were giving their families money, often to the detriment of their own ability to afford educational materials.

In the face of strained family finances, parents sometimes turned to their college-going children to help with expenses. Camila Rios Echeverria, a US citizen, admitted that her undocumented parents have on occasion "asked for a little bit of money to pay the rent" and $3,000 for the lawyer who was helping her mother secure a green card. Though she was able to cover these expenses—"thankfully, through whatever job I was working at, I could afford to help them out"—she admitted that "it hurt a little bit, just because I had to think about whether I am going to struggle to pay for books." Likewise, Gael Yepez Correa remarked that his parents "depend on me paying most of their bills throughout the month with my own money and then reimbursing me like, pretty later, later on." Most commonly, students volunteered to provide financial support to their families, making the difficult zero-sum decision to contribute time and money toward their family's financial security rather than their own educations.

Many students reported that their efforts to mitigate family financial strain by contributing to the household economy resulted in personal food insecurity. Gabriel Ballón, a DACA recipient, explained that his family needed him to come home during the weekends to help with their landscaping business. At first, this shared expectation of work was perceived as mutually beneficial because he "needed the money and they needed help." However, this collective financial arrangement pulled Gabriel away from campus on weekends and did not provide enough money to cover his basic needs on campus during the week. He recalled:

> In college it was like, shit, how am I going to pay for food, how am I going to buy my books, gas, and parking? Yeah, it was a lot . . . They say like freshman in college you gain some weight, but honestly, I think I hardly gained any weight because I hardly ate because it was like, "Damn, I can only eat this today because I don't have enough money for that." And if I do [have enough], I'll eat this [part] and save it for tomorrow.

For many students like Gabriel, their contributions to cash-strapped families were prompted by an understanding that their families' financial situations were indistinguishable from their own.

The food insecurity that resulted from students' financial trade-offs led them to struggle academically. Julia Soto explained how it was "just sometimes being hungry" that caused her academic strain:

> I wouldn't think about being hungry. I would just go to sleep. I would just be like, "You know what? Not today." I would just go to sleep, but if I went to sleep, obviously I couldn't study, I couldn't do my readings and then that meant being unprepared the next day. And when you have a small class, that's the worst thing because then you have to partner-share or sometimes you're asked [to answer a question] out of nowhere. And then I wouldn't attend those classes; I would be like: You know what? I'm not prepared. Why am I going to sit there if I'm not even going to understand the lesson?

Julia experienced cascading consequences from personal food insecurity that ultimately compromised her ability to pass her classes.

Others were unable to afford educational materials, which also affected their studies. Lucia Ortega, a DACA recipient, admitted: "I've had to drop classes because the class required several books that were pretty expensive that I couldn't find online, or they were just not the right version, or things like that. I just had to drop it so that I don't have to spend the money on it." The cost of an up-to-date, reliable computer was also a challenge. Sylvia Molina Santoyo, a DACA recipient, identified going without a computer as her biggest challenge all through high school and her first two years of college at a community college. After transferring to the UC system, she used a loaner computer, but when she had to return it she only could afford a tablet. She explained: "I remember it was always a struggle because teachers and professors would sometimes assign online homework and it was difficult for me because sometimes, I had a computer, but I didn't have wi-fi at home. To this day, I still go to the library." The tough choices these students made under precarious financial circumstances compromised their ability to do well in classes and risked setting them back in meeting graduation requirements or completing certain majors.

All in all, family financial strain associated with family legal vulnerability culminates in several cascading consequences that adversely affect immigration-impacted students' college experiences and academic outcomes. They stress about securing sufficient financial aid to maintain enrollment, struggle to balance work and school commitments, and feel pressure to prioritize financial contributions to families. While they find ways to make ends meet, they are haunted by the academic trade-offs: reduced attention spans, less study time, limited academic engagement, and poor performance. Notably, other low-income students likely share similar academic strains if they do not receive sufficient financial aid or face similar family financial demands. However, their own and their parents' lawful statuses may increase their eligibility for or willingness to access resources—such as loans, campus resources, or supplemental nutrition programs—to mitigate such strains.

Skirting the Edges: Competing Responsibilities, Social Exclusion, and the Costs to Campus Life

Immigration-impacted students shared that they sometimes limited their time or engagement on campus, leading them to experience social exclusion. As discussed in chapter 1, avoiding or withdrawing from events and activities helped to minimize the risks of exposing themselves and/or family members to legal vulnerabilities including deportation and family separation. Social isolation also served as a strategy to save money; extracurricular activities require disposable income. While social exclusion may thus be protective, it is not always a self-imposed, direct response to family legal vulnerability. It can also be a result of the competing responsibilities imposed by family legal vulnerability and limited time available to participate in campus life. Indeed, we find that immigration-impacted students confronted social exclusion as a cascading consequence of family legal vulnerability that threatened their ability to capitalize on their education and pursue postcollege mobility.

Missed Connections and Thin Social Networks

As they prioritize work and family responsibilities, students must limit the time they spend on campus, compromising their ability to build meaningful connections with faculty and peers. For Clara Dominguez, her campus schedule limited her ability to attend office hours or socialize with classmates (apart from a standing lunch date and walk). As an undocumented fourth-year transfer student who lived at home, Clara started her campus commute at 5 a.m. to make an 8 a.m. class, followed by two more classes. During lunch she visited with "the one friend that I have for my third class—that was my company." Following lunch, she attended a final class before leaving for home at 3 p.m. This compressed schedule was related directly to her need to commute and work, and Clara was aware that it constrained her social interactions, her ability to attend instructors' office hours, and her opportunities to participate in extracurricular activities. Given such a schedule, the likeliest time for her to attend office hours would have been after 3 p.m., but the prospect of hitting traffic just to talk to a professor at 5 p.m. was daunting. She also was working in the evenings. Clara further explained that, due to her commute, busy class schedule, and the difficult transition from her community college's semester system to the quarter system, "I didn't have the time to join a club or something like that, or even to use the rec center, or the gym. . . . I always wanted to go to the undocumented student center, and I didn't have time. I would love to go." She admitted that she felt "sad" and "bad" about missed opportunities: "I didn't do anything [in the way of extracurriculars], and I really feel bad, I should have." When asked to explain why she felt this way, she shared: "Because I didn't get to meet more people, more people to have memories, good memories, to share something with people in the rest of the UC Riverside community." Many immigration-impacted students who make it to class but have time for little else on campus feel that they had missed out.

Over time students realized that their social isolation might compromise their postgraduation plans. Valentino Peña, a US citizen with undocumented parents, had just finished his fourth year when we interviewed him. He confessed that, for most of his time in college, he never met with his instructors or participated in discussions with students or faculty after class. Instead, he admitted how "I've been more focused on my job and making sure I'm financially stable within that sense." He planned to apply to law school but decided first to take a year off to improve the competitiveness of his application, including securing letters of recommendation. Somewhat anxiously, he acknowledged that he needed the extra time to become "more used to building relationships with my professors." He conceded that his reticence to engage in relationship-building with faculty and students was at least in part rooted in "the trade-off of being a first-gen student," which required him to "give up some things to get other things."

The costs associated with rushing through college without taking the time to build social relationships and professional networks could also hinder students' career prospects. As a US citizen with undocumented parents, Paloma Montoya reflected on the limits of her undocumented family members' ability to help with career preparation and planning:

> All of [my family] work in manual labor, construction, and gardening, and being seamstresses. They've never worked in an office or anything like that, in my immediate family, there's no one I can turn to. And professional connections? I don't have any professional connections.

Paloma's realization reflects the reality of many immigration-impacted students and the Latino second generation in general. In her study of young adult Latino children of immigrants, sociologist Maria Rendón shows how thin social networks lead to class convergence; specifically, the children of Latino immigrants turn to their working-class social networks to find employment, negating the potential boost a college education can play in one's job prospects.[13] For many participants, limited social engagement on campus prevented them from diversifying their social networks. Paloma, for example, faltered in her response when asked about professors or classmates to whom she might turn for such advice or guidance: "No, I don't have—It's not—No, it's not like—I'm not on a—I can't reach out to anyone for help, for professional help. If I wanted to ask for advice on [job] interviews from other students, or from students who had already graduated, there's really no one I can ask."

Students like Clara, Valentino, and Paloma realized the importance of building social networks while at college late in their college careers. They had been largely unaware of this aspect of the "hidden curriculum," or the unspoken cultural norms and values of the mainstream.[14] Arranging tight class schedules left little room for co-curricular or extracurricular activities, including attending office hours, participating in professional development opportunities, building relationships with professors and classmates, or socializing with friends. Ultimately, such trade-offs can diminish immigration-impacted students' academic performance, college experiences, and postgraduate career opportunities.

Making Time for High-Impact Opportunities

Internships and research experiences offer critical opportunities to build social networks, develop marketable skills, and pursue career-related experiences. Educational researchers refer to these as "high-impact educational practices" because they offer significant educational benefits to participants, especially those who are traditionally underserved by higher education.[15] Indeed, research suggests that undocumented students' participation in professional development opportunities facilitates their successful career transitions.[16] Recognizing the challenges posed by legal vulnerability to future mobility, several participants sought out high-impact opportunities to compensate for and overcome such constraints. But participation in such opportunities was itself conditioned on whether they could find the time to do so given the collective constraints of family legal vulnerability in the first place.

Undocumented students in particular sought to acquire additional skills that would help them overcome limitations associated with individual legal vulnerability. For example, Violeta Perez, a DACA recipient, was working in an internship at the campus women's resource center. She described the internship as helping her prepare for a future career in nursing but also said that she participates in such activities to compensate for her immigration status:

> I'm always trying to make plans on getting my life together and figuring out little backup plans if something doesn't work out, which comes from being always on temporary status. I have one plan and I have another plan just in case the first plan doesn't work out. I'm just trying to be positive, and trying to be like, "Oh yeah! This is what I'm excited for in the future."

For students like Violeta, the vulnerability that comes from being undocumented—whether or not they have the temporary benefits of

DACA—drives them to seek out professional development opportunities to enhance their competitiveness in the labor market.

For others, participating in an internship program could open the door to graduate school. Sabrina Soriano Trejo, another DACA recipient, participated in a paid internship opportunity at the career center to strengthen her skill set, earn a bit of money, and secure a letter of recommendation from the director. She explained:

> The most impactful part of my internship was my relationship with the career counselor overseeing my internship. He wrote the letters of recommendation for my graduate program. I'm very shy like I said, so I don't go to office hours or anything like that. So I was always really scared of applying to grad school and not having that letter of recommendation. So connecting with him was very awesome.

Like Sabrina, immigration-impacted students often engaged in internship or research opportunities to increase their chances of being admitted to graduate or professional school. Importantly, Violeta and Sabrina were able to make time for their internships because they received financial compensation. However, such paid opportunities are few and far between, especially for those without work authorization. While many students reported finding unpaid opportunities, their individual and family financial strain often prevented them from being able to take these; for most, forgoing paid work was simply not an option if they wished to stay afloat.

US citizen students with undocumented parents also sought out professional development opportunities to improve their career outlook as well as the circumstances of their parents and larger community. Rubén Huerta-Diaz, a US citizen, initially sought out an internship at a nonprofit organization to hone his professional writing skills, his knowledge of civic engagement, and to "become a more competitive applicant for grad school." He added that his internship was also for "unselfish reasons—to help members of my community." He shared that his internship had unexpectedly turned into a job. He planned to prepare for graduate school, help his parents "with their papers," and pursue his newfound purpose of "helping members of my community" while

continuing in the job. Though participating in professional development is a positive form of academic engagement, it remains rooted in
the collective constraints of family legal vulnerability; as such, not all
immigration-impacted students had the opportunity to participate in
similar opportunities.

In sum, immigration-impacted students' attempts to cope with challenges related to family legal vulnerability may prompt self-imposed
social exclusion. Some may choose to save money by living at home
rather than in the dorms or in an off-campus apartment with roommates, thereby increasing social isolation. Others may prioritize their
contributions to family finances or responsibilities at home, thereby limiting their time on campus and forgoing opportunities to deepen social
networks and engage in professional development opportunities. In centering the safety and financial security of their families, social exclusion
can become a necessary concession for immigration-impacted students
to persist in higher education. However, simultaneously it compromises
academic performance and engagement.

Academic Disparities: Comparing Immigration-Impacted Students to Peers

Thus far we have traced how family legal vulnerability unleashes a
myriad of cascading consequences as immigration-impacted students
find their attention and resources drawn away from academics. We
turn now to our quantitative survey data to determine if these experiences contribute to unequal outcomes. Specifically, we compare the
academic outcomes of undocumented students and US citizen students with undocumented parents to US citizen students with lawfully
present parents. Regression analyses consider to what extent these two
groups of immigration-impacted students differ from their peers and
whether family legal vulnerability explains any disparities. We examine
four measures—*low GPA, course failure, academic engagement,* and *participation in professional development opportunities*—that represent both
short- and long-term outcomes that have implications for retention and
postcollege success. Appendix C provides full details on the regression
models.

Low GPA

Grade point average, which is the sum of course grades divided by the total number of credits, is a widely used measure of student academic achievement. Low GPA can be understood as a long-term measure of compromised academic performance, as poor performance must accumulate over multiple courses and terms. This matters because poor grades can influence persistence, with GPAs below 2.0 prompting academic probation and ineligibility for most university scholarships. Further, employers and admissions officers perceive GPA as an indicator of success in graduate and professional school as well as in the workforce. A recent survey of employers indicated that almost one-quarter planned to screen job applicants by college GPA, with a cutoff of 3.0, the equivalent of a B average.[17]

Descriptive analysis suggests that immigration-impacted students' GPAs are lower than those of US citizen students with lawfully present parents. Figure 3.1 presents descriptive characteristics of students' cumulative GPA. US citizen students with lawfully present parents were less likely to report low GPAs and more likely to report higher GPAs than immigration-impacted students. Whereas 11 percent of undocumented students and 12 percent of US citizens with undocumented parents reported a cumulative GPA below 2.5, only 7 percent of US citizens with lawfully present parents did so. By contrast, almost 30 percent of US citizen students with lawfully present parents reported a GPA above 3.5, compared to 24 percent of US citizen students with undocumented parents and 23 percent of undocumented students.

Regression analyses revealed that, after controlling for demographic characteristics, immigration-impacted students have a higher likelihood of having a low GPA than US citizen students with lawfully present parents. This is indicated in Figure 3.2, which graphs the predicted probability of having a low GPA after controlling for demographics (i.e., at baseline). However, the only statistically significant difference is between US citizen students with undocumented parents and those with lawfully present parents. Prior research by sociologists Amy Hsin and Holly Reed has established undocumented college students' hyperselectivity, suggesting

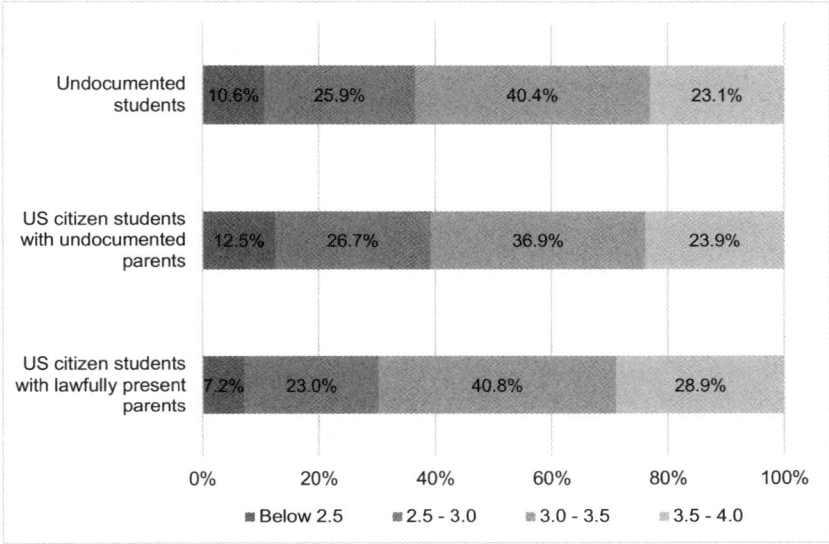

Figure 3.1. GPA of survey respondents by self and parental immigration status.

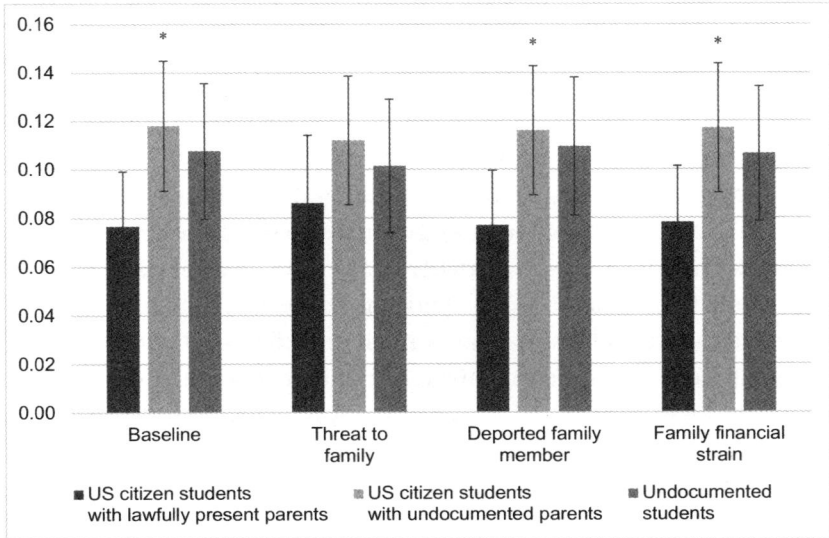

Figure 3.2. Predicted probability of having a low GPA when controlling for family legal vulnerability.
NOTE: Statistically significant differences from the reference group are indicated by * when p<.05.

that a lack of difference between them and their US citizen peers with lawfully present parents may be explained by their greater academic preparation.[18]

With this in mind, we considered the role family legal vulnerability may play in driving group differences in GPA. Specifically, we examined whether group differences in GPA changed as we accounted for three dimensions of family legal vulnerability: *immigration-related threats to family, having a family member who had been deported,* and *family financial strain.* This sequential modeling approach allowed us to see whether and how unique conditions associated with family legal vulnerability shape immigration-impacted students' academic profiles relative to their peers who do not experience these same stressors. Figure 3.2 graphs the predicted probability of having a low GPA when controlling for each dimension of family legal vulnerability. Comparing each model to baseline allows us to determine whether each dimension of family legal vulnerability contributes to academic disparities.

We find that perceiving threats to family due to the exclusionary immigration policy context is an important driver of low GPA among immigration-impacted students. This measure broadly captures the threat of deportation alongside a range of interrelated policy threats by assessing how frequently participants worried about the impact immigration policies have on them or their family, feared that they or a family member would be reported to immigration officials, and worried about family separation. Once we accounted for this perceived threat, we saw a decrease in the probability of having a low GPA among both undocumented students and US citizens with undocumented parents. The decrease was substantial enough among US citizens with undocumented parents to eliminate statistically significant differences between them and their peers with lawfully present parents. This suggests that, if immigration-impacted students did not experience the burden of immigration policy threat, they would be no less likely to have a low GPA than their US-born peers with lawfully present parents. Accounting for whether a student had an immediate or extended family member who was deported and family financial strain did not explain group differences in low GPA.

Failed a Course

Failing a course can be understood as an indicator of short-term compromised academic performance within a specific school term. Descriptive results indicate that almost half of undocumented students (47 percent) reported ever having failed a course, which is higher than the proportion of US citizen students with undocumented parents (at 42 percent) and those with lawfully present parents (38 percent) (see figure 3.3). There is almost a 10 percentage point difference in failing a course between undocumented students and US citizen students with lawfully present parents. This reinforces our interview findings, in which many immigration-impacted students shared that they had failed a course or been placed on academic probation.

Figure 3.4 displays the predicted probability of course failure across the three student groups. The left-most set of bars compares the three student groups at baseline. It reveals that undocumented students had a statistically significant higher likelihood of course failure on average compared to their US citizen peers regardless of parents' status. As with GPA,

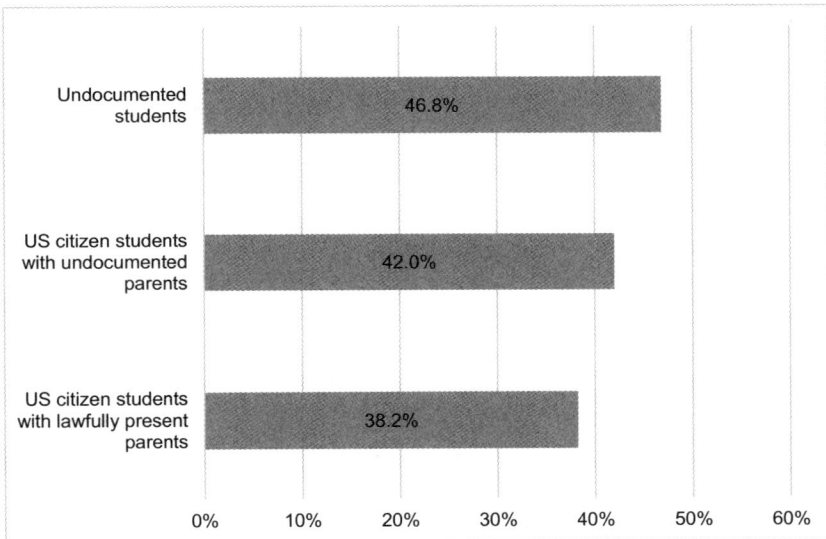

Figure 3.3. Course failure of survey respondents by self and parental immigration status.

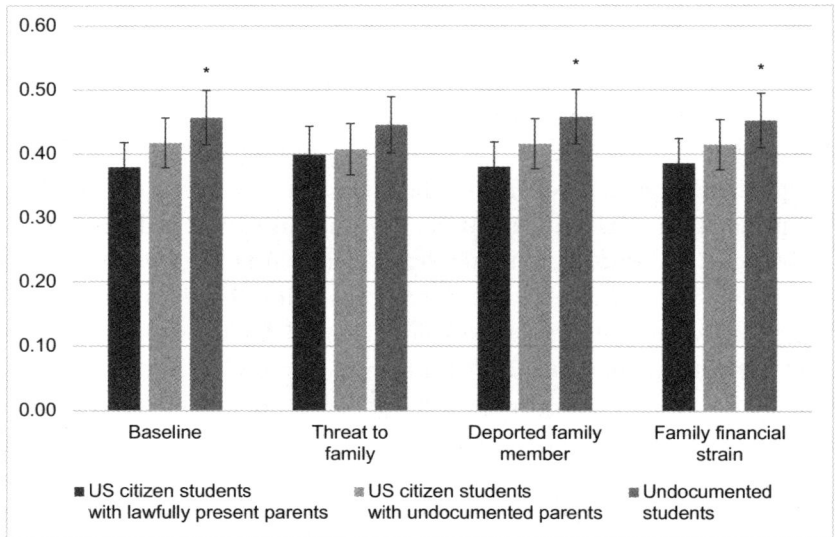

Figure 3.4. Predicted probability of course failure when controlling for family legal vulnerability.
NOTE: Statistically significant differences from the reference group are indicated by * when p<.05.

accounting for perceived threats to family due to exclusionary immigration policy was the only dimension of family legal vulnerability to decrease the probability of failing a course among both undocumented students and US citizens with undocumented parents. The decrease was substantial enough for undocumented students to eliminate statistically significant differences between them and their peers with lawfully present parents. These findings underscore the extensive reach of deportability and threats of family separation into students' academic lives to the point that it compromises their long- and short-term performance.

Academic Engagement

Academic engagement signifies the extent to which students are absorbed in class-related activities and is associated with academic achievement.[19] Academic engagement can be negative—that is, students may be disengaged academically, which may be evident in skipping class; or positively engaged, such as by contributing to class discussions. Because negative and positive academic engagement capture different and unique aspects of dis/engagement (rather than the presence or absence of the same behavior), we investigate these two aspects separately.[20]

Immigration-impacted students appear to have elevated levels of negative academic engagement. Figure 3.5 displays the mean negative engagement scores by self and parental immigration status; undocumented students and US citizens with undocumented parents reported a mean of 1.29, compared to 1.20 for US citizens with lawfully present parents. This is equivalent to responding either rarely (1) or sometimes (2) to three actions: failed to turn in a course assignment, attended class unprepared, and skipped class.

Figure 3.6 compares the mean scores of the three student groups after controlling for demographic characteristics and family legal vulnerability. Findings show that, at baseline, US citizens with undocumented parents reported significantly higher levels of negative engagement than their peers with lawfully present parents. Notably, all three dimensions of family legal vulnerability—threat to family, the deportation of a family member, and family financial strain—decreased

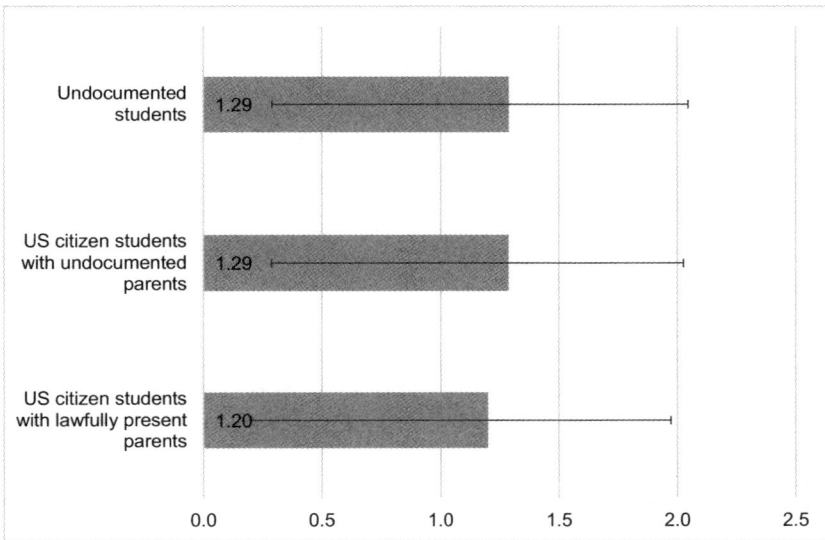

Figure 3.5. Mean negative academic engagement scores of survey respondents by self and parental immigration status.

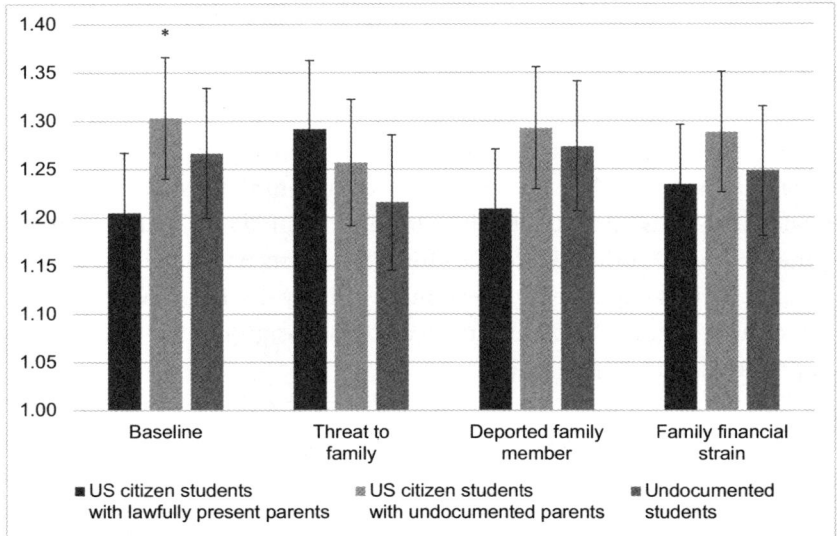

Figure 3.6. Predicted mean negative academic engagement scores when controlling for family legal vulnerability.
NOTE: Statistically significant differences from the reference group are indicated by * when p<.05.

negative academic engagement among US citizens with undocumented parents. This outcome may result from this student group being uniquely called upon to deploy their citizenship privilege on their parents' behalf to the point of pulling them away from academic tasks more frequently. Like the other academic outcomes, immigration-related threats to family had the most profound impact on eliminating differences, as it achieves the largest reduction in mean negative academic engagement scores for both US citizens with undocumented parents and for undocumented students.

Turning to a consideration of positive academic engagement, descriptive findings reveal that undocumented students reported slightly higher mean scores than their US citizen peers. Figure 3.7 displays the mean positive engagement scores by self and parental immigration status; undocumented students had a mean of 1.58 compared to a mean of 1.54 among US citizens with undocumented parents and 1.52 among US citizens with lawfully present parents. This is equivalent to responding rarely (1) and sometimes (2) to four actions: sought academic help from instructor or tutor when needed, studied with a group of classmates outside of class, contributed to a class discussion, and communicated with the instructor outside of class about issues and concepts derived from a course. Figure 3.8 compares the mean scores of the three student groups when controlling for demographic characteristics and family legal vulnerability. Findings show that, at baseline, undocumented students reported significantly higher levels of positive academic engagement than US citizen students with lawfully present parents.

Exploring the relationship further suggests that undocumented students' higher rates of positive engagement relative to other groups are explained by family legal vulnerability. Accounting for perceived threat to family reduces immigration-impacted students' positive engagement scores and eliminates statistically significant differences between undocumented students and US citizens with lawfully present parents (see figure 3.8). Further, controlling for family financial strain also eliminates statistically significant differences between undocumented students and their US-born peers with lawfully present parents. This suggests that immigration-impacted students' positive academic engagement,

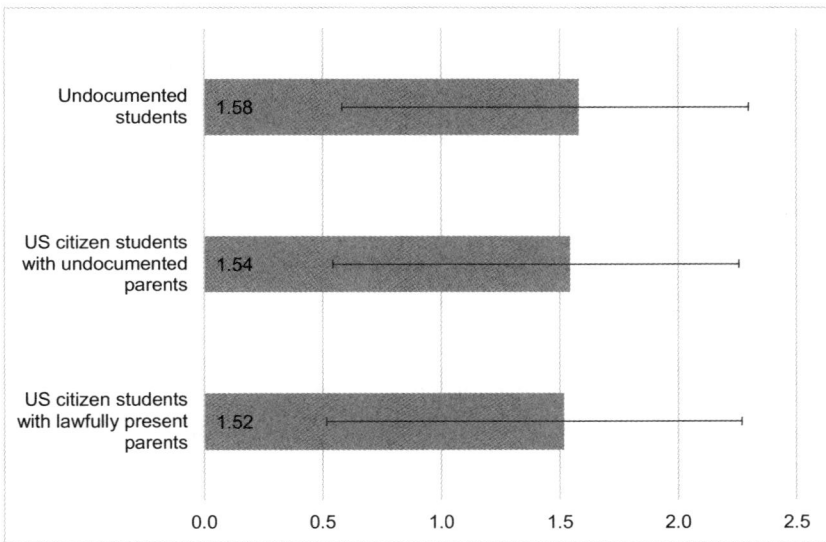

Figure 3.7. Mean positive academic engagement scores of survey respondents by self and parental immigration status.

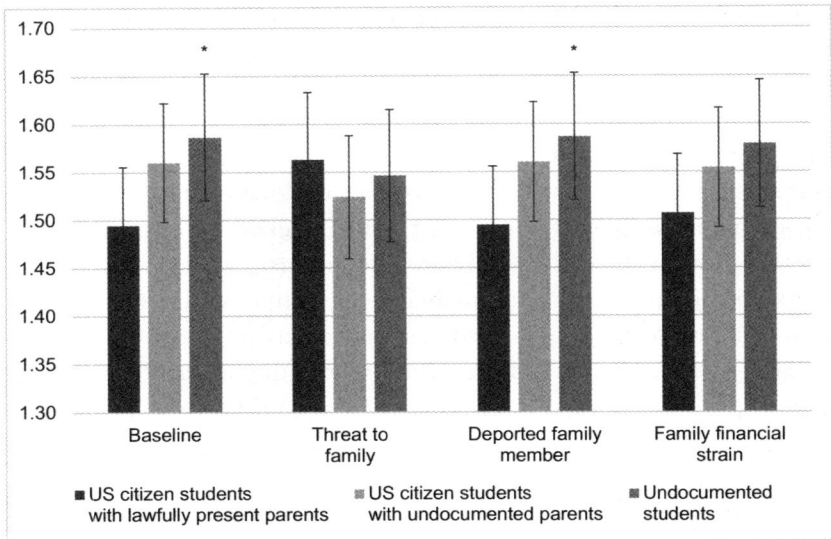

Figure 3.8. Predicted mean positive academic engagement scores when controlling for family legal vulnerability.
NOTE: Statistically significant differences from the reference group are indicated by * when p<.05.

particularly that of undocumented students, is linked to these two aspects of family legal vulnerability. It may be that they are seeking out additional support from faculty and peers to make up for the times in which family-related deportation concerns and financial considerations pulled them away from their studies.

Professional Development

Professional development is the final measure of academic engagement we assessed, which includes taking part in an unpaid or paid internship, credit-based internship, practicum, field experience, or career-relevant job. Figure 3.9 shows that undocumented students outperformed US citizen students on this measure; fully 45 percent reported participating in such activities, compared to 35 percent of US citizens with undocumented parents and 38 percent of US citizens with lawfully present parents. Figure 3.10 compares the predicted probability of participating

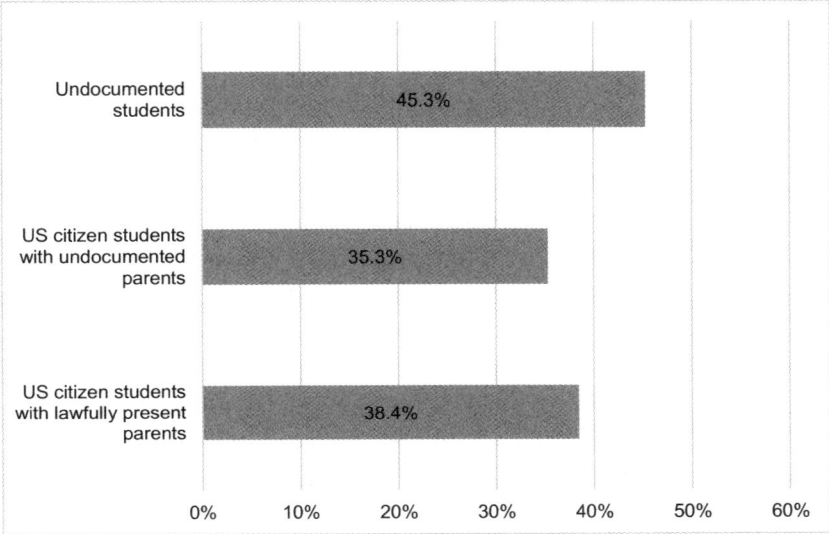

Figure 3.9. Professional development participation of survey respondents by self and parental immigration status.

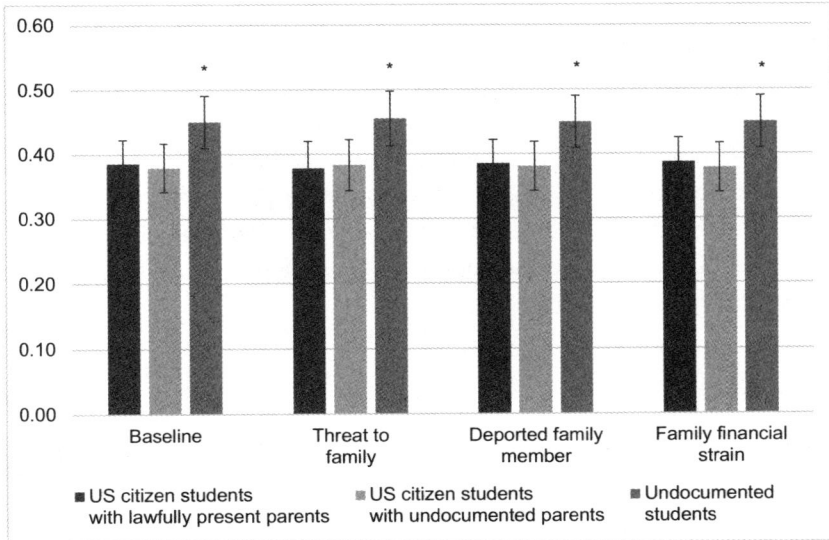

Figure 3.10. Predicted probability of professional development participation when controlling for family legal vulnerability.
NOTE: Statistically significant differences from the reference group are indicated by * when p<.05.

in a professional development opportunity across the three student groups when controlling for demographic characteristics and family legal vulnerability. Findings confirm that, at baseline, undocumented students have significantly higher likelihood of participating in one of these opportunities than their US citizen peers. Furthermore, this statistically significant difference is maintained even after accounting for all three dimensions of family legal vulnerability.

These findings suggest that undocumented students are more likely to participate in professional development opportunities than US citizen students with lawfully present parents. However, their reasons for doing so may have more to do with their own undocumented status than with family legal vulnerability, because controlling for family legal vulnerability does not alter their participation. This finding is reflected in our interview findings and prior research wherein undocumented students expressed a distinctive need to engage in professional development opportunities to counteract their individual legal vulnerability.[21]

In sum, our quantitative analysis provides ample support for the notion that family legal vulnerability influences the academic outcomes of immigration-impacted students. These students consistently have a greater likelihood of negative academic outcomes when compared to US citizen students with lawfully present parents. Further, perceived threat to family due to the immigration policy context consistently eliminates group differences, with the exception of undocumented students' persistent participation in professional development opportunities. Although undocumented students are more positively academically engaged than their US citizen counterparts, this seems driven by family legal vulnerability.

Conclusion

This chapter reveals that the collective constraints and cascading consequences associated with family legal vulnerability adversely affect academic outcomes. Interviews highlight how undocumented and US citizen students with undocumented parents frequently worry about the security and safety of their families while also taking on greater family responsibilities and often working for wages to help make ends meet. Such actions are necessary to sustain family security but simultaneously pull students' attention away from their academic journeys by compromising the time and energy they have to devote to academic success. Indeed, quantitative analyses illustrate the cost of family legal vulnerability on common markers of academic success. Reinforcing our findings regarding mental health in chapter 2, we find that perceived threats to family consistently explain immigration-impacted students' increased odds for lower academic performance and higher positive academic engagement. Further, family financial strain plays a significant role in explaining group differences in positive and negative engagement, speaking to the role of financial strain as both a motivating and constraining factor within immigration-impacted students' educations. Ultimately, these findings direct attention to the deep power that restrictive immigration policies and family legal vulnerability have over immigration-impacted students' academic lives.

4

"We're Trying for People That Can't"

Political Engagement

"I haven't gone [to a protest] because my parents, they don't want me to go. I really want to go, but . . . I don't know. I think some people feel more like they're free in terms of, 'I can go to a protest and my parents won't like it, but at the end of the day, they'll be okay with it.' Whereas with mine . . . they don't want me to go to a protest at all."
—Ava Cornejo

Ava had few memories of traversing the boundaries of her Los Angeles neighborhood when she was a child. Because of their fears of being detained—or even deported—Ava's undocumented parents always moved through their lives with caution. Though she and her family lived within driving distance to the beach, Ava didn't see the ocean until she was an undergraduate college student participating in an international internship program in Michoacán, Mexico.

Attending college, especially doing the coursework for her minor in Chicano/a and Central American Studies, showed Ava how immigration policies shaped her parents' lives and her own. She began to contemplate how political engagement could affect policy. As a US citizen, she knew that she had options for participating in the political life of this country when her parents did not. Because she knew that they would deeply disapprove of her participation in any kind of political protest, she began by voting.

For Ava, however, voting was more than an individual action at a ballot box. She wanted to include her parents in the electoral process through ongoing conversations. She regularly talked to her parents about issues on the ballot, especially those related to immigration, and how she planned to vote. She said: "I like to let them know what it is that

I'm voting for just to give them peace of mind. And just to know that, you know, people like me and you and other people are trying to make the difference here. We're really trying for people that can't."

Ava felt like her parents' undocumented status increased the stakes of her political participation, and she aspired to be more engaged to effect social change. Immigration laws and practices were not just something she learned about in the classroom; they defined the parameters of her family's life. In particular, the ever-looming threat of her parents' detention and deportation cast a shadow over her everyday life, with cascading consequences for her current and future actions. While in college, Ava joined the Chicanx/Latinx political advocacy group Movimiento Estudiantil Chicano de Aztlán (MEChA). She hesitated to participate in any large-scale political protests but instead looked for other ways to engage. She traveled to her parents' home state in Mexico for an internship offered through the Mexican government. The program was available to DACA recipients and Mexican American citizens who had undocumented parents or grandparents. It aimed to teach students about Mexican policies, particularly those related to migration, and the connections between the United States and Mexico. Soon after, she volunteered to work on a political campaign for a candidate running for a seat on the Board of Education for the Los Angeles Unified School District. The candidate had previously been undocumented, and she felt that their experience would provide the perspective needed to advocate for families like her own.

Although Ava was one of the most politically engaged of our participants, many were paying attention to the political landscape and participating in ways that they could. This chapter explores their political engagement, which was often a response to an anti-immigrant political climate. Students looked for ways to learn about political processes and to leverage their education for the public good. This motivation to engage was particularly salient during the years of Donald Trump's first presidential administration, when proposed and implemented restrictive and exclusionary immigration policies exacerbated feelings of individual and family legal vulnerability. Though the desire to address problems or concerns rooted in individual and family legal vulnerability often sparked political engagement, accumulating knowledge and emerging feelings of agency set the stage for greater political involvement. As with Ava, however, many hesitated to participate in protest activities due to family legal vulnerability. Our quantitative survey analysis examines the impact of such cascading consequences and reveals that, in general, immigration-impacted students reported more political engagement than their US citizen peers with lawfully present parents. This pattern strongly suggests that family legal vulnerability encouraged immigration-impacted students' political engagement, but it also confined that engagement, discouraging more risky forms of engagement.

Motivation to Engage: Political Threats and Restrictive Immigration Policies

Immigration-impacted students in our study were engaged in a variety of political issues, ranging from gun control to climate change to affordable textbooks. However, the majority placed at least some of their energy in political issues that directly affected the immigrant community. Our participants came of age during the first Trump administration, and most were attending high school during his 2016 presidential campaign. Many noted that his campaign and presidency were key to their political formation. Beginning in 2015, Trump campaigned on a platform that was anti-immigrant—promising to build a wall between the United States and Mexico, characterizing Mexican immigrants as drug dealers, criminals, and rapists, and announcing that he would ban migration from Muslim-majority countries.[1] In fact, beginning in January 2017, he used his executive power to try to ban migration from certain Muslim-majority countries, allocate money for a more robust border wall, expand the capacity of Immigration and Customs Enforcement for immigration raids, and eventually to rescind the DACA program. Family legal vulnerability—particularly the specter of deportation and social exclusion—began to loom more heavily in students' lives against the backdrop of Trump's unique brand of "legal violence."[2] Attentive to these growing personal and collective threats, both undocumented students and US citizen students with undocumented parents were motivated to engage politically.

As anti-immigrant rhetoric was fomented and the potential for increasingly restrictive immigration policies seemed imminent, immigration-impacted students were motivated to become politically involved to protect their families. Benjamin Ponce, a US citizen whose mother was a legal permanent resident and whose father was undocumented, framed his growing involvement as a response to his family's legal vulnerability during Trump's first presidential campaign. He recalled:

> [My family] did have times where we did want to speak out on certain issues and share our voice and whatnot. And one instance in particular was the first time that Donald Trump was running. He had a lot of language that was negative toward immigrant communities, and my parents recognized that. And they were like, well, what can we do to help the candidate that was running against him, that wasn't . . . bad-mouthing . . . immigrant communities? What can we do to help them?

Benjamin and his parents recognized a collective threat to their family's well-being, especially because his undocumented father was the household's main breadwinner. Thus, the financial strain of family separation would have been significant.[3]

Family legal vulnerability motivated all family members to want to become involved, but it also presented risks. As a US citizen and the person with the most security, Benjamin felt the obligation to act politically on his parents' behalf. He explained:

> Having immigrant parents, and me having someone in my family be directly affected by legislation that focuses on immigration, kind of encourages me to want to take more action in certain ways. So I think those [who] are just more affected directly tend to be the ones that take action, and I think that's just the case for me. My parents are affected by those laws. So that would encourage and push me to want to speak out within that realm.

Many participants expressed a motivation to engage on behalf of their families. Their political motivation was not individual; it was collective. This sense of responsibility to fight for their families' collective stability and well-being cascaded to encourage individual political participation.

Threatening political moments, like those endured under Trump's first presidential administration, inspired some students' initial forays into politics. Ignacio Padilla Cortes, a US citizen whose undocumented parents have Temporary Protected Status, was a first-year student living in the dorms during the fall of 2016, when Trump was elected. He was watching the votes come in on election night in disbelief alongside his dormmates. He remembered:

> Everybody was shocked that the racist, sexist person won. Who didn't really win [the popular vote], right, because of the electoral college or whatever. But we were just all stunned. And on my floor, it's an international floor, where it was mixed by international students and half US students. So it was, it was emotional. My RA [resident assistant], I remember her, she was undocumented. She got all of us into a little circle to all . . . just express our feelings. And just process what was happening. And I remember folks were just crying. They were just really upset. I was more like, Oh shit. I still couldn't believe it.

Ignacio recalled the collective shock at the results of the election but also his subsequent motivation to mobilize: "And then after that . . . you just heard like a crowd outside [on] the campus. And everybody just started joining it. And we just went all around the campus, just protesting. And I think that was my first ever kind of protest that I would join." Living in the dorms and having time to engage in student organizations opened opportunities for reflection and political participation in the wake of perceived threats. In this instance, Ignacio's dorm community, including his undocumented resident assistant, helped him to process his shock and emotions. The impromptu campus protest allowed him to join in a collective action when the threat, and his motivation, were fresh. That protest was Ignacio's first, but he would go on to become a community organizer. Notably, opportunities to turn motivation into engagement were more limited for students whose family legal vulnerability required them to work, live off campus, and/or commute.

Other immigration-impacted students who were already politically involved found that the threatening actions promised by the Trump administration shifted their advocacy to immigration politics. Belinda Avila, a DACA recipient, was a student intern for the Los Angeles nonprofit California Public Interest Research Group (CALPIRG), a nonpartisan organization whose goal is to build political engagement among college students. As an intern, Belinda helped to register people to vote, and followed her passion for environmental sustainability by seeking signatures on a petition to save bees and to advocate for renewable energy. Because of the organization's nonpartisan stance, she never tried to influence anyone in terms of how to vote. Her passion was sustainability, and CALPIRG was a good place for her to advocate for the environment. When Trump announced his 2020 run for reelection, she began to work in a more partisan way. She recalled: "[Before] I was just trying to help people vote. [The first Trump administration] motivated me to like, you know, go there." At that moment, Belinda was galvanized to try to influence people to vote for a candidate who would enact more inclusive immigration policies.

Despite high motivation, practical barriers created by family legal vulnerability made it difficult for other students to engage politically. Camila Rios Echevarria, a US citizen with undocumented parents, had joined a campus organization that focused on increasing the Latino vote. But she found that, in light of attending classes, her on-campus job, assisting her mother with her work cleaning houses, and the expensive and time-consuming process of petitioning for her parents' immigration status, she had to stop her involvement. The COVID-19 pandemic had made all her obligations even more difficult to meet. She said: "I feel like this happens a lot with students, we want to do everything and it's just hard. . . . I would try to do at least one community club or organization every quarter, sometimes I was able to finish. Sometimes, unfortunately, I wasn't able to." Camila felt that her parents' safety and security was her "primary responsibility or obligation." Likewise, Ava Cornejo also cited family responsibilities as restraining her ongoing involvement with MEChA. She said:

> I knew that being involved was very important, but I didn't have [time]. Like I said, I would come back home every week or every time that I could. So it was really hard to stay active. So I'm like, It's best if I just don't join because I'm just going to look really bad not being able to attend all the time.

Of course, many students face challenges in joining formal political organizations due to constraints on their time. But for immigration-impacted students, it was family legal vulnerability that suppressed political engagement, even as it motivated some to greater involvement.

As with immigration-impacted students' mental health and well-being (see chapter 2) and academic engagement and performance (see chapter 3), family legal vulnerability also complicates political engagement. Initially it can motivate increased political engagement. Such motivation can be characterized as a beneficial cascading consequence, as political awareness and involvement are understood as desirable outcomes. However, feeling the need to be politically engaged in order to protect one's family may come at the expense of other activities that may help students flourish and may compromise students' mental-health outcomes.[4] Further, family legal vulnerability may strain students' ability to act on their motivation.

From Knowledge to Action: Political Agency in the Age of Trump

Highly motivated by family legal vulnerability, immigration-impacted college students sought to keep abreast of the emerging immigration policy climate. Camila stated plainly: "I can't afford to not care about an issue or not pay attention." Interviewed a few months after the 2020 election of Joe Biden to the presidency, Camila explained how she sought to keep herself politically informed: "I hear a lot [of people saying], like, 'Oh, I didn't have time to watch the debate. I haven't seen the news.' And it's like, I can't afford to not know what's happening. So I think that's a big part of why I watch the news every day or I watch these debates, or I keep up with the polls and stuff like that." Like Camila, many immigration-impacted students explained that staying informed about immigration policy was of utmost importance to protecting and advocating for their own and family members' safety and well-being. Students' efforts to stay informed had cascading consequences for their political engagement as they used their knowledge to inform immigration-related political participation in their surrounding community.

Immigration-impacted students often sought to use their knowledge to protect and advocate for their families. For Camila, this meant using the political knowledge she gleaned from the news and social media to make sure she was an informed member of the electorate. Much as Ava did, she described a sense of collective responsibility she felt as a US citizen who enjoyed the right to vote: "When I'm voting, I'm voting for my parents as well because they can't vote. So I'm their vote as well." Amaya Martinez, a US citizen with an undocumented single mother, also emphasized the importance of voting:

> What motivates me is just the fact that I am lucky to have a voice in this country, especially when it comes to voting. I see that as a tool and consider myself very lucky, so I might as well just take full advantage of that. [I have to] know what I'm voting for and be very informed.

Like many of the other US citizen children of undocumented immigrants we interviewed, Amaya recognized her right to vote as a unique privilege and opportunity to exercise her political voice on behalf of her family and community. She also sought to make sure that her vote reflected her mom's needs and opinions: "I try to get that input from her, or just if I know how she stands on certain issues, then I know what way to vote so I definitely take it into account for that." Like Amaya, US citizen students with undocumented parents framed voting as an action they took on behalf of their families with the intention of ensuring their collective well-being.

As an undocumented student without lawful status, Nicole Robles could not vote. But she shared how she used her political knowledge to keep her family informed about the immigration policy context:

> My sister and I engage in conversations with my parents about what's happening, just so they're aware. Because they are becoming more aware of the situations that are happening around us. So here and there we've talked to them about it because they are trying to understand why my sister and I aren't eligible for DACA. So just trying to explain the process and eligibility requirements and things like that.

Nicole and her sister, both of whom were college-educated, relied on social media to learn about immigration policies that affected their family. They kept an eye out for news about what was happening in their community in addition to policies like DACA. Nicole emphasized that she was sharing this information with her undocumented parents so that they all could collectively guard against impending threats. Their combined political awareness felt particularly necessary given the uncertainty and instability of the immigration policy context where it seemed like laws and policies were constantly being introduced, rescinded, or winding their way through the judicial system.

Students who stayed informed also found themselves in a position to raise awareness about immigration policies in their communities. Nicole did not stop with her parents but took to social media to circulate political information to others in her social networks. She asserted:

> I am aware of the policies and bills that we need to push for and advocate for. So just becoming more knowledgeable about it. I am able to share it even if I'm not directly in action with it or either protesting or things like that, I am able to share on social media so people will become more aware.

Nicole viewed both informing herself about policies and sharing that knowledge with others as political engagement. She compared it to protesting, noting that helping people become aware of the issues is also a part of the collective action needed to achieve immigration reform. Similarly, Lucia Ortega, a DACA recipient, recounted how she leveraged her influence on social media to amplify her political voice. She explained wanting to share her knowledge when she learned about the horrors experienced by migrant children who were being detained at the United States–Mexico border and then separated from their families. She did not feel safe enough to travel to the border to protest against border militarization or the detention of migrants. She explained: "I wish I could be able to go to the border and try to bring awareness to how severe people are being treated and stuff. [But] I do bring awareness of that in different ways." Indeed, she had raised awareness and exercised her political agency in several other ways: "I told my friends. I posted on social media. I try to donate as much as I can as a struggling person. I try to tweet the links, try to help spread them so that people can know the information." Many other immigration-impacted students also exercised political agency online. This reflects an emerging pattern of young adults turning to social media to engage in participatory politics, including starting an online political group, sharing commentaries about political issues, and /or circulating other political information among friends and followers.[5]

Some students translated their political knowledge into action in the communities surrounding their universities and homes. Most did this type of work within the context of on-campus student organizations or community-based immigrant rights organizations. These organizations worked to educate students about immigration policy and advocacy work and to provide opportunities for students to do this work. For example, Belén Mesa, a DACA recipient, joined a student organization on her campus that aimed to help (im)migrants understand their rights. They would go to nearby Mexican and Salvadoran consulate offices and offer information and support to people there. She explained:

> We do outreach there where we talk to people and let them know that we are offering these services. We are helping people with the process; if they're doing that application for the first time, we'll help them with that. Or if they're not being paid overtime at their work, we help them with that. A lot of their worker rights. It's mostly like their worker rights and immigration stuff.

Belén was intimately aware of the obstacles undocumented workers faced to claim rights. Her own father, a construction worker, had the experience of not being paid for his labor from certain employers. While he and their family knew that this was unlawful, he hesitated to report it because of his undocumented immigration status. Through this student organization, Belén was able to share her knowledge with immigrants like her father so that they would know their rights, become connected to resources, and reduce the negative impacts of their legal vulnerability.

In other instances, students focused their attention on their college campus as a space where they could affect immediate change to counter the exclusionary immigration policy context. As an undocumented student without lawful status, Arely Barajas felt "very alone" and "very, very stressed" about securing enough funding to pay for college. Connecting with the undocumented student services office and the undocumented student organization on her campus linked her to a community of student activists. These spaces opened opportunities to become involved in a campaign to advocate for more paid professional development opportunities for undocumented students like herself who did not benefit from the DACA program. She reflected on how students could affect change through collective action:

> I think every single thing that's available to [undocumented] students, it's because of students. . . . I mean, it's crazy how a ton of [university administrators] didn't even know what DACA or non-DACA was. And they don't even realize why it's so important to have non-DACA opportunities, because obviously, more and more students aren't going to have DACA because the requirement for DACA hasn't changed and now it's closed again.

Arely and her peers drew on their political and experiential knowledge to launch a campaign to educate campus administrators about the DACA program, its rescission under the Trump administration, and the needs of undocumented students without DACA. The campaign helped raise campus awareness and paved the way for the establishment of a fellowship program focused on providing professional development and funding to students without employment authorization.

Maribel Aranda, a DACA recipient attending another campus, recognized that she benefited from the efforts of student activists like Arely. She said:

> The only reason why I was able to receive [undocumented student resources and services] was because of the work that previous students did to make sure that there was a physical space for us. And just student advocacy throughout, or before me, is what really made the university see that we are valued and that we are needed and that we do deserve these resources.

Maribel's inclusive campus experience speaks to the importance of undocumented students' collective action. She became involved in a range of student and community organizations aimed at improving immigrant communities on campus and off, including the Center for Community Action and Environmental Justice, where she canvassed for environmental and get-out-the-vote efforts, and the Coalition for

Humane Immigrant Rights in Los Angeles (CHIRLA), where she landed a part-time job phone-banking.

Focusing on their immediate communities allowed students like Arely and Maribel to feel a sense of agency in an exclusionary political context. Maribel was gratified by seeing the positive impact of advocacy work on immigrant communities, but her participation was also personal. She explained: "Doing advocacy work and just talking to peers and other organizations who are helping the immigrant community is something that I do to help myself feel better; not necessarily focused on the bad aspects of being undocumented." She saw her political engagement as a way of coping with the strain of her undocumented status. At the same time, she was aware of the collective impact she was making by participating in immigrant rights organizations, "creating space for communities to learn about their rights," and looked forward to continuing to do so "once I graduate from law school or even as I work toward that goal."

Motivated to advocate for themselves and their families in an exclusionary immigration policy context, immigration-impacted students sought to keep themselves informed about immigration policies. Many deployed this information to raise awareness within their families and communities; others also began to engage in direct action. Social media and on-campus and community-based organizations played an important role in creating opportunities for students to practice their political agency.

Participating in the Electoral Process

In light of the first Trump administration and the rise of similarly aligned politicians at the state and local levels, many immigration-impacted students also saw electoral politics as a particularly important avenue for effecting political change that could usher in more inclusive immigration policy. Interviewing students on the heels of the 2020 presidential election, such actions were fresh in their minds. Maribel explained that she was prompted to participate in the electoral process: "A lot of the time, I feel that because we're not able to vote, other people are basically making decisions for us." Through participation in a community-based undocumented student organization during high school and then her campus's undocumented student organization, Maribel became empowered by the idea that, "even though we may not have a legal status, [you] can still advocate for yourself and not necessarily be at the mercy of others." Maribel's statement illustrates the ways that some immigration-impacted youth come to see themselves within the political system. Understanding the exclusionary political context through this perspective, immigration-impacted students sought to engage in the electoral process through a range of activities.

Whereas only US citizen students could vote, talking to others about voting was accessible to all immigration-impacted students regardless of their own immigration status. Sylvia Molina Santoyo, a DACA recipient, focused such efforts on her own family. She recalled:

> I've attempted to convince some of my family members who can vote to vote. Especially my sister since she's a US citizen, she can vote. I know there was a time in my life a couple years back . . . when I would try to persuade her to vote to try to make a difference. I would tell her from my viewpoint, I would tell her, "Well, you have a mother who doesn't have status the same way you have it."

At the time of our interview with her, she had not yet succeeded, but she continued to open those conversations. Amaya likewise encouraged others to vote. She said that her motivation for political engagement stemmed from having an undocumented mother:

> Just my experience growing up, and just being a child of an immigrant and being Latina. For example, getting people engaged and making sure that they do vote, that stemmed from seeing my mom not being able to vote and just making sure that people do take full advantage of their privilege to be able to vote.

By talking about voting with others, immigration-impacted students like Amaya and Sylvia sought to encourage US citizen family members and friends to keep their families in mind when deciding how to cast their votes and to multiply the number of people voting for candidates, laws, and propositions that would lessen their individual and family legal vulnerability.

Some students also engaged in the electoral process by participating in formal get-out-the-vote campaigns or canvassing for candidates. Gael Yepez Correa, an undocumented student with no lawful status, had worked with a Los Angeles–based immigrant rights organization. He recalled that he and the other volunteers were:

> trying to convince people to . . . go out and vote. Because the communities we were targeting were mainly like low-income Latino communities. And so just telling them to go out and vote. We weren't necessarily trying to say, vote this or vote that person in or vote this bill. . . . It was just more of like, please go out and vote. Like, your vote matters.

Aside from this organization, he also canvassed for local political candidates that he felt would represent effectively the needs of the immigrant community. Other students had participated in phone- or text-banking for candidates or ballot issues.

Some of the most politically active students were also engaged in lobbying elected officials to enact laws and policies that would advance inclusion for immigrant families and communities. Most had first become aware of community-based organizations when they were seeking resources and support to pursue their college educations and subsequently volunteered. Catalina Paz Flores became involved in the Inland Empire Immigrant Youth Coalition (IEIYC) in this way. She learned about support structures like the California DREAM Act that enabled her to access state and institutional financial aid, and simultaneously she became plugged in to their advocacy network. She took her younger sister, who was also undocumented, to organization meetings where they learned about resources, their rights, and proposed bills. Eventually they joined IEIYC during lobbying visits to state elected officials in Sacramento.

Similarly, during high school Maribel participated in CHIRLA's WiseUp! program. As the organization's website states, members, "attend local and national workshops, conferences, presentations and rallies to learn how to participate in policy debates, analyze power maps, and encourage leadership actions in their own schools."[6] Once in college,

Maribel became involved in several other community and student organizations. Much like Catalina, she traveled to Sacramento to lobby for progressive state-level immigration policy with these groups. She recalled: "I was able to go to the capital, share my experience about being an undocumented student and just trying to help our stories be heard. . . . [I would share] my thoughts and kind of persuade [them] to vote a certain way instead of another, or just share my lived experience to influence [their] decision." Through organizational participation, Catalina and Maribel found opportunities to further influence electoral politics by engaging directly with elected officials and their staff members. In this way, they extended their electoral reach beyond their immediate social circles to influence the way that lawmakers crafted and voted on public policy.

Immigration-impacted students participated in the electoral process in a range of ways. Those with citizenship made it a priority to vote; those without talked to others about voting. With the support of on-campus or community organizations, students found additional ways to engage the electoral system, such as by canvassing or phone-banking for political candidates and by lobbying elected officials. Such organizational structures were critical to support students' agency in leveraging their political voices to affect the electoral process.

Public Protests: Navigating the Collective Risk of Police Presence and Deportability

The first Trump administration was marked by public protests advocating for just treatment for a range of marginalized groups, including (im)migrants, racial minorities, and women. Immigration-impacted students were concerned that participating in such activities could put their families and, for those without documentation, themselves at risk. Students with no lawful status felt these constraints most intimately; they feared for their own personal safety, expecting that any arrest by police could lead to deportation. Those with DACA feared that an arrest would jeopardize this temporary protection; a conviction for a felony, a serious misdemeanor, or posing a "threat to national security" would disqualify them from renewal.[7] Though US citizen students did not perceive a threat to their citizenship if they were arrested, they were aware that one could bring unwanted attention to their family. For example, parents' immigration status could be exposed if they were called on to bail them out of jail. In this way, family legal vulnerability constrained the protest participation of citizens and noncitizens alike, although some members of both groups ultimately decided to engage.

Our participants were in elementary school during the May Day marches of the mid-2000s, a watershed moment in the history of US Latino politics.[8] Several major US cities including Los Angeles and Oakland saw mass mobilizations of immigrants and their allies. Once called a "sleeping giant" because of its size, potential political influence, and its general failure to exert that power, the Latino community was awake and engaged in US politics. The protests were a response to the so-called Sensenbrenner Bill of 2006, which passed the House of Representatives but ultimately did not pass in the Senate. One of the provisions of the bill (formally House Resolution 4437) was to reclassify improper entry into the country from a misdemeanor to a felony and to criminalize those who aided undocumented immigrants. These marches were community and family events; it was not uncommon to see children holding protest signs that read, "My parents are not criminals."

Gabriela Ortiz, a US citizen, had attended some of these demonstrations with her undocumented parents at age six or seven. She recalled these early lessons in collective political power:

> We were doing *las marchas* [the marches], trying to change the immigration policies. So my parents would take me sometimes. Because sometimes it would be like, I didn't have school, or they would pull me out of school. Not like, frequently. But just enough that I was part of it. Yeah. And it was just kind of like, Wow! Like, it's not just us who are in this situation.

Gabriela found it empowering to recognize the size of the immigrant community and its collective mobilization. But she also witnessed that participation could be risky. After attending a series of peaceful protests in 2006 that contributed to the defeat of the Sensenbrenner Bill, her family attended the May Day marches in 2007. They witnessed the beginning of what would come to be known as the "May Day Melee" in MacArthur Park, located near downtown Los Angeles.[9]

Gabriela recalled a "pretty chill day" with family friends. But as she and her parents were walking to their car, they saw signs of what was to come:

> I remember we were crossing the sidewalk and . . . I just see the LAPD lining up with shields and stuff. And I pointed to my dad, like, what the heck is that? And so my parents rushed us to the car. . . . Then on the ride home, we hear it on the radio. Like, oh, they've thrown gas bombs, they're hitting people, all this. We get home, my brothers have the TV on, we're watching this. We're getting calls from the East Coast, from our family in Mexico. We're calling people from LA as well. And they're calling us to make sure everyone's fine and stuff. . . . It was pretty scary.

This was a formative memory for Gabriela about the relationship between the immigrant community and the police. More than a decade later, she was afraid to engage in protests because of what had happened.

Few participants recalled the 2006 immigrant rights marches but instead focused on the most active protests at the time of our 2021 interviews: the Movement for Black Lives. Many students in our study had wanted to show their support for the Black Lives Matter movement through participation in these protests. Some also saw this as a form of coalition-building that would signal the importance of dismantling interlocking systems of oppression that were shared among communities of color.[10] However, they were conscious that police presence was common at these protests, and they were fearful of risk to themselves and family members. Even though they were aware that public protest is protected speech in the United States, students knew that protest sometimes involved acts of civil disobedience (e.g., blocking traffic, disturbing the peace) that could lead to arrest. Belén Mesa, a DACA recipient, recalled:

> I wanted to go to the Black Lives Matter protests in downtown LA [in the summer of 2020], but [my mom] did not allow me to go. She's like, "No, like, what if the police stop you? . . . They're going to send you back to Mexico." In that sense, they do worry for me, and I'm not allowed to do protests and stuff that involve the police just because it scares my parents.

Concerns about her family's legal vulnerability and subsequent fears and anxieties motivated her to stay home. Similarly, Elena Moreno Gomez, also a DACA recipient, reflected: "I try to refrain from protests because I also think if something happened to me, it's not just happening to me, it's going to happen to my family as well. And I don't ever want to do things that are going to put my family at risk." Because family members are often situated within a delicate nexus of responsibility and obligation, one person's detention and/or deportation could reverberate to other family members, thereby destabilizing the entire family.

Other students referenced more directly the problem that if they were arrested their families would be made vulnerable. Camila shared that she had wanted to join protests being held outside detention centers when she was in high school. Her parents, however, refused to allow her to attend:

> I would always want to go but my parents always said no, because they were worried that, one, something would happen to me, I would get hurt. Protests can sometimes turn violent. But their main concern was [that] people get arrested: "What if you get arrested? They're going to call me, how am I going to be able to pick you up? You're putting me in danger, by putting yourself in danger too." And so that was something I didn't argue too much about because it was true. I was being a little bit selfish in wanting to go do that because they would call my parents and if they wanted to, they would ask questions.

Camila said she "didn't argue" the point because she knew it was valid; her parents were responsible for her as a minor. Even though the goal of protest was political change to help a collective group of undocumented people, that change would be in the long term. In the short term, Camila was convinced that it was "selfish" to put her political desires ahead of her family's immediate safety.

While family legal vulnerability played a major role in the way that immigration-impacted students assessed the risks associated with public protest, other students emphasized the risks to their own individual legal vulnerability. For some students this was specifically because DACA protections felt fragile; any arrest on their record would place them into a gray area of eligibility for DACA renewal.[11] Gabriel Ballón, a DACA recipient, shared about his desire to participate in the Black Lives Matter protests following George Floyd's murder. He explained his DACA-related concerns: "I feel like I have a lot to lose. So if I were to do stuff [like protesting], or I do it wrong, . . . [I risk] going to jail or that being in my record. . . . I'm not a citizen or a resident yet, so I got to figure out my stuff out first before I can actually take on those big risks." Gabriel was particularly concerned about an arrest appearing on his record, which might preclude him from renewing his DACA protections or prevent an application to adjust his immigration status. Gabriel believed in public protest and supported the Black Lives Matter movement. Of participating in a public protest, he stated: "It could help." He wished he could participate but felt he could not.

As an undocumented student without lawful status, Edgar Lopez Linares was also concerned about his own deportation. However, he was the only person in his immediate family living in the United States, so deportation would have involved family reunification in Mexico rather than family separation in the United States. Nevertheless, he felt a sense of responsibility to remain in the United States to secure future job and career opportunities that would support his family's financial well-being. He stated frankly: "I'm scared to be deported. I feel like if you go in any march, or in a protest, like you don't know if it's going to get out of control. You don't know if the police are going to grab everyone. So for me, that was the [risk]." Edgar assumed that he would have little legal recourse if he were detained.

Edgar's family did not have the same legal vulnerability of others who were living undocumented in the United States. But he worried what his family would say if he were deported for attending a protest. Specifically, it was:

> the stigma of "What were you doing there? You know that you are [undocumented]." Like a bad thing happens and then it's like the family . . . is like, "Damn, you actually just went to a protest, and you just get deported for that. That's stupid." That's the family stigma as well.

As the only member of his family who was able to live and study in the United States, Edgar did not experience family legal vulnerability in the same way as many of our other respondents did. He was, however, influenced by their perceptions about his choices and felt responsible for their economic stability. The well-being of his family, in particular his role in supporting his family by achieving his educational and career goals, revealed that they were never far from his mind; this prompted him to play it safe with regard to public facing political engagement.

While most immigration-impacted students we interviewed avoided protest, others found ways to manage their safety concerns. Some were able to draw on their circle of friends to provide help if a protest were to go badly. Once she became a student at UCLA, Camila participated in public demonstrations because she established a community of friends who would be there for her if she were to be arrested. "That's how I started going to protest because I didn't have to worry my parents about [picking me up from the police station]. I can call somebody else," she said.

Other students felt an increased sense of security engaging in public protest alongside community advocacy groups. Immigrant rights organizations and student organizations with civic/political engagement goals were invaluable to students' sense of purpose and safety. Catalina Paz Flores, a DACA recipient, reflected on how she became comfortable attending IEIYC's protests of the Adelanto Detention Facility:

> I trust them. You know what I mean? They're a group that I trust, and I know they're not going to do something that's going to put us in danger. But they also let you know of course, "It's okay if you don't want to turn up" or things like that. Because each person is different, some people could be more scared to attend protests or things like that. . . . I know the type of protest that they are: they're not like civil disobedience, they're just peaceful protests. So I know that. . . . I know other people could be scared of attending and stuff. But me, I mean, I feel with them I'm more comfortable.

Catalina trusted IEIYC and believed that the organization's leaders would not consciously place her at risk. She also appreciated the honesty of the organization in terms of informing students about the risks of particular political actions and allowing young people to choose how they wanted to participate based on their personal levels of comfort.

Ultimately, however, the majority of immigration-impacted students that we interviewed did not participate in protests because of their individual and family legal vulnerability, sometimes in spite of very much wanting to do so. They anticipated heavy police presence at protests and believed warnings about cooperation between police and immigration enforcement, which signaled that an arrest at a protest could end in family separation. While the security of friends or established community organizations could mitigate this sense of threat to some degree, family legal vulnerability nonetheless constrained political expression.

Heightened Political Engagement: Comparing Immigration-Impacted Students to Peers

Thus far we have traced the cascading consequences of family legal vulnerability on political participation as it shapes immigration-impacted students' motivation and forms of engagement. We turn now to our quantitative survey data to determine if these experiences contribute to unequal outcomes. Specifically, we compare the political engagement of undocumented students and US citizen students with undocumented parents to US citizen students with lawfully present parents. Regression analyses consider to what extent these two groups of immigration-impacted students differ from their peers and whether family legal vulnerability explains any disparities. We examine three types of political engagement—*talking to others about voting, participating in a protest*, and *participating in an organization to solve a problem*—that represent a range of activities. Appendix C provides full details on the regression models.

Talking to Others About Voting

Voting, and talking to others about voting, is a quintessential measure of political engagement. Our survey found that four out of every five survey participants had talked to others about voting, as depicted in Figure 4.1. A slightly higher percentage of US citizen students reported engaging in this activity often or always, with 38 percent of US citizens with lawfully present parents and 36 percent of US citizens with undocumented parents reporting doing so, compared to 34 percent of undocumented students. Regression analyses revealed that, after controlling for demographic characteristics, all three student groups reported similar levels

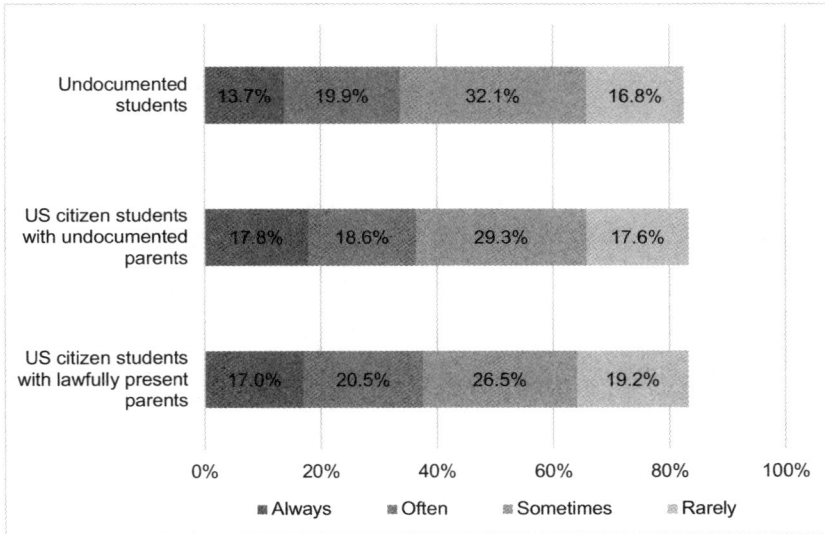

Figure 4.1. Frequency survey respondents talk to others about voting by self and parental immigration status.

of talking to others about voting. This is indicated by the left-most set of bars in Figure 4.2, which graphs the predicted probability of talking to others about voting when holding demographics constant (i.e., at baseline).

With this in mind, we considered the role that family legal vulnerability may play in shaping one's motivation and willingness to participate in this way. Specifically, we examined whether group differences in talking to others about voting changed as we accounted for three dimensions of family legal vulnerability: *immigration-related threat to family, having a family member who had been deported,* and *family financial strain.* This sequential modeling approach allowed us to see whether and how unique conditions associated with family legal vulnerability shape immigration-impacted students' political engagement relative to peers who do not experience these same strains. Figure 4.2 graphs the predicted probabilities when controlling for each dimension of family legal vulnerability. Comparing each model to baseline allows us to determine whether each dimension of family legal vulnerability contributes to differences in political engagement.

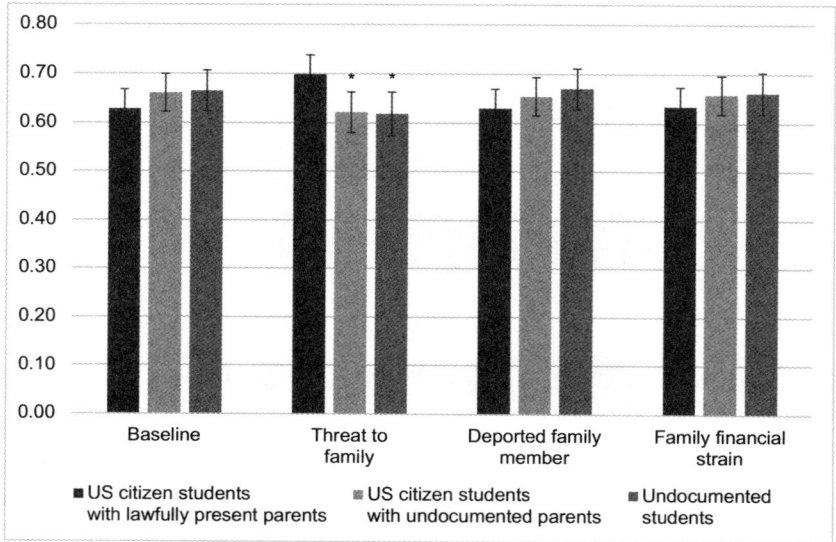

Figure 4.2. Predicted probability of talking to others about voting when controlling for family legal vulnerability.
NOTE: Statistically significant differences from the reference group are indicated by * when p<.05.

We find that perceived threat to family due to the exclusionary immigration policy context is an important driver of talking to others about voting among immigration-impacted students. This measure broadly captures the threat of deportation alongside a range of interrelated policy threats by assessing how frequently participants worried about the impact immigration policies have on them or their families, feared that they or a family member would be reported to immigration officials, and worried about family separation. Once we accounted for this perceived threat, we saw changes in political engagement among immigration-impacted students. In other words, if immigration policy threat was not a factor, both undocumented students and US citizens with undocumented parents would talk to others about voting less than their peers with lawfully present parents do. These findings suggest that immigration-impacted students who talk to others about voting are motivated at least in part due to policy-related threats to their families. Accounting for whether a student had an immediate or extended family member who was deported and family financial strain did not change the baseline pattern; this suggests that these two forms of family legal vulnerability do not play a role in motivating or dissuading immigration-impacted students from engaging in this form of political participation.

Participating in a Protest

Protest participation provides a window into a more public and potentially risky form of political engagement.[12] A national poll of youth social movement and protest activities found an increase in protest among youth during the first Trump administration, consistent with activities reported by our interview participants.[13] Further, a recent study of youth protest participation found that, whereas 5 percent of US youth participated in a protest in the year before the 2016 election, by 2020 that percentage had increased sixfold, to almost 30 percent.[14] Descriptive results indicate that protest participation is highest among US citizens with undocumented parents, of whom 51 percent reported ever protesting, compared to 46 percent of undocumented students and US citizens with lawfully present parents (see figure 4.3). A higher percentage of this group also reported protesting often, both on and off campus.

Figure 4.4 displays the predicted probability of protest participation across the three student groups. At baseline, US citizens with undocumented parents reported significantly higher levels of participation than their peers with lawfully present parents. However, controlling for perceived threat to family due to the exclusionary immigration policy decreases protest participation among both groups of immigration-impacted students. Specifically, US citizens with undocumented parents now have a lower likelihood of protest, and significant differences emerge between undocumented students and US citizens with lawfully present parents. These findings suggest that protest participation among immigration-impacted students is motivated in part by immigration-related threat to family. This motivation is so strong for US citizens with undocumented parents that they protest at higher levels than their peers with lawfully present parents. It is likely that undocumented students would protest at higher rates, similar to US citizens with undocumented parents, if not for their concerns about their own legal vulnerability.

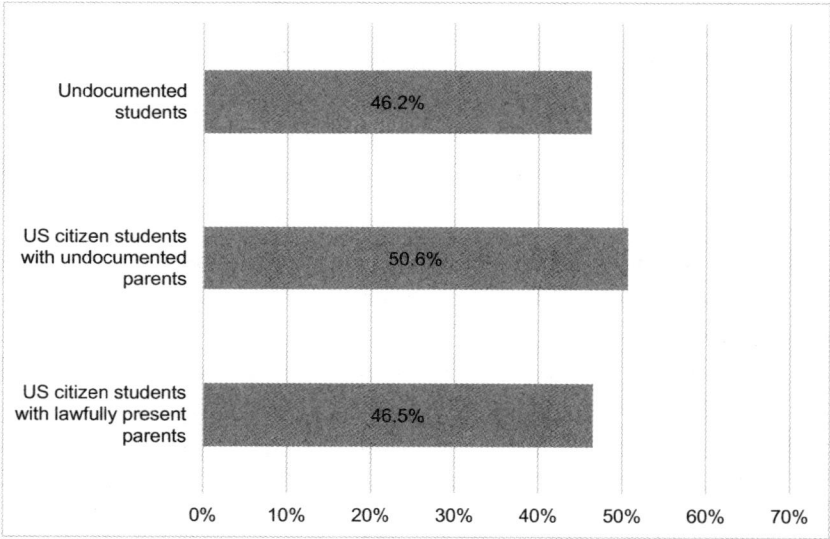

Figure 4.3. Protest participation of survey respondents by self and parental immigration status.

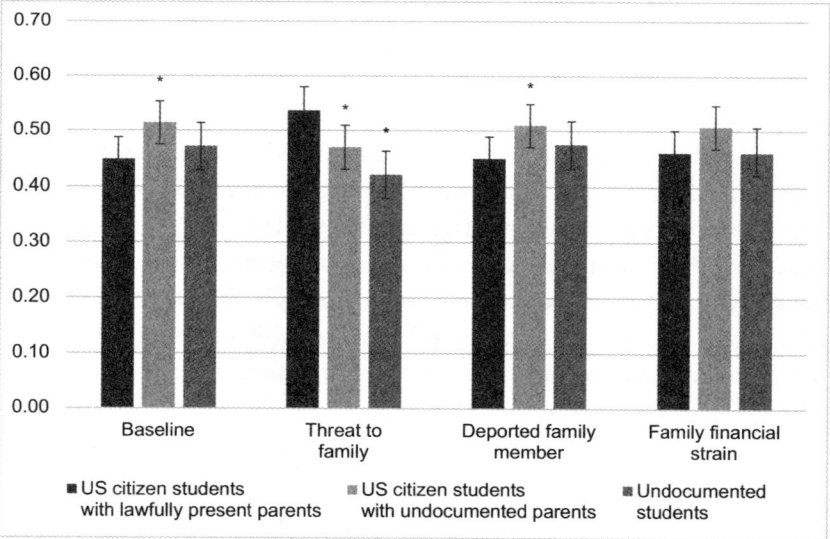

Figure 4.4. Predicted probability of protest participation when controlling for family legal vulnerability.

NOTE: Statistically significant differences from the reference group are indicated by * when p<.05.

These results suggest that the undocumented interviewees who engaged in protest, like Ignacio and Catalina, are unique, although it is also possible that organizations like the Inland Empire Immigrant Youth Coalition, which made Catalina feel safe protesting, have untapped potential to encourage others to participate.

Accounting for family financial strain eliminated significant differences observed at baseline so that US citizen students with undocumented parents were no more likely to participate in protests then their peers with lawfully present parents. This finding suggests that experiencing family financial strain encourages US citizen students with undocumented parents to participate in political protest. Experiencing the deportation of a family member did not change the baseline pattern, suggesting that this form of family legal vulnerability does not play a role in motivating or dissuading protest participation; again, the lack of significance observed here may have more to do with the specific experiences reported by our respondents including deportations that had occurred in the distant past, been resolved, or affected an extended family member.

Participating in an Organization to Solve a Problem

Finally, organizational participation is a distinct form of political engagement that involves an ongoing commitment to advocate for a specific cause. A national survey revealed that over half (55 percent) of Latino youth are affiliated with "a group or movement that will vote to express its views," suggesting that a majority of Latino youth participate collectively in groups that share the same political ideologies and who, as individuals, express that shared ideology by voting.[15] Relatedly, a survey of California young adults aged 18 to 26 found that 27 percent were working with others to address an issue impacting their community.[16] Our study asked a related but narrower question: whether students participated in an organization with an aim to solve a problem. Undocumented students were most likely to say "yes," with 55 percent having participated in such an organization compared to 44 percent of US citizens with undocumented parents and 45 percent of US citizens with lawfully present parents (see figure 4.5).

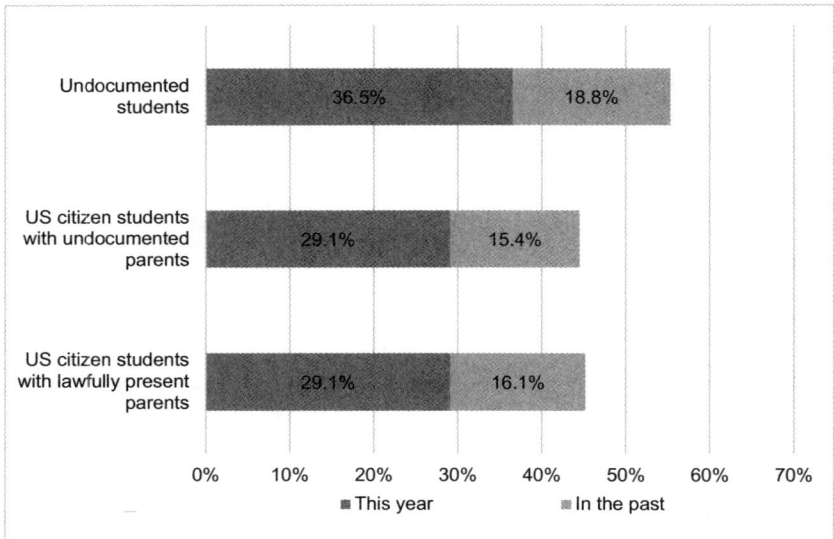

Figure 4.5. Organizational participation of survey respondents by self and parental immigration status.

Once we control for demographic characteristics, undocumented students remain significantly more likely to participate in an organization than US citizen students with lawfully present parents (see figure 4.6). As with the other two forms of political engagement, threat to family explained group differences—that is, if undocumented students did not experience immigration-related threats to their family, then their organizational participation would be on par with that of their US citizen peers. When we accounted for having experienced a family member's deportation and family financial strain, the baseline pattern remained the same. Overall, this suggests that immigration-related threat to family is a consistent motivator of political engagement for immigration-impacted students. Further, organizational participation is a potentially safer and more readily accessible option for undocumented students, contributing to their higher rates of participation in this form of political engagement. These differences may also reflect the availability of organizations aligned with addressing immigration-related issues. At the University of California, such advocacy is often championed by each campus's undocumented student organization.

Although US citizen students are welcome to participate, these organizations may pave the way for undocumented students experiencing individual and family legal vulnerability to become involved.

Conclusion

This chapter reveals how family legal vulnerability plays a substantial role in immigration-impacted students' political engagement, both in terms of their motivation and approach. Students became more aware of political issues and were motivated to politically engage during the first Trump administration when there was an upsurge in anti-immigrant rhetoric and policy. They kept abreast of immigration policy changes to protect themselves, their families, and communities. Many drew on their knowledge and political agency to address their concerns and, in the process, became politically engaged to alleviate family legal vulnerability. Students understood that even small actions could make a difference in the political landscape. They shared

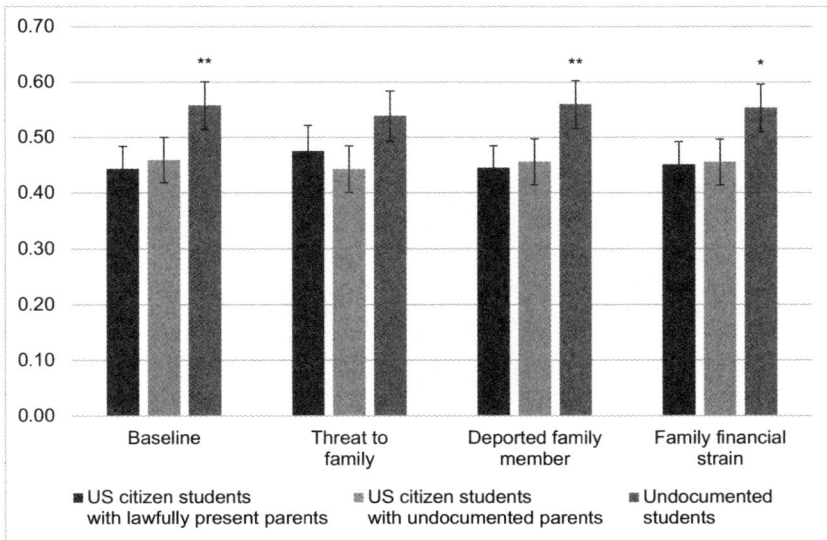

Figure 4.6. Predicted probability of organizational participation when controlling for family legal vulnerability.
NOTE: Statistically significant differences from the reference group are indicated by ** when p<.01 and * when p<.05.

information on social media, joined organizations, registered and encouraged people to vote, lobbied politicians, and went to protests. Yet individual and family legal vulnerability also constrained which activities they chose to engage in, as undocumented students did not have the right to vote and both groups of immigration-impacted students worried about the collective threat of deportation associated with protest. Nevertheless, students asserted their political voices in an effort to build political power.

PART III

Achieving Equity by Centering Family

5

What Can Universities Do?

How Campus Resources Can Alleviate the Effects of Family Legal Vulnerability

"When I would use these resources, my mental health would go up. My productivity would go up. My work would go up."
—Ryan Zepeda

As an undocumented student without lawful immigration status, Ryan Zepeda had encountered a number of obstacles during his college career. With two undocumented guardians (his sister and brother-in-law), he felt that his family's shared undocumented status was "the biggest block for my family's growth." They struggled financially, and Ryan perceived their quality of life to be slipping as "the capacity to keep sustaining that . . . just keeps on getting lower." This family reality framed Ryan's college experiences as he struggled with food insecurity. He stuck to a tight budget and watched how much he ate at each meal. Sometimes he ran out of food and there were nights he went to bed early to ignore the hunger pangs.

Educational institutions can embrace inclusionary policies to promote the incorporation of undocumented immigrants by lowering the everyday consequences of individual and family legal vulnerability.[1] When a basic needs center opened on Ryan's campus, it became "a humongous resource line" that "definitely was a huge, huge help." In addition to providing fresh vegetables and other healthy food items, it connected him to other resources on campus: "If I would want to do a seminar on finances, then my diet would get better because I was able to afford better food. . . . They referred me to a dietician at the student health center, then that also helped me figure out that, Okay, I should better myself physically and start going to the gym." He felt that "there was a ripple effect that these referrals would have," noting how receiving such resources boosted his mental health and academic performance.

Ryan found the undocumented student services office to be another important source of support. Established through funding allocated by the University of California Office of the President, by 2014 all UC campuses had undocumented student centers with at least one full-time professional staff member and had access to systemwide free immigration legal services. These institutionalized resources sought to advance equity and inclusion for undocumented students by providing academic, social, emotional, financial, and legal support.[2] The office connected Ryan with a paid fellowship program that placed him in a campus site where he dedicated 10 hours per week to working on a project with a mentor and received a scholarship that was equivalent to being paid minimum wage for his time. In addition to the value of this financial assistance, the existence of a program designed to meet the needs of students without employment authorization felt validating to Ryan. He acknowledged that the undocumented student services office was "the biggest [resource] when it comes to status," but he also sensed its limited ability to address underlying legal vulnerability. Ryan felt that "the legal services that help undocumented students, . . . you don't really get help but rather a reality check." Speaking with the campus immigration attorney, he learned that there were no options available to adjust his immigration status: "It was really heavy news." Contrary to the other campus resources that made him "feel better," this one highlighted the legal constraints he faced with no immigration relief in sight. He confronted the limits of the campus bubble that failed to insulate him from these structural inequities.

This chapter turns attention to institutions of higher education as a site of intervention for the inequalities we have documented throughout this book. We glean important lessons for alleviating family legal vulnerability by focusing on the University of California system as a relatively inclusionary institution within a distinctly inclusionary state context. We show that the services and resources the UC provides helped immigration-impacted students alleviate some of the collective strains associated with family legal vulnerability, including economic insecurity and concerns about deportation and family separation. Campuswide services, including mental health services, academic support services, and identity-based centers, also helped students address the cascading effects of family legal vulnerability on their mental health, academic performance, and political engagement. Undocumented student services offices, which serve undocumented students as well as other immigration-impacted students, created and offered many of these resources; however, US citizens with undocumented parents vastly underutilized these services. Based on such findings, we offer recommendations for how institutions can strengthen campus resources to alleviate the collective constraints and cascading consequences of family legal vulnerability on students' success. In light of persistent political gridlock, universities and colleges seeking to advance equity, inclusion, and justice must act within their realm of power to support all students' success, including those impacted by restrictive immigration policy.

Alleviating Family Legal Vulnerability

The immigration-impacted students we interviewed accessed campus services with the purpose of obtaining information and resources to support their personal and academic success and well-being. Many drew on campus resources to help alleviate two prominent dimensions of family legal vulnerability: economic insecurity, and concerns about deportation and family separation.

Economic Insecurity and University Financial Support

As we documented in the preceding chapters, family legal vulnerability prompted shared financial strain among immigration-impacted students and their family members. Given their low-income status, participants received financial aid that covered major educational expenses, including tuition and fees and most housing costs; these financial aid packages were integral to maintaining enrollment. Yet not all expenses were covered, and students were frequently called on to help manage their family's collective financial need. They subsequently cut corners in personal living and college-related expenses, often at a cost to their well-being and academics. Many drew on financial aid and campus safety-net resources to alleviate cascading individual financial strains.

FINANCIAL AID

Financial aid aims to expand access to higher education for low-income students by relieving the barriers posed by economic insecurity. And whereas the US citizen children of undocumented immigrants are eligible for federal financial aid, undocumented students are not.[3] However, a series of California state laws have expanded undocumented students' access to more affordable higher education. Assembly Bill 540 and subsequent extensions allow undocumented students to pay in-state tuition rates if they attended a California school for three full-time years (or part-time equivalent) and received a high-school diploma or associate's degree (or equivalent).[4] The California DREAM Act granted undocumented students access to institutional grant aid and need-based state grants. At the University of California, institutional aid is critical to making attendance affordable for low-income students. Specifically, the UC system draws on a mix of federal, state, institutional, and/or private funding sources to guarantee that all systemwide tuition and fees are covered for California students whose families earn less than $80,000, regardless of their own or their parents' immigration status. Students with greater financial need receive additional aid to cover expenses such as housing and educational materials without regard for immigration status.[5] These UC system policies ensure that undocumented students receive need-based grant aid on par with their US citizen peers. This financial aid is critical to supporting immigration-impacted students' enrollment and persistence in higher education.

Despite eligibility, immigration-impacted students disclosed the strains of trying to apply for financial aid every year. Undocumented participants recalled attending annual workshops to fill out the California Dream Act application. Catalina Paz Flores, a DACA recipient, noted, "the tax portion is really confusing. . . . Especially being an undocumented family, you don't know what to put, because my mom, she never really has a job-job. It's more like her doing her own thing like selling *comida* [food] or working, but on the down-low. I don't even know what to put. Am I supposed to put her [income on the form]?" Meeting with an adviser from the financial aid office who was partnering with undocumented and immigration-impacted student services helped Catalina get answers to her questions and feel confident in her application. US citizen students recalled similar complications with reporting their undocumented parents' employment and tax information. Other students struggled with what to put on the form when it prompted them for social security numbers, nine digits that their undocumented parents did not have. In these cases, staff often helped immigration-impacted students navigate the financial aid process to secure the financial aid they were entitled to.

Once awarded, students' financial aid packages often included loans that could help bridge the gap between their grant aid and their total educational costs; however, many students expressed concern and confusion about these loans. Xochitl Amador, a US citizen student with undocumented parents, explained that she had for a long time declined the loans offered to her because she was afraid of acquiring too much debt, even though it was federally subsidized. Years into Xochitl's college career, a friend explained that she could accept a portion of the loan:

> She was like, "Why don't you accept it? And then just take out, instead of like the full loan, just take out what you need for rent? . . . You shouldn't have to worry about a loan of that amount too much in the future." So she kind of like, pushed me toward getting it. But I didn't know that you could ask for like, a smaller amount. I just thought that whatever was on your financial aid letter was what you had to take out.

Xochitl was grateful for this advice but wished it had come sooner, perhaps as a financial aid crash course that would include information on loan types and lending processes. Edgar Lopez Linares, a DACA recipient, was similarly loan-averse when he learned about the California DREAM Loan, a state program that allows eligible undocumented undergraduate students to access up to $4,000 per year in institutional/state loans with a maximum of $20,000 over their educational careers.[6] Taking out one of these loans prompted new worries: "Now, I am concerned because I created a loan. . . . It's like, how am I going to pay for the loans? I'm ashamed to ask for money from my uncle, so I had to start working on anything [I could get]." The pressure to repay loans compromised Edgar's ability to seek out jobs and opportunities that would have been more related to his planned career path. As with any economically disadvantaged student, loans helped relieve immigration-impacted students' financial strains, but could also create new ones.

RECOMMENDATION #1: PROVIDE EQUITABLE
FINANCIAL AID AND ESTABLISH SUPPORT FOR
FINANCIAL AID PROCESSES THAT SERVE
IMMIGRATION-IMPACTED STUDENTS.

Universities and colleges must provide comprehensive financial aid awards that support the full breadth of educational expenses for immigration-impacted students. This means ensuring that the amount of financial aid awarded accounts for all educational and cocurricular costs and accurate living expenses. The case of the University of California shows that inclusive state and institutional policy can effectively support this goal; however, larger financial aid awards are needed to make college fully affordable. More comprehensive aid will benefit all low-income students who are struggling to cover expenses given the gaps in their financial aid packages.[7]

Considering undocumented students' ineligibility for federal financial aid, institutional funding must be allocated to scholarships that can meet demonstrated financial need. Scholarship requirements could be reviewed to expand and explicitly note eligibility for undocumented students. In states where undocumented students are not eligible for in-state tuition rates and/or non–federally funded financial aid, universities and colleges can advocate for such inclusive state policies, for example through organizations such as the Presidents' Alliance on Higher Education and Immigration.[8] University regents may also establish institutionally specific policies along these lines.[9]

Universities and colleges are advised to establish financial aid support tailored to immigration-impacted students' unique financial aid processes and concerns. Institutional support should be readily available to help students fill out financial aid applications. This could include detailed FAQ sections on their websites, designated point people to contact within the financial aid office, and sessions dedicated to supporting immigration-impacted students when filling out financial aid forms. Targeted financial aid counseling, through individual meetings or group workshops, could explain loan options and help immigration-impacted students understand the repayment process in light of individual and family legal vulnerability. Such counseling should include information such as the possibility of accepting a loan but choosing to receive only part of it. Partnerships between the financial aid office, undocumented student services, and other relevant campus offices could help ensure that these resources reach intended student audiences.

SAFETY-NET RESOURCES

Despite receiving substantial financial aid awards to support their education, immigration-impacted students still had to navigate their families' collective economic insecurity. Many attempted to do this by minimizing the costs they placed on their families' earnings, often by limiting their own personal expenses, particularly around food. We assessed survey participants' food security based on US Department of Agriculture definitions: "very low food security" means experiencing disrupted eating patterns and reduced food intake due to limited resources, while "low security" means reduced quality, variety, or desirability of diet without reduced food intake.[10] As Figure 5.1 shows, 61 percent of the undocumented students, 60 percent of the US citizen students with undocumented parents, and 58 percent of US citizen students with lawfully present parents had low or very low food security, with very low food security representing 42 percent, 36 percent, and 32

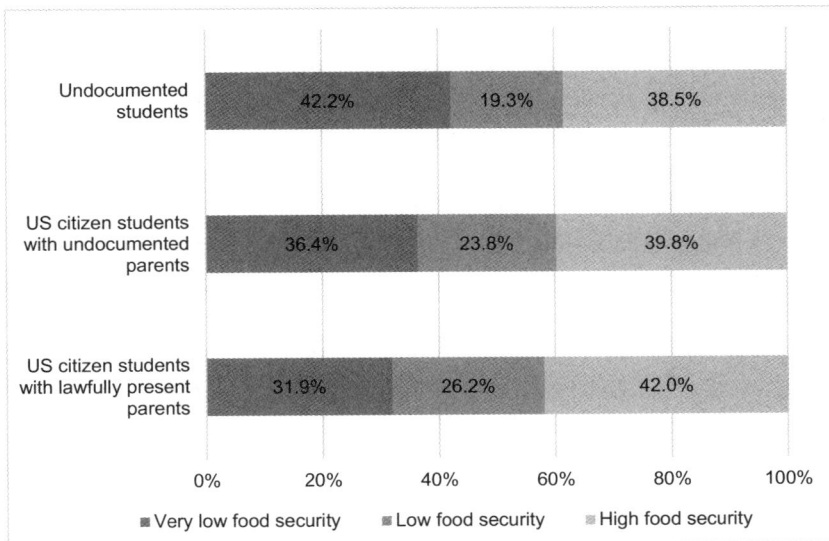

Figure 5.1. Food security levels of survey respondents by self and parental immigration status.

percent of each student group, respectively. While all these numbers are concerningly high, analyses indicate that there are statistically significant differences among the three groups.[11]

In light of research linking food insecurity and poorer academic engagement and performance outcomes,[12] UC has instituted food pantries and basic needs centers at every campus. Our interviewees indicate that these essential campus resources play a critical role in disrupting the effects of collective economic insecurity within undocumented and mixed-status families. Julia Soto, a US citizen with undocumented parents, explained that she had relied on her campus center for feminine hygiene products and other necessities like sample-size toothpaste, deodorant, and laundry detergent. A food pantry provided three free ready-to-eat food items on each visit. She remembered the *sopitas de maruchan*—also known as "cup-o-noodles"—fondly as something quick and "super easy" to eat when she did not have enough food. Gabriel Ballón, a DACA recipient, noted that savings from his receipt of campus resources snowballed, that they "helped me save money on food, and in turn helped me pay for parking, pay for gas, all those types of stuff."

Notably, basic needs centers were the most-used campus resource in our survey and were more likely to be used by immigration-impacted students. Figure 5.2 displays the frequency with which our survey participants visited basic needs centers during the academic year. Overall, 67 percent of undocumented students and 60 percent of US citizen students with undocumented parents reported visiting basic needs centers, compared to 52 percent of US citizens with lawfully present parents. Immigration-impacted students were also more likely to access such resources frequently; more than half of those who visited the center did so once per month or more. Regression analyses confirm that, after controlling for demographic characteristics, undocumented students and US citizen students with undocumented parents visited basic needs centers more than US citizen students with lawfully present parents. This is indicated by the left-most set of bars in Figure 5.3, which graphs the predicted probability of visiting the basic needs center when holding demographics constant (i.e., at baseline).

Regression analyses also suggest that family legal vulnerability motivates immigration-impacted students' use of basic needs centers.

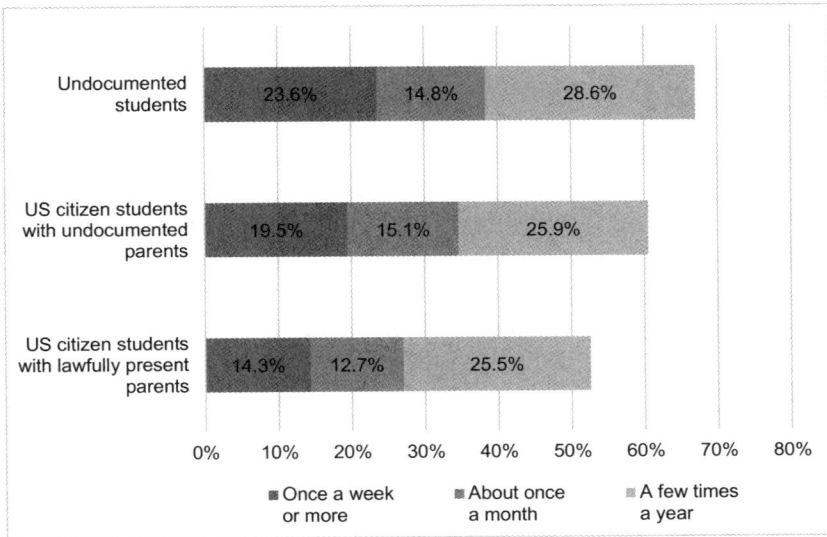

Figure 5.2. Frequency survey respondents visited the basic needs center by self and parental immigration status.

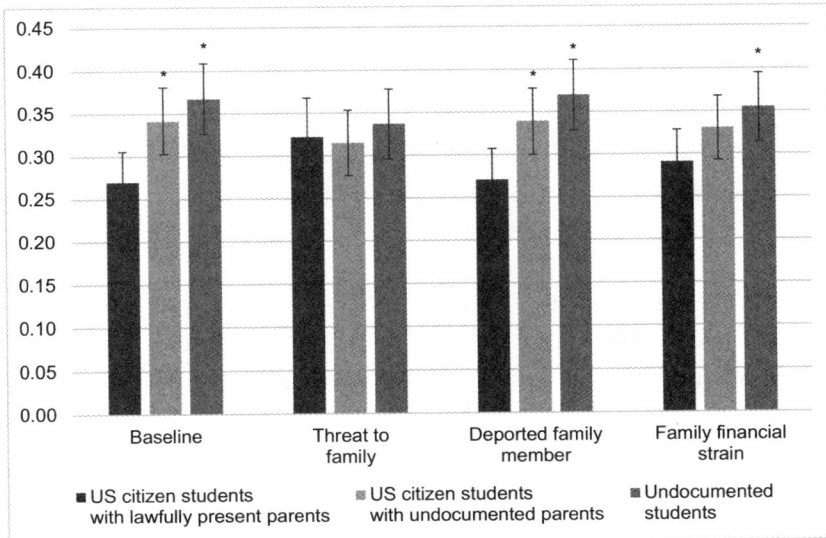

Figure 5.3. Predicted probability of visiting the basic needs center when controlling for family legal vulnerability.
NOTE: Statistically significant differences from the reference group are indicated by ** when p<.01 and * when p<.05.

Specifically, we examined whether differences in visiting a basic needs center changed as we accounted for three dimensions of family legal vulnerability: immigration-related threat to family, having a family member who had been deported, and family financial strain (see figure 5.3).[13] Controlling for perceived threat to family eliminated differences in visiting a basic needs center for both undocumented students and US citizens with undocumented parents compared to US citizens with lawfully present parents. Stated another way: If immigration-impacted students did not experience the burden of immigration policy threat, their use of this campus resource would be on par with their US-born peers with lawfully present parents. After controlling for family financial strain, undocumented students remained more likely to visit than US citizens with lawfully present parents, likely due to their need for help managing individual financial strain as well. However, accounting for family financial strain was enough to eliminate statistically significant differences between US citizen students with undocumented parents and their peers with lawfully present parents. Collectively, these findings suggest that immigration-impacted students are turning to basic needs centers for support with managing family legal vulnerability.

Yet our interviews suggest that students may still not visit a basic needs center as frequently as their needs might require. Viewing resources as finite, students were sometimes hesitant to access basic needs resources that they perceived others to need more. Madeline Salinas, a US citizen with an undocumented parent, explained that she used her campus food pantry infrequently:

> I didn't like to go too often. Because I was like, "Oh gosh, what if I'm taking food away from people that actually need it?" . . . I knew the resources were available to me, but I think because I wasn't starving, I didn't consider myself okay to use them as much. I was like, Well, I can just take a couple more shifts [at work]. There was never any major food insecurities. It was just like, I'll just eat sandwiches straight for this week. But I had food. So it wasn't like that. So I think it just felt improper to use, kind of.

What Madeline describes suggests she had "low" but "not very" low food security by the US Department of Agriculture's definition. Madeline imagined specific archetypes who might be struggling more—a pregnant student, a graduate student with a family, or "kids that were here on scholarships like me, but maybe they didn't have the part-time job that I had." This perception that students should minimize their demands on these centers to protect the collective good was common.

Emergency grant aid programs were another safety-net resource that helped students manage unexpected expenses that threatened their family's precarious financial balancing act. Catalina Paz Flores, a DACA recipient, had received an economic crisis response grant from her campus financial aid office. Paying for her undocumented mother's medical treatment had depleted her savings:

> If you need help with your rent or any bills like that, they will give you the money for it. The way I put it was, "I had to use some rent money for my mom's medical emergency. She doesn't have health insurance. So . . . now I'm a little short on rent," something like that. Because otherwise I believe they don't give it to you. It has to be specifically for [your] rent and bills.

Catalina's request was approved, and she received funds for two months of rent, totaling $800. She recalled this news brought huge relief, "I was like, Wow! And I wanted to cry." Though small, these emergency grants provided significant relief to students like Catalina when there was no other way to make ends meet. Yet Catalina's explanation hinted at the difficulty of translating her individual and family financial strain in a way that is legible to the university. In particular, individualistic institutional logic required that these emergency funds addressed personal, not family, financial needs. She was aware she could not have asked for money to help her mother directly—even though that was the underlying source of the emergency.

The undocumented student services office was a third strand in the campus safety net. Gael Yepez Correa, an undocumented student without lawful immigration status, had worked as an intern at his campus undocumented student services office and was well acquainted with its slate of targeted financial support programs. He described the emergency grant and scholarship programs for undocumented students administered by the office in addition to other programs. As he said, the undocumented student services office established a committee to "lend textbooks to students who can't afford it." The committee had copies of many of the textbooks assigned on campus, and, he said, it would buy textbooks they didn't have if he could not afford it. "You just return it to them at the end of the [academic] quarter," he explained. Gael also described the office's push to supplement campus efforts to address food insecurity, establishing a partnership with campus and community partners to distribute food vouchers for a local grocery store. Gael noted that it was designed to match Cal-Fresh, a governmental supplemental nutrition program for which undocumented students are not eligible. Belen Mesa, a DACA recipient at another campus, explained that she was also a beneficiary of her campus paid fellowship program for undocumented students. Receiving $4,500 over the course of the academic year as a fellowship stipend helped her cover many of the expenses not covered by financial aid.

Ultimately, these campus resources benefited students' education by relieving financial strains and creating space for academic and social engagement on campus. Benjamin Ponce, a US citizen with an undocumented parent, recalled that the growing burden of educational expenses was harming his academic performance and that additional financial resources had helped cover expenses, making it "one less thing to worry about when I'm doing my classes." J. D. Armenta, a DACA recipient, noted that one of the offices on his campus helped cover club fees. He was able to get help paying for his rugby fees and ensured access to a space where he built a peer support network: "I think through rugby, I definitely had a place where I can move and connect with people. Later on, we all became friends and we studied together and stuff." Similarly, Fernando Medina, a US citizen with undocumented parents, found that being able to access fresh food through the campus food pantry allowed him to learn that he enjoys cooking: "[It] takes my mind away from other things that I'm able to do. I'm able to not only afford yummy food, but I'm able to cook yummy food. And while I cook the yummy food, my mind is taking a break from everything." In addition to the physical and psychological benefits of healthy cooking, prior research suggests that students with food security have better academic engagement and performance outcomes.[14] Such instances suggest that campus financial assistance removed immediate stressors, created mental space for academic engagement, fostered physical and psychological well-being, and also helped students engage in spaces where they could build social capital. All of these positive impacts support improved academic outcomes.

RECOMMENDATION #2: ESTABLISH, EXPAND, AND RAISE AWARENESS ABOUT CAMPUS SAFETY-NET RESOURCES.

As our findings illustrate, institutions must establish, expand, and raise awareness about the availability of safety-net resources. Given the remarkably frequent use of basic needs centers on UC campuses, similar facilities should be established on other campuses that serve immigration-impacted students, and funding needs to be robust to safeguard against feelings of competition for limited resources. Campuses that do not have emergency grant aid programs should establish them with enough funding to meet student demand. Such programs should be publicized so that students are well aware of their availability and purpose. Institutions could also confirm that their emergency grant application process acknowledges the collective nature of financial strain within families; explicitly acknowledging how family financial strain can exacerbate individual financial strain to encourage students to make and explain these connections. Partnerships between undocumented student services, basic needs centers, and other related offices could see to it that safety-net resources reach intended student audiences.

In light of students' expressed reluctance to access safety-net resources, university faculty and staff must anticipate this and work to empower students by reframing and raising awareness of such services. Our conversations with UC undocumented student services staff reveal their efforts to reframe students' zero-sum perceptions. They explain to students that their use of resources and applications for aid actually help staff make the case for the allocation of additional funds due to high student demand. Such logic frames resource use as a form of advocacy rather than as a competition.[15] Students may also benefit from educational campaigns that define food insecurity so that students are empowered to recognize their own basic needs and then access resources as needed.

Fear of Family Separation and University Legal Services

Santos Castro, a US citizen with an undocumented father, shared that he wished there was campus support to help with his fears of family separation. As he said: "Because when my father does get deported, who do I ask for help?" He was well aware of the impact of these concerns on his academic performance and felt that the institution should be supporting his success by alleviating them:

> Because I can't focus in school knowing that my father could be deported one of these days. . . . Who protects my family? Where's . . . UC when these things happen? Will they support lawyers? Will they help my father get out [of] detention centers? That's definitely the resource that we need, UC being there to back us up and our families in times of need.

Immigration-impacted students wanted immigration legal services and programming that would address the cascading consequences of deportation threats—the strain on their mental health, disruption to their academic participation, and deterrence of their political engagement. Our findings suggest that UC's free legal immigration services were immensely valuable and should be expanded.

IMMIGRATION LEGAL SERVICES

The University of California established the UC Immigrant Legal Services Center in 2014 to provide free immigration legal services to students and their immediate family members.[16] Services include free legal representation if they are detained or placed in deportation proceedings as well as legal consultations and assistance with applications for immigration relief programs like DACA, U visas (which are available to victims of certain crimes), or adjustment of status. Importantly, these legal services take into account how family legal vulnerability is experienced collectively by explicitly serving all students—not just undocumented students—and their immediate family members.

Our interviews reflected the value of the UC Immigrant Legal Services Center. Several interviewees had consulted campus immigration attorneys for themselves, their parents, and/or siblings through the center. DACA recipients often relied on these attorneys to file DACA renewal requests. These free services had ensured the timely and cost-effective submission of applications. Some campuses also covered students' US Citizenship and Immigration Services (USCIS) filing fees, which could range from $600-plus to nearly $3,000 at the time of our interviews; this essentially eliminated financial barriers to renewing DACA or applying for other forms of immigration relief and reducing students' stress. Other students recalled seeking legal advice for family members. Catalina Paz Flores, a DACA recipient, explained: "I've gone to the lawyer to talk to them about my sister and things like that and what their advice would be on her case." Her undocumented older sister had been deported years before and returned to the United States by clandestinely recrossing the United States–Mexico border. Having access to free legal advice was "really, really, really, really helpful" for Catalina and her family to understand her sister's legal options.

Free legal services were indispensable when students or their family members required attorney representation. Madeline Salinas, a US citizen with an undocumented father, recalled finding out about UC Immigrant Legal Services during the end of her sophomore year:

> My dad got arrested and he was really close to getting deported so that became really big. . . . I had to go home just because of everything that was happening, and there was just a lot going on. And I remember I missed my classes for two weeks, not going to lie. And I remember taking care of my little brother. It was just an intense time and we sort of had to scramble to get a lawyer.

Madeline was so thankful for the UC Immigrant Legal Services Center because "I would have freaked out if all that stuff had happened to me and I wouldn't have had anybody." Having access to a qualified and free attorney allowed her to understand the complexities of the deportation proceeding process and possible outcomes. This support helped Madeline transition from panic to preparation: "She did help me calm down. . . . Because I was over there thinking the worst and she was like, 'No, legally that can't happen.' So she just provided an anchor." This support allowed Madeline to minimize the impact that this experience could have had on her academics. Her father was not deported, and while it is impossible to know if her father would have been spared deportation without representation, research suggests that having an attorney improves the odds that detainees will be granted bond and be allowed to remain in the United States.[17] In the end, Madeline was shielded from the worst catastrophic socioemotional and economic strains that deportation places on families and its negative impacts on students' academic performance, educational retention, and mental health.[18]

Some students found relief simply in knowing that immigration legal services were available. Ryan Zepeda, the undocumented student whose story opened this chapter, anticipated that he could find himself in a situation like Madeline's father. Despite feeling that his conversations with UC immigration attorneys had thus far been a "reality check" about the difficulties he faced, knowing legal services existed was "a humongous stress relief because I knew if I were to ever get into something with law enforcement, I have them. . . . Having someone give you their cell phone number is a humongous help." In such hypothetical situations, students experienced emotional relief that reduced the cognitive load associated with deportability concerns.

Despite their explicit eligibility for utilizing the UC Immigrant Legal Services Center, US citizens underused this service, according to our survey. While 69 percent of undocumented students reported accessing campus immigration legal services, only 13 percent of US citizen students with undocumented parents had used them.[19] Yet most would have benefited. As we discussed in chapter 1, many US citizens were eagerly awaiting their twenty-first birthday, when they would become eligible to petition for their undocumented parents to adjust their immigration status and become lawful permanent residents; they often dedicated valuable time and savings to pay for legal consultations and fees. The center's free and reputable immigration legal services could have defrayed these costs. Our interviews suggest most of our US citizen participants did not know this resource was available to them.

It is important to note that some of the students who accessed immigration legal services in an attempt to alleviate legal vulnerability did not get the material relief they desired due to the limitations of immigration law. As Bianca Mercado, a DACA recipient, elaborated: "I remember sitting down with one of the UC lawyers and we were talking about citizenship options for my parents. But I mean, the options weren't really something that . . . applied to my family." The handful of adjustment programs available in the United States, such as for victims of domestic abuse, did not apply for many students or their families. Rather, in legal consultations students often learned that the clandestine modes of entry into the United States they or their families had taken would complicate family-based immigration petitions by requiring them to leave the country to process their petitions and possibly facing a ten-year bar on their return.[20] In some cases parents' past detentions or deportations would make adjustment of status nearly impossible. Some students looked for other legal representation following such news, opening themselves up to scams and predatory "service providers" who promised legal loopholes that did not exist.

RECOMMENDATION #3: PROVIDE FREE IMMIGRATION LEGAL SERVICES TO STUDENTS AND THEIR FAMILY MEMBERS AND ENSURE THAT THERE ARE NO BARRIERS TO ACCESSING THESE SERVICES.

Universities and colleges should follow the example of the University of California to provide free immigration legal services to all students and their immediate family members. UC's immigrant legal services model—directly employing multiple staff attorneys and support staff—may work for some institutions. Others might look to the California State University system, which contracts with local immigration legal service providers to arrange for services.[21] Legal service providers could be readily available for on-campus consultations and provide virtual appointments to accommodate family members and online students. Services should be widely advertised to ensure that US citizens with undocumented parents are aware of them. Staff could highlight the benefits of accessing legal services through their campus immigration attorney, including no attorney fees and fraud protection. To guard against the risk of fraud in cases when immigration relief is not available, providers of campus legal services could help students understand why they do not qualify for relief and facilitate referrals to qualified attorneys who can provide second opinions. Campuses could also establish funds that students can access to pay for the USCIS filing fees associated with various immigration relief applications.

PROGRAMS TO MANAGE DEPORTATION CONCERNS

While campus legal services proved helpful for managing Ryan's anxiety about deportation, other students felt that their campuses lacked resources to help manage this stressor. When asked about if such programming exists, Emilia Negrete Romero, an undocumented student without lawful immigration status, answered plainly: "Not really. No." She added that she recognized that the university can do little to mitigate these risks: "Because I would feel that's more closer to the root problem, which they can't really do anything about." As Emilia bluntly acknowledged, there are limited ways to provide material relief through legal representation. Thus, immigration-impacted students identified a need for programming to help them manage their fear of family separation and the cascading effects of these concerns on their mental health and academic success.

Undocumented students asked for the recurring provision of "know your rights" information that would prepare them to navigate interactions with police or immigration authorities. Gael Yepez Correa, an undocumented student without lawful immigration status, felt that he had benefited from "know your rights" information distributed by campus undocumented student services staff, and he highlighted the advantage of "red cards," a resource formatted as a bright red business card that lists what to do when encountering immigration enforcement. "They're also pretty helpful," he said. Designed to fit in a wallet or otherwise be kept with one at all times, red cards are a critical resource at moments of intense danger. Having them made students feel prepared.

However, the provision of such information was intermittent and varied by campus. Arely Barajas, a third-year undocumented student without lawful immigration status, said that she had "never heard anyone have a conversation about" the rights of undocumented immigrants. She longed for workshops: "That would really help, because if I was to be detained, I have no idea what that looks like, what you're expected to do. I know it's like, you shouldn't sign stuff, but that's all I heard. I don't know what that means." Notably, many of the students longing for more information did not benefit from DACA and were thus less protected from deportation threats. This is notable for institutions given that over time fewer and fewer students will be DACA recipients. Further, students may perceive stronger threats in more exclusionary state and local contexts.

Immigration-impacted students appreciated the few programs that existed to help them process and manage their deportation concerns. Some had attended healing circles, which were typically run by undocumented student services, undocumented student organizations, and/or in partnership with campus mental health services. Attendees valued these spaces. Gabriel Ballón, a DACA recipient, described the healing circle he had attended as helpful for managing deportation concerns and fear of family separation "because you're talking about it and you feel like you're not the only one. [You're] all in the same boat. . . . And it felt good because you feel like you're not alone. [You're] in this fight together." Perhaps because US citizens with undocumented parents rarely sought help from the undocumented student services office, they typically had not attended such sessions—and yet they yearned for them. Santiago Zaragoza Zamora, a US citizen anxious about the vulnerability of his undocumented parents, wished for such a space to "just open discussions about it. . . . Let out your concerns."

Students also highlighted a practical measure that mitigated their deportation anxiety: students attending campuses far from home were concerned about asking their parents to drive long distances to pick them up for weekends or holiday breaks. They associated driving with increased risk of deportation. They also were conscious of financial barriers associated with purchasing gas or taking time off work. Marcos Villaseñor, a DACA recipient from Southern California attending UC Santa Cruz, approximately six hours away, recalled that the campus had previously offered special holiday transportation options that helped meet these needs:

> When there was a big break like Thanksgiving . . . or winter break, you would buy a ticket through the university, and then they would have these charter buses take all these students to LA. That was very useful for students who were new to Santa Cruz who didn't really know how to get around that much or needed to get back home. It was also cheaper.

Although this program was open to all students, it has particular value for immigration-impacted students because of their families' financial constraints and concerns about deportability. Such programs might help students feel more comfortable attending colleges farther from home.

RECOMMENDATION #4: OFFER PROGRAMMING THAT
EMPOWERS STUDENTS' MANAGEMENT OF DEPORTATION
THREATS AND CONCERNS.

Universities and colleges must offer programming that empowers students with information and strategies to manage their concerns about the possibility of their own and/or family members' deportation. Workshops could include traditional "know your rights" presentations, which provide information about the deportation process and undocumented individuals' rights when interacting with police and immigration agents.[22] These workshops could also guide students on how to pass along information to family members and prepare family deportation plans for real-word scenarios. Workshops could also provide strategies that immigration-impacted students can use to manage deportation concerns; this could include trauma-informed training and strategies to monitor deportation threats through social media without letting it overwhelm them or disrupt their academic engagement. To reinforce consistent availability of information, workshops should be offered annually; recordings and fact sheets could also be made available on campus websites. Such programing is especially critical in exclusionary state and local contexts in which law enforcement collaborates with federal immigration enforcement. Every effort should be made to establish that US citizen students with undocumented parents are aware of and invited to participate.

The development of transportation assistance programs would help immigration-impacted students traverse spaces perceived to be risky. Programs could include charter buses to major cities throughout the state. Institutions that draw large out-of-state student bodies, such as private colleges and universities, should identify innovative ways to virtually or physically accompany students who must travel across the country to provide a sense of security. Such programs will be especially important with the implementation of REAL ID requirements to board airplanes, which make it difficult and risky for undocumented immigrants to fly. These programs should be advertised year-round, especially during admissions and recruitment, to help immigration-impacted students feel more comfortable enrolling in campuses farther from home.

Overall, we identified four meaningful campus resources that support immigration-impacted students' efforts to directly manage family legal vulnerability: financial aid, campus safety-net resources, immigration legal services, and deportation threat management programming. Creating and strengthening these campus resources can promote student success by helping lessen the effects of collective economic insecurity and concerns about deportation and family separation. Such university resources can address or reduce the salience of family legal vulnerability in everyday life.

Addressing Cascading Consequences

In addition to providing resources that alleviate legal vulnerability, university services can also address the cascading effects of family legal vulnerability on students' mental health, academic success, and political engagement. Academic support services help students who are struggling academically or want additional support to transition successfully to college. Mental health counseling supports student well-being, a necessary condition for academic success.[23] Multicultural and identity-based centers provide tailored resources and safe spaces to aid historically excluded groups and promote their campus belonging and integration, including through organizational and political engagement.[24] In the University of California system, all campuses offer comparable services in these areas. Here we examine the extent to which immigration-impacted students accessed these campus services and how institutions can strengthen them to support students suffering the consequences of family legal vulnerability.

Supporting Mental Health

All nine UC undergraduate campuses have on-campus mental health counseling services with staff psychologists. They provide free short-term counseling services to enrolled students, including eight to ten individual therapy sessions, group therapy, and mental health workshops. Figure 5.4 displays the frequency with which our survey participants visited campus mental health services during the academic year. Overall, 32 percent of undocumented students reported visiting campus mental health services, compared to 24 percent of US citizen students with undocumented parents and 25 percent of US

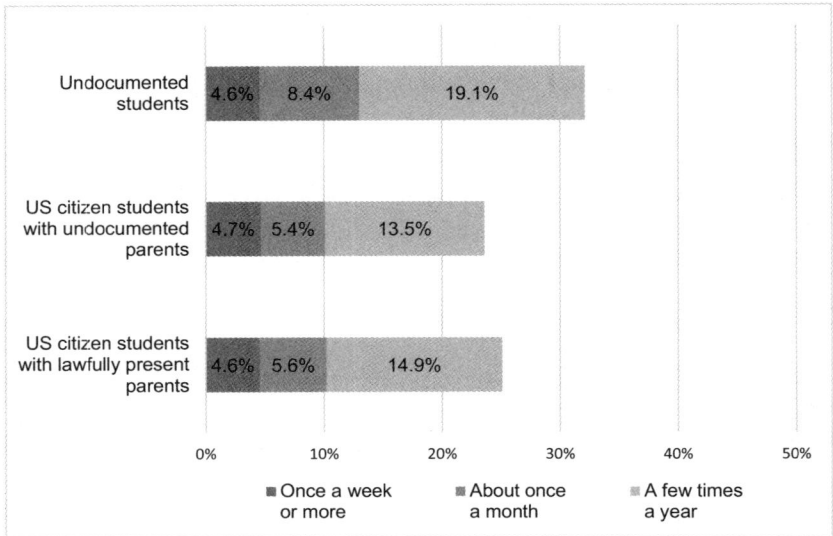

Figure 5.4. Frequency survey respondents visited campus mental health services by self and parental immigration status.

citizen students with lawfully present parents. The majority of these visited intermittently—a few times per year.

Our regression analyses identified no significant group differences in students' use of mental health services once controlling for demographic characteristics (see figure 5.5). That is, undocumented students and US citizen students with undocumented parents were as likely to use on-campus mental health services as US citizen students with lawfully present parents. This is not surprising given our findings in chapter 2 that there were no significant differences in depression and anxiety symptomatology across the three student groups. Although no group differences emerged once we accounted for measures of family legal vulnerability, threat to family and family financial strain were significant predictors that increased the chances of mental health service use. This suggests that the immigration-related mental health strains we documented in chapter 2 are contributing to immigration-impacted students' use of campus mental health services, just not to the point that they use services above and beyond their peers with lawfully present parents.

Despite their need for and modest use of services, our interviewees suggest that immigration-impacted students underutilize mental health services. Students who gained access to on-campus providers found that they could not accommodate the long-term therapy needed to address the mental health impacts of chronic family legal vulnerability. Ignacio Padilla Cortes, a US citizen with undocumented parents, explained the limitations he had faced: "I went to therapy for a bit but then I ran out of like therapy credits. . . . We have a certain amount of days a semester or a quarter to go to a therapist and then you're done. I do feel like I'm way better than last year because I understand . . . how to . . . manage [my emotions]. But I'm still struggling just with unprocessed trauma that I have." Many others similarly highlighted limited access to services due to high demand, insufficient staffing, long wait times, and the focus on short-term treatment.

Some of our interviewees sought out and found value in workshops aimed at expanding their mental health coping strategies. Aimee Bañuelos, a US citizen with undocumented parents, mentioned she had gone to "a few" such events. She said it had been a way "to learn a little bit more about how to deal with stress and different things like that."

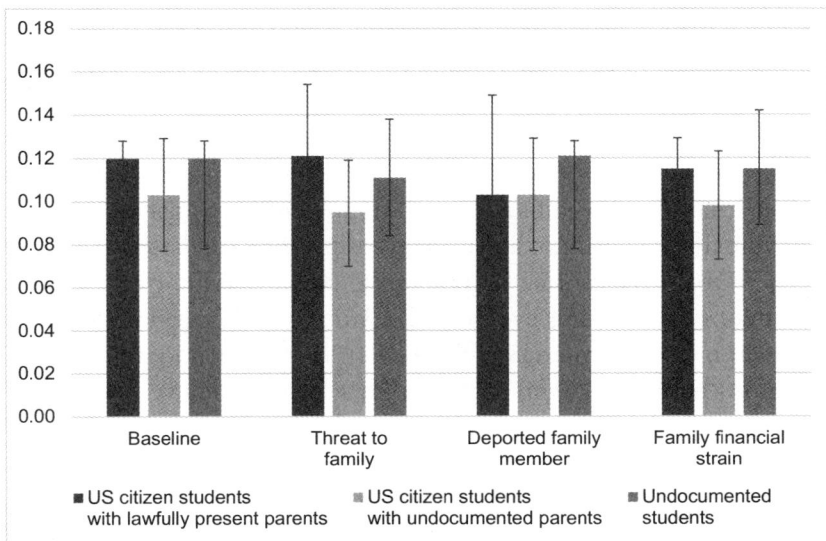

Figure 5.5. Predicted probability of visiting campus mental health services when controlling for family legal vulnerability.

Diana Mora, who is also a US citizen with undocumented parents, said: "The Women's Center, they offered a lot of workshops about mental health. They have this little library where you could go and check out [related] books and stuff, and I'm a fan of that." Although these workshops were not focused on family legal vulnerability, they helped students refine the tools they had available to protect their mental health in light of the many stressors they faced.

Undocumented students identified successful support groups run by their campus's undocumented student services office, often in collaboration with campus mental health services. Maribel Aranda, a DACA recipient, described the undocu-circles that the campus undocumented student services office hosted:

> There's a therapist there where we can talk about our feelings about things that are going on. So that was helpful too and I think that helped kind of alleviate my feelings with folks who are also undocumented or allies. . . . A counselor . . . would come to basically just kind of help navigate the conversation, kind of like group therapy.

These spaces varied in their structure and could address a range of topics, including deportability and family separation, as mentioned above in this chapter. Students like Catalina Paz Flores, a DACA recipient who attended a different campus with a similar program, explained that she joined a few sessions when the topics resonated with her: "It helped a little bit because I was able to vent and stuff and just express myself. It's basically just expressing yourself and venting and talking about it with your other peers, getting each other's perspectives on the issue." These types of less formal support group programs not only provide a space for processing family legal vulnerability but also can help students build a peer support group and establish relationships with campus counselors, potentially easing their transition into formal therapy if needed.

RECOMMENDATION #5: EXPAND ACCESS TO AND
TYPES OF MENTAL HEALTH SERVICES AVAILABLE TO
ADDRESS FAMILY LEGAL VULNERABILITY.
Taking into consideration the mental health strains we documented in chapter 2, universities and colleges must make certain that on-campus

mental health services are readily available to promote help-seeking among immigration-impacted students. Institutions must invest in expanded mental health services by hiring more counselors, extending the number of short-term therapy sessions offered, and making long-term therapy available on campus. Prior research on undocumented college students' mental health help-seeking suggests that on-campus mental health services must also address psychosocial barriers to use. Undocumented students, and likely US citizen students with undocumented parents, may normalize their mental health strain due to its chronic nature or perceive treatment to be futile because it does not address underlying structural barriers.[25] Education campaigns should help immigration-impacted students recognize their mental health strain and understand the purpose and utility of therapy and other mental health services. In addition, undocumented students expressed concerns about facing immigration-related stigma from mental health service providers, and those who perceive more social exclusion due to the immigration policy context are less likely to use on-campus mental health services.[26] Institutions must ensure that counselors are culturally competent and receive professional development training to understand family legal vulnerability.

In addition to expanding mental health counseling services, institutions could invest in programming that empowers students with skills and strategies to care for their mental health. Workshops can help students reflect on the impact of immigration policies on their lives and develop strategies for managing the specific strains associated with family legal vulnerability. Institutions could also establish informal support groups that hold space for immigration-impacted students as they reflect on and process individual and family legal vulnerability. Collaborations between campus mental health services, undocumented student services, and other relevant student services may be particularly useful for ensuring that programming reaches the intended audience. These programs can form a bridge to help students understand when, how, and why they should access more formal mental health services.

Promoting Academic Success

All UC undergraduate campuses offer a vast range of academic support. Academic counselors or advisers associated with the school or

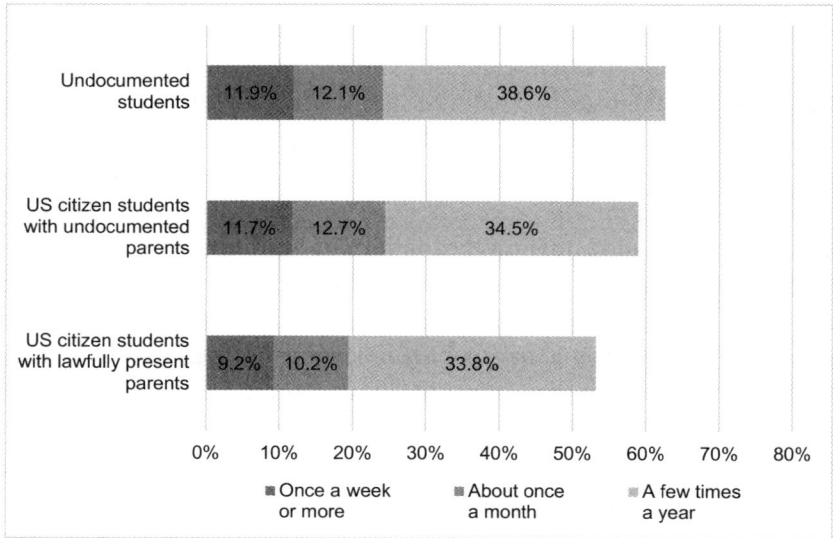

Figure 5.6. Frequency survey respondents visited academic support services by self and parental immigration status.

one's specific major provide guidance on meeting academic requirements. Academic support services promote student success through workshops and individual meetings; some, like writing and tutoring centers, help students strengthen particular academic skills or support them with specific classes. All campuses have dedicated offices that aid students who have been historically underrepresented in higher education through holistic programming including academic, personal, and career counseling, workshops, cohort and peer-support programs, tutoring, peer mentoring, study spaces, and scholarships. Figure 5.6 displays the frequency with which our survey participants visited academic support services during the academic year. Overall, 63 percent of undocumented students reported visiting campus academic support services, which was comparable to 59 percent of US citizen students with undocumented parents. US citizen participants with lawfully present parents had the lowest rates of use at 53 percent. About two out of every five students who accessed these services did so frequently, once per month or more.

Family legal vulnerability motivates undocumented students' higher propensity to use academic support services. Regression analyses confirm that, at baseline, undocumented students were more likely to use these campus resources than US citizen students with lawfully present parents (see figure 5.7). This reflects findings in chapter 3 wherein undocumented students practiced higher rates of positive academic engagement. Differences between these student groups were eliminated once we accounted for two aspects of family legal vulnerability: perceived threat to family, and family financial strain. That is, if undocumented students did not experience these forms of family legal vulnerability, their use of this campus resource would be on par with their US-born peers with lawfully present parents. Collectively, these findings suggest that that undocumented students are turning to academic support services for help managing family legal vulnerability.

Our interviews reveal that immigration-impacted students felt unsupported by academic support services staff due to limited understandings of legal vulnerability. Undocumented students often encountered professional and peer staff members that did not understand the

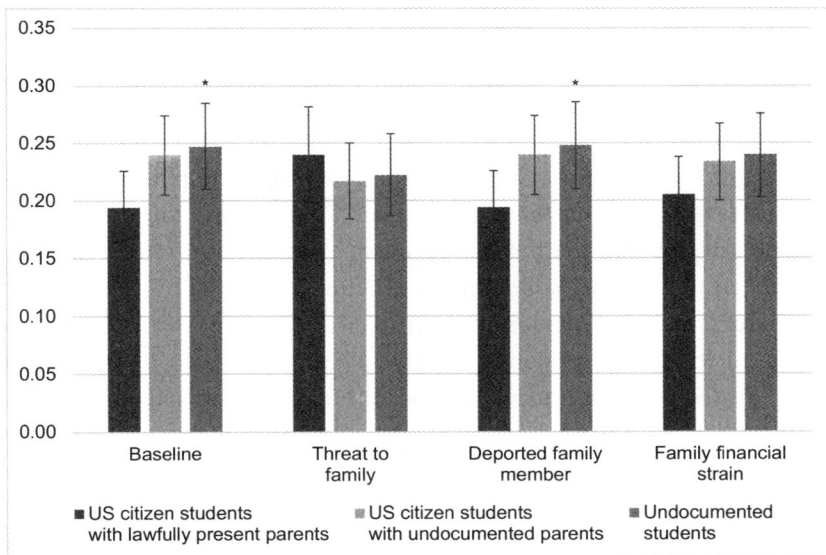

Figure 5.7. Predicted probability of visiting academic support services when controlling for family legal vulnerability.
NOTE: Statistically significant differences from the reference group are indicated by * when p<.05.

constraints associated with their immigration status. Mateo Olivares Galvan, a DACA recipient, explained: "I had a [peer] tutor . . . and I remember telling him about my startup [company plan]. . . . He was telling me, 'You go to UCLA, you have all the skills I have. Why can't you work?' So there's a huge portion of people that just don't know what it really means [to be undocumented]." Mateo's tutor did not understand legal vulnerability or its consequences. As a result, attempts at encouragement landed flat, making such support ineffective. Similarly, Benjamin Ponce, a US citizen with an undocumented parent, recalled an academic counseling experience in which the counselor did not take family legal vulnerability into account:

> I was a transfer student, I was [living] at home, I had immigrant parents at home that I was supporting, and that kind of obligated me to work. And the whole situation of having to work and go to school at the same time, the counselors really didn't want to pay attention to that. They were kind of just stuck on the ways of: we're only going to recommend what we recommend to traditional students. And if you can't put those recommendations [into practice], it's your fault that you're failing.

Benjamin tried to explain his situation, but he found that counselors were not listening. He stopped seeking academic support as a result. While our survey results suggest that immigration-impacted students do access academic support services, Mateo's and Benjamin's experiences suggest that they may do so less frequently than they need or desire because of these alienating experiences.

Students felt that academic support was more effective when they worked with counselors and staff who displayed an ethic of care and understanding of their individual and/or family legal vulnerability. Julia Soto, a US citizen with undocumented parents, recalled meeting with an academic adviser when she was at risk for dismissal for poor academic performance: "It was more like: 'What are you trying to do?' 'What are your worries?' 'How are you doing?' And then from there a plan was built." This counselor made her feel like an active participant in the planning process and tried to understand underlying constraints and issues that were contributing to her poor performance. Similarly, Maribel

Aranda, a DACA recipient, recalled positive experiences with a career-center counselor who worked closely with undocumented students. She explained: "You can say, 'Hey, I'm undocumented,' and so they assign you to her. . . . And that's who I turned to when I was trying to look for jobs; that was really helpful." There is a clear need for more counselors with the training to offer such an approach. Further, identifying dedicated counseling staff who students know will understand their specific individual and family legal vulnerability can increase willingness to state their needs, thereby improving the support provided and increasing the odds they will return.

Indeed, holistic counseling encouraged immigration-impacted students to return to academic support offices and become more integrated on campus. Rocio Carrillo Guerra, a DACA recipient, summarized her visits to the academic support services office that focused on providing holistic services to historically underrepresented students. She initially formed a relationship with the office through a summer bridge counselor and then as a participant in a cohort-based program that supported incoming undocumented students through peer and professional staff support:

> I think having the counselors there, . . . being able to go in there and cry in their office was always—it made me feel so much more relieved and so much better. Having the peer educators helped me make my schedule, figure out how to study, . . . having the printing services, being able to print my study guides and use the computers. They would have snacks. . . . Just overall, the environment was . . . really welcoming. I felt productive and I had somewhere to go. . . . I remember how it felt my first year, not knowing where to stay or what to do, where to study. Knowing that I had a place where I could just go and sit was nice.

Similarly, Valentino Peña, a US citizen with undocumented parents, traced his support system of "people that I can talk to during my problems" back to the same office Rocio had described. "That's where I built relationships with the staff and created mentorship relationships." Through programs and holistic academic counseling services, these offices promote a sense of belonging and integration.

RECOMMENDATION #6: STRENGTHEN THE CULTURAL
COMPETENCY AND BELONGING OFFERED BY ACADEMIC
SUPPORT SERVICES WHEN WORKING WITH
IMMIGRATION-IMPACTED STUDENTS.

In light of the academic disruptions that we documented in chapter 4, academic support services should be enhanced to meet the needs of immigration-impacted students. Institutions should provide professional development for academic counselors and related student affairs professionals to expand the toolkit they have available to understand and address individual and family legal vulnerability. This could include understanding underlying concerns as well as identifying campus resources to which they can refer students. Offices could also identify a point person who is best prepared to receive and serve undocumented students. This person should be given the necessary time and resources to develop relationships with their campus undocumented student services office and create crossover programs focused on the immigration-impacted student population. Academic support programs that focus on historically underrepresented and/or immigration-impacted students, such as summer bridge programs and cohort-based retention programs, can also be effective ways to foster campus belonging—a key factor that can encourage academic success and retention.[27]

Empowering Political Participation

Identity-based centers and student organizations provide opportunities to build leadership skills, explore politicized identities, and develop a sense of empowerment, which can lay the groundwork for political engagement.[28] Figure 5.8 displays the frequency with which our survey participants visited identity-based centers during the academic year. Overall, 46 percent of undocumented students reported visiting these centers, compared to 33 percent of US citizen students with undocumented parents and 34 percent of US citizens with lawfully present parents. About half of the students who visited these centers did so once per month or more. Regression analyses confirm that, after controlling for demographic characteristics, undocumented students in our survey visited identity-based centers more frequently than US citizen students with lawfully present parents (see figure 5.9).

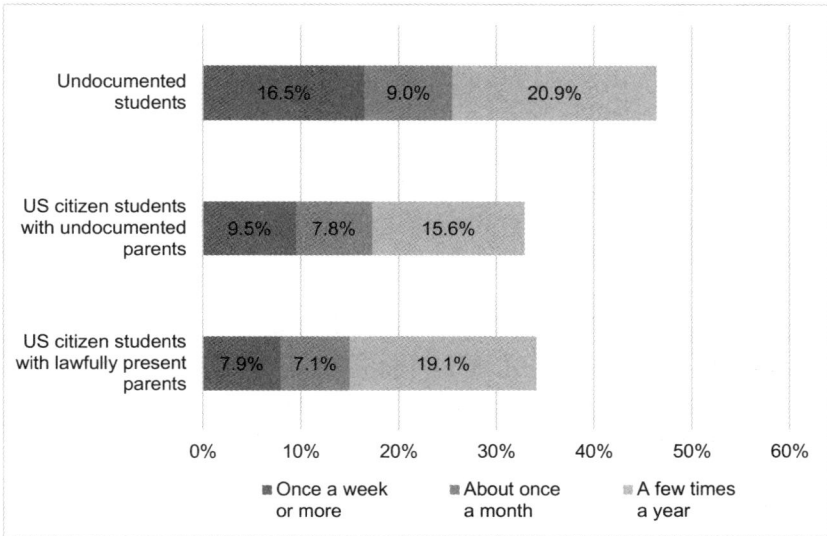

Figure 5.8. Frequency survey respondents visited identity-based centers by self and parental immigration status.

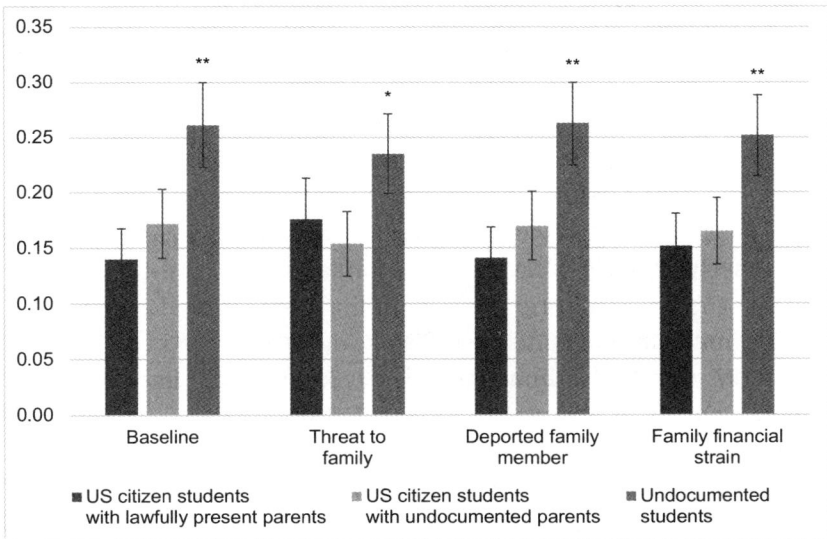

Figure 5.9. Predicted probability of visiting identity-based centers when controlling for family legal vulnerability.

NOTE: Statistically significant differences from the reference group are indicated by ** when p<.01.

Differences between undocumented students and US citizen students with lawfully present parents were reduced once we accounted for threat to family and family financial strain; however, undocumented students still remained significantly more likely to visit than their US citizen peers with lawfully present parents. Both measures were significant predictors that increased the chances of visiting such centers. In other words, family legal vulnerability partially explains undocumented students' higher visitation rates relative to US citizen students with lawfully present parents, but other factors also drive group differences. It seems likely that individual legal vulnerability may help explain this trend, as undocumented students may seek out identity-based centers to meet like-minded students and manage the legal vulnerability tied to their own immigration status.

Identity-based centers are important spaces that promote community empowerment and engagement among immigration-impacted students. Bianca Mercado, a DACA recipient, recalled that her campus's Chicanx/Latinx student program sponsored a weeklong series of events to support Chicana/Latina women:

> I would attend those events and I would talk to people from [the program] and I found a community there. . . And I talked to them and I told them that I was undocumented and I was also Mexican and I felt solidarity with them. I feel like it's that thing where you talk with people who are like you, and you just feel proud for them. They were telling me, oh, I'm proud of you. And then likewise, vice versa. And it was a very nice community to be a part of.

Finding this community inspired Bianca and strengthened her sense of purpose. However, she simultaneously realized that these identity-based centers were under resourced: "I knew that [my campus] did not fund those programs the way that they should be funded. Also kind of sad that, for each department, their room is . . . tiny." When there was finally a "huge push on funding for those programs," she participated. As a member of her campus newspaper staff, she wrote articles highlighting the importance of the work performed by these centers. She felt "it wasn't fair for a program so helpful . . . to not have funding." In addition to promoting a sense of individual and community empowerment, students found opportunities to advocate for themselves and their communities through identity-based centers.

Identity-based student organizations also fostered student political empowerment and engagement. Arely Barajas, an undocumented student without lawful immigration status, traced her growth within her campus undocumented student organization. She recalled feeling "very alone" her first year and "stressed about not having DACA. And I was very stressed with financial stuff because . . . if my parents can't help me and if I don't get enough financial aid, then I can't really help myself." Visiting the undocumented student services office, she learned about a student-run advocacy campaign to increase campus support for students without employment authorization. She joined an email list and then an advocacy workshop and before long "started going to the meetings that they were holding with deans and school administration." The next year she participated in an internship program, where she was paired with one of the organization's leaders to build up advocacy skills and received a small scholarship. The following year she was elected advocacy director and the year after co-chair. Throughout her four years with the organization, she met several role models, developed leadership skills, and had opportunities to empower herself and others to advocate for resources to meet the unique needs of undocumented students. Student-run organizations like these are critical spaces where undocumented and other immigration-impacted students can find opportunities for political engagement and growth.

RECOMMENDATION #7: DEDICATE RESOURCES TO
FACILITATE IMMIGRATION-IMPACTED STUDENTS'
POLITICAL EMPOWERMENT AND ENGAGEMENT.
In light of the constrained political participation we document in chapter 5, universities and colleges could dedicate resources to support campus and student-run spaces that empower and engage immigration-impacted students. Institutions could invest in identity-based offices to fund programs that can support student empowerment and leadership. They could also support the establishment and development of immigration-impacted student organizations that are dedicated to empowering and advocating for this specific student population. Both identity-based centers and student organizations could in turn

work to develop their members' political knowledge and skills, including through workshops, advocacy actions, and mentored leadership opportunities. Scholarship or fellowship funding could be offered to individuals who are participating in programs or longer-term commitments to offset the opportunity costs associated with participating in such leadership building opportunities.

Overall, we examined three meaningful campus services that immigration-impacted students can access to address the cascading effects of family legal vulnerability: campus mental health services, academic support services, and identity-based centers and student organizations. Both the UC and institutions nationwide should strengthen such campus services to ensure that they can provide targeted resources and programs that directly address the needs of immigration-impacted students and acknowledge the role of family legal vulnerability in their educational journeys. Such interventions would help mitigate the cascading consequences of family legal vulnerability on students' mental-health, academic, and political engagement outcomes.

Investing in Holistic Support for Immigration-Impacted Students

In addition to campuswide services, all UC campuses have undocumented student services offices that provide a welcoming and supportive environment with resources dedicated to advancing educational access and equity for undocumented students as well as other immigration-impacted student populations. These offices emerged out of mobilization by, with, and on behalf of undocumented students, and their initial mission was to support undocumented students.[29] However, over time these spaces have come to implicitly and sometimes explicitly serve a wider group of students impacted by immigration policy. They offer a range of holistic resources and programming to alleviate the effects of legal vulnerability, including many of the innovative and collaborative programs and resources discussed in this chapter so far.[30] While these services may provide support to US citizens with undocumented parents, most of their work focuses on supporting undocumented students by addressing individual legal vulnerability. Undocumented and immigration-impacted student services offices are singularly prepared to help ease family legal vulnerability, and institutions should invest in their development to maximize their impact.

In contrast to many experiences of general campus services, interviewees often identified undocumented and immigration-impacted student services as a site to find support. Adrian Villagomez, a DACA recipient, explained how the undocumented student center increased his sense of belonging on campus:

> [Visiting the undocumented student center] had a positive effect, just because I knew I had a place where I belong. I knew where I could go and meet other people who are going through the same struggle that I'm going through, or someone who could relate to my experience, because I couldn't talk with my classmates from my majors about these topics, because I don't feel they will understand. But at this place, that wasn't an issue.

For some students just knowing the office was there was powerful. Maribel Aranda, a DACA recipient, explained:

> When I first came to [campus] just knowing that there was a physical space made me feel more comfortable and welcome at this university. . . . Just knowing that there was not only help for me, but for my family really helped me feel more welcome and at ease and that I actually belong at this university regardless of my status.

Importantly, Maribel highlights how feelings of belonging are informed by the fact that staff members recognize that she is embedded in a legally vulnerable family. In part this is indicated by their recognition of and provision of resources to help mitigate family legal vulnerability.

The positive reputation of undocumented and immigration-impacted student services also helps integrate students into the campus's larger resource network, where they could access crucial resources. Among undocumented students who visited undocumented and immigration-impacted student services during the academic year, 50 percent had spoken with a campus partner (e.g., an academic counselor or mental health counselor) at the office. Undocumented student services staff also helped integrate students into the larger campus resource network:

76 percent reported that they were referred to at least one other person on campus who could provide needed support, services, or resources. These referrals and partnerships capitalize on the trust that undocumented and immigration-impacted student services staff cultivate with students to link them to relevant campus resources. Such referrals are integral to helping students identify staff members across campus who are informed about legal vulnerability and have professional expertise in providing needed resources and support.

Given the unique role that undocumented and immigration-impacted student services provide within the campus resource ecosystem, institutions should work to expand their use by all immigration-impacted students. In our survey, 70 percent of undocumented students reported visiting an office, such as undocumented student services, that focused on supporting undocumented students and/or students with undocumented family members. In contrast, 11 percent of US citizens with undocumented parents and 5 percent of US citizens with lawfully present parents had visited such an office.[31] Of the US citizens with undocumented parents who had not visited this office, 49 percent agreed that this was because "these resources are not for students like me," and 69 percent agreed that this was because they did not know it existed. These results suggest that such services are not effectively reaching a substantial segment of immigration-impacted students.

These services were underutilized by US citizen students with undocumented parents because they perceived such resources to be limited. Rubén Huerta-Diaz, a US citizen with undocumented parents, explained that he did not seek services out of a concern about scarcity of resources:

> I never went to the actual, . . . like DACA resources. . . . It didn't feel necessary to take up the seats for other students who are struggling. I felt like mine were less important. Just being a citizen, I think I reflected and realized that I'm in a privileged spot and these students are more concerned about themselves and I'm concerned about my parents. It's two different aspects and I think I wanted to respect that.

Much like food-insecure students who did not obtain support from the basic needs center, Rubén assumed that this was a zero-sum game and did not want to monopolize resources. But Isaiah Avalos, another US citizen with undocumented parents, recognized that the mission of the undocumented student services office was also to serve him. Nevertheless, he was concerned about scarcity:

> While their name was undocu-student services, and even though when you read the description . . . they do say that we can help students whose parents are also [undocumented]. . . . I know that there are other people that can help me with this, . . . contrary to other people who are completely in the dark about this. So I kind of ended up thinking . . . I shouldn't go because then I'd probably be taking it away from somebody else who actually needs it.

Many US citizen students struggled to see themselves as part of the intended audience for undocumented student services. Reflecting on their privilege relative to undocumented students, they sought to leave these resources for those who they perceived to need them more but simultaneously cut themselves off from important sources of support.

On top of this, family legal vulnerability had taught students to guard against the risks of revealing their own and/or family members' immigration status. Violeta Perez, a DACA recipient, explained that she had primarily sought support from the women's center rather than the undocumented student services office: "I always was intimidated to go . . . into that space because it's just public. I don't know! It's like, publicly you're outing yourself in a way." US citizens with undocumented parents also had to consider that they were not revealing their own immigration status but rather a family member's. Edgar Lopez Linares, an undocumented student without lawful immigration status, explained that he never accessed immigration legal services on his brother's behalf. His brother had been denied entry when reentering the United States on a tourist visa and was barred from returning to the United States for five years. Edgar mentioned it to his UC Immigrant Legal Services attorney once, but "my brother was like, 'Don't talk about it.' Because he didn't give me that permission, . . . I don't want to feel like I'm involving him in something that he didn't want to do." Both undocumented and US citizen students shared concerns about revealing their own or family members' immigration status, potentially exposing them to

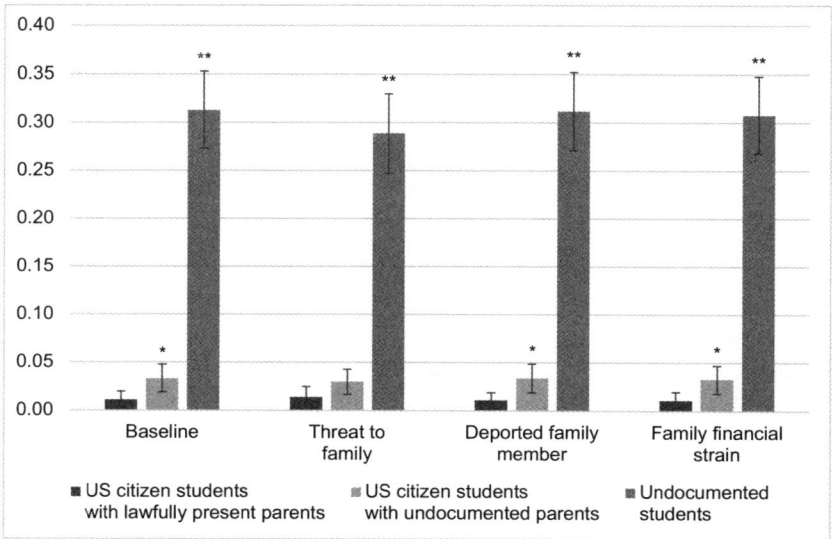

Figure 5.10. Predicted probability of visiting undocumented student services when controlling for family legal vulnerability.
NOTE: Statistically significant differences from the reference group are indicated by ** when p<.01 and * when p<.05.

stigmatizing and/or risky interactions. These concerns raised barriers to students' resource use as they sought to balance the risks and benefits of resource-seeking.

Regression analyses suggest that family and individual legal vulnerability informs students' use of undocumented and immigration-impacted student services. Figure 5.10 shows that, when controlling for demographic characteristics (i.e., at baseline), undocumented students and US citizens with undocumented parents used undocumented and immigration-impacted student services more than US citizen students with lawfully present parents. These differences were eliminated for US citizens with undocumented parents and reduced for undocumented students once we accounted for threat to family due to the restrictive policy context. Family financial strain was also a significant predictor, although not to the point of eliminating group differences. Immigration-impacted students appear to seek out services to manage family legal vulnerability. However, persistent differences remain for undocumented students because individual legal vulnerability plays a substantial role in guiding them toward this unique campus resource.

RECOMMENDATION #8: INVEST IN UNDOCUMENTED
AND IMMIGRATION-IMPACTED STUDENT SERVICES.
Universities and colleges should follow the UC system's example by establishing undocumented and immigration-impacted student services, and these offices must be funded to ensure that they can create innovative programming to help ease individual *and* family legal vulnerability. To encourage all immigration-impacted students to access these services, these offices could consider using terms that clarify that they serve all immigration-impacted students, including US citizens with undocumented family members, as we found that calling these offices "undocumented student services" discouraged some students who had citizenship. Clarifying mission statements for such offices may also be effective. For example, UC Irvine's center revised its mission statement shortly after the beginning of the first Trump administration to explicitly include all people "impacted by immigration policy." All staff members are trained to frame services in this way, and relevant programs are advertised accordingly. Such offices could also evaluate if their location, logistic processes like check-in documentation, and other day-to-day actions signal their commitment to protecting the privacy of students wishing to conceal their legal vulnerability; virtual meetings, online information, and alternative meeting places or more discrete locations may be effective means to initiate relationships with students who hesitate to access public office space. Students may realize that anyone who sees them entering such an office will know—or think they know—that the students are undocumented.

Undocumented and immigration-impacted services offices are not simply an identity-based center but are rather a holistic service provider that requires a substantial staff to offer a meaningful range of targeted resources and programming. Indeed, undocumented and immigration-impacted student services spearheaded many of the examples of innovative resources mentioned in this chapter. Institutions must provide sufficient funding to make certain that these offices can develop and expand resources and programming that responds to immigration-impacted students' economic, legal, academic, social, and emotional needs. In the University of California system, funding for these services has historically been distributed based on the size of each campus's undocumented student population; however, this does not take into account the size of other immigration-impacted student populations. Additional funding is needed to cover the increased staffing and programming costs that come with expanded programming for this broader student body.

Cross-campus and community partnerships are critical for deepening the accessibility and impact of undocumented and immigration-impacted student services. Programs and resources could be offered in partnership with other campus offices to maximize access and avoid duplication; care should be taken to ensure that immigration-impacted students feel permitted to access these services. Hiring staff into cross-unit positions could facilitate this. For example, a mental health counselor could be hired with an appointment in campus mental health services with a dedicated percentage of time to be spent each week on immigration-impacted student services. Such cross-unit appointees would be well positioned to facilitate referrals between these two offices and develop targeted programming that responds to students' needs by drawing on appointees' professional expertise and deeper understanding of legal vulnerability. Such positions would also allow for collaborations to emerge from true partnerships across units.

Conclusion

Campuswide, undocumented, and immigration-impacted student services provide invaluable resources that can alleviate the negative effects of the collective constraints and cascading consequences of family legal vulnerability. To date, most attention and campus resources have focused on undocumented students; however, throughout this book we have established that family legal vulnerability exposes a broader group of students to the negative repercussions of restrictive immigration policy. Undocumented students indisputably need targeted services to support their educational equity and mitigate their individual legal vulnerability. The UC system and other institutions that have such offices can build on campuswide resources and undocumented student services by expanding offerings to explicitly address family legal vulnerability and by ensuring that services are accessible and impactful for all immigration-impacted students. By examining the inclusionary case of the University of California system, we have shed light on potential pathways to improve campus policies, programs, and practices at the UC and elsewhere. Our recommendations throughout this chapter are meant to aid stakeholders in identifying ways their campuses can expand existing services to more effectively support all immigration-impacted students and alleviate family legal vulnerability.

Conclusion

Family Matters for Immigration-Impacted Students

"You don't know what's going to happen."
—Leticia Tzoc

Leticia always assumed that she would go to college. However, having grown up as an undocumented youth with undocumented immigrant parents, she figured that she would go to a more affordable community college or maybe directly to a California State University school if her family stretched their dollars. Two weeks before the application deadline, her teacher persuaded her to also apply to the University of California despite its higher price tag. Leticia was accepted to several campuses, and she picked one she felt was balanced between being close enough to home to visit regularly but far enough to gain some independence. Almost four years later, preparing for her final year of college, she shared with us stories about the stress caused by her own and her family members' undocumented immigration status.

Leticia began meeting with a therapist to support her mental health during her first year. But she got the impression that the therapist might report that she or her parents were undocumented, so she stopped going. While likely she had misunderstood a standard disclosure about reporting immediate threats to self, others, or children, Leticia's decision was shaped by her family's legal vulnerability: "I didn't want to overshare something or get my family in trouble," she explained. Her sophomore year, a dispute between her father and his friend led to her father being reported to immigration enforcement. Leticia had to meet frequently with the UC immigration legal services attorney who was representing her father during deportation proceedings, and she recorded her lowest GPA. As her parents' oldest child, she regularly served as their language interpreter and cultural broker, and she stepped in to watch her siblings, often to the detriment of her academics: "Whenever I try to do my homework or try to focus, I can't really do that because I have to think about other things. Or I receive a phone call from my parents saying, 'Hey, I need to take your dad to court' or 'Hey, we have to go to see the lawyers, take care of your siblings.' And stuff like that. So I guess sometimes, even though I try to focus, I can't." She missed class frequently to take whatever appointments were available in the attorney's packed schedule. She never explained this to her professors because she assumed they would not understand. She did not internalize her poor grades, knowing she wasn't lazy and that she cared about school. She saw her academic struggles for what they were: a consequence of the uncertainty and stress of her family's legal vulnerability.

Recognizing the impact that immigration policies had on her academics, Leticia decided to major in education and aspired to pursue a PhD. Her original career goal had been to become a Spanish teacher but she feared it would not pay well enough and decided not to pursue it. She linked this to her family's legal vulnerability: "I just had to prepare myself in case anything happens. I do want to support my family. And that's one of the reasons why I didn't want to go into teaching anymore, because I know with the salary, I won't be able to support my family." Recognizing that her parents' undocumented status would bar them from ever owning a home, she wanted to use her privileges as a DACA recipient to buy a home for her family. She saw herself "moving back in with my family and having a home, a home that we own. . . . That's literally my dream, moving in with my family. And hopefully the rest of my siblings live with me, too."

A college degree is the most reliable vehicle for individuals from low socioeconomic backgrounds to achieve upward mobility.[1] However, students' experiences while on campus—including the extent to which they engage in extracurricular opportunities and build social capital that will facilitate their post-college trajectories—also shape their chances for mobility.[2] By these metrics, Latinos are doubly disadvantaged, as they display lower rates of degree completion and lower returns on their college degree compared to other groups.[3] Leticia's college experiences show that family legal vulnerability plays a critical role in curtailing the educational attainment and mobility opportunities of Latino students from undocumented and mixed-status families.

In 2016, the children of undocumented immigrant parents made up nearly one in twelve primary and secondary school students in the United States. These 4.1 million immigration-impacted K–12 students included 3.5 million US citizens and 600,000 undocumented youth. In California, the share is even higher, with 13.3 percent of students having at least one undocumented immigrant parent.[4] This is equivalent to four students in a class of 30. The chances of encountering immigration-impacted students are even higher in Latino communities given that a quarter of Latino children in the United States have at least one undocumented parent.[5] As these children age into young adulthood, university and college campuses will be home to a growing population of immigration-impacted students.

Immigration-impacted students don't leave behind their families when they walk into a college classroom. Rather, they carry their families with them—their hopes, dreams, fears, and strains crowding into their backpacks to accompany them on their journey. In this book, we have captured how undocumented and US citizen students with undocumented immigrant parents negotiate the two worlds of education and family. Their experiences growing up in their families shape their educational trajectories and life chances. Their memories and experiences of family legal vulnerability propel them to college and push them to strive for a degree on their path to collective upward mobility. Household finances determine their eligibility for financial aid and whether parents can help students cover costs or if, instead, students will be called on to help families manage financially. Fears about family separation seep into their minds, creating anxiety, distracting them from academics, and pulling them away from public forms of political engagement. Family responsibilities compete for their time. The stories we have documented in this book highlight how families, and family legal vulnerability, matter deeply in the educational journeys of immigration-impacted college students.

We look beyond individual immigration status not because it is unimportant but because family legal vulnerability is integral to understanding the experiences of Latino college students from immigrant families. We have shown that undocumented students and US citizen students with undocumented parents share many similar experiences. They confront the collective constraints that the immigration policy context imposes on their families as members share in the material barriers and emotional turmoil produced within it. Cascading consequences ensure that family legal vulnerability unleashes a torrent of individual strains that shape students' everyday lives and compromise their mental health, academic success, and political engagement. Ultimately, these outcomes are similarly compromised, leaving immigration-impacted students struggling to obtain the same college education as their US citizen peers with lawfully present parents.

Placing Legal Vulnerability in Context

Most research on undocumented immigrants and mixed-status families draws on theories of immigrant illegality to define the contours and consequences of immigration-related laws and policies for undocumented immigrants and their family members. Building on this, we contend that legal vulnerability is a distinct part of the illegalization process. As a social position in which there is risk of unequal experiences and outcomes because of exclusionary immigration laws and policies, it is the cause that gives way to the effect that is illegality. It is structured by deportability, economic insecurity, and social exclusion, constraints that are exacerbated by an unpredictable immigration policy context that leaves all family members with feelings of uncertainty about the future. By focusing on the risks associated with undocumented status, legal vulnerability allows us to examine the process through which individuals experience, interpret, and respond to the law, establishing their unique experience of illegality. This process unfolds within nested contexts of family and place.

Centering Family Legal Vulnerability

Families are sites of social reproduction where immigration policies are made consequential for undocumented immigrants as well as their US citizen family members.[6] Part I of this book theorized this context by conceptualizing family legal vulnerability as a distinct form of legal vulnerability. Family legal vulnerability is not merely the sum of individual-level vulnerability across undocumented family members but is activated when close family is under threat, regardless of one's own immigration status. It captures how undocumented and mixed-status families are exposed to immigration policies that perpetuate educational, economic, and social harm.

Our findings highlight that the family is a critical context that conditions individual experiences and outcomes. Immigrant family members share linked lives wherein their life chances are intertwined through the intergenerational transmission of material, cultural, social, and emotional resources.[7] Prior research by Laura Enriquez has documented that immigration policy imposes multigenerational punishment in which US citizen children of undocumented immigrants suffer because of their (inter)dependence on undocumented family members.[8] These collateral consequences extend into young adulthood as young adults with undocumented parents step up to help families navigate illegality, such as by contributing to household incomes.[9]

For Latino college students, undocumented immediate family members, particularly parents, play a central role in fostering feelings of family legal vulnerability. We refer to students who experience this form of vulnerability as immigration-impacted students; this includes both undocumented students and US citizen students with undocumented parents. Conceptually, this recognizes the shared experiences of family legal vulnerability in their lives and allows us to center how immigration policies constrain their trajectories, despite their differing immigration statuses. It uniquely captures the precarious position of the family as a collective unit, as all members are exposed to legal violence through the immigration policy context.

Our qualitative interviews revealed that collective constraints are the primary pathway through which individual legal vulnerability is translated into a lived experience of family legal vulnerability. Specifically, the strains associated with one family member's undocumented immigration status affect all family members as they experience shared material and emotional consequences. In other words, collective constraints are the process through which multigenerational punishment unfolds and continues to be experienced into young adulthood. Further, we show that the undocumented children of undocumented immigrants also experience collective constraints and multigenerational punishments shared within undocumented and mixed-status families.

Students' experiences of family legal vulnerability reflect the enduring consequences of growing up in undocumented and mixed-status households headed by undocumented immigrants. As children and adolescents, our participants depended on their parents. They lived in financially unstable households where the precariousness of their parents' employment left them struggling to pay for basic necessities. They were taught to protect the family by hiding their own or family members' undocumented status. They witnessed and internalized discriminatory experiences and were subjected to anti-immigrant narratives aimed at themselves, their parents, and their families. They avoided social interactions that they feared might put their family's well-being at risk. They grew up knowing that their family's security depended on the implementation of immigration policies that could create opportunities for inclusion; a continued policy trend toward social marginalization and structural exclusion would compromise their well-being. These experiences and memories did not disappear once they left for college. Rather, as college students and young adults, our participants occupied a liminal space in which they were simultaneously expected to be dependent upon and independent from their parents. Most often they felt as if they were growing into a space of interdependence where they continued to feel a sense of responsibility to support and protect their families.

Placing legal vulnerability within the family context has implications for how scholars theorize illegality when researching undocumented immigrants. The "master status" framework that pervades much of the early research on undocumented young adults contends that individual immigration status overwhelms all other characteristics to become the predominant identity.[10] Scholars have since criticized this framework as obscuring the importance of other identities, such as race and gender, that intersect with and mutually construct unique experiences of illegality.[11] Our work similarly suggests that a master status framework is inadequate because it does not capture collective experiences of family legal vulnerability. Its exclusive focus on individual immigration status disregards the collective family legal vulnerability that also structures the experiences of undocumented young adults. Doing so presumes that undocumented young adults would have similar experiences regardless of their parents' or other family members' immigration status; however, our work suggests that is not the case. The immigration status of our participants' parents plays a substantial role in their experiences of illegality.

Alternatively, legal vulnerability captures the complexity through which both individuals' and their family members' immigration status structures everyday life. It also lends itself to intersectional analyses by creating space for future work to interrogate how race, class, gender, sexuality, age, and other social locations may impact how individual and family legal vulnerability manifests and can be negotiated. Such an approach is critical for tracing how contemporary illegality and legal vulnerability contributes to Latinos' substantial exclusion over generations.

Recognizing the Significance of Policy Context

In addition to placing students within the family, we also place them and their families within the policy context that shapes their lives. Immigration policy, including federal, state, local, and institutional policies, can promote either the inclusion or exclusion of undocumented immigrants by determining the extent to which undocumented status is salient in everyday life.[12] Acknowledging the exclusionary federal context, we situated our study in a state and within a university system that are both national leaders in advancing inclusive policies for undocumented and mixed-status communities. California has created one of the most inclusive contexts for undocumented immigrants and their family members by limiting cooperation with immigration enforcement, creating access to higher education, and providing access to health and public services.[13] The University of California is a premier public institution that has pioneered supporting upward mobility for first-generation students and advancing educational equity for undocumented and immigration-impacted students.[14] Thus, our specific findings regarding how immigration-impacted students experience family legal vulnerability likely represent a best-case scenario.

Consistent with prior research in California, our participants reported occupying protective social and spatial locations that insulated them from fears about their own deportability but made them attuned to the risks their parents faced.[15] Such fears are stronger in states and localities where immigration enforcement activity and/or collaborations with local law enforcement is greater.[16] The financial strains reported by our undocumented participants were also less severe than those reported by their peers attending the California State University system or institutions in other states where there are fewer opportunities for financial assistance.[17] Although our participants contended with social exclusion and constrained mobility as they navigated legal constraints, research suggests that such experiences may be more frequent and severe in more exclusionary state policy contexts like Arizona and Florida.[18]

Arizona offers a useful case comparison for understanding severe family legal vulnerability, as it implemented exclusionary policies at a time when California was moving toward inclusion. In the 2010s Arizona implemented laws that criminalized undocumented status, limited access to a driver's license or identification card, restricted access to jobs and health services, and promoted exploitative employment practices and enforcement strategies, with the stated goal of convincing undocumented people to leave the state. Cecilia Ayón has documented the destructive consequences of this exclusionary policy context for Latino immigrant families. Undocumented Latino parents reported that because of these policies they leaned into social isolation and changed family practices, such as restricting travel and work, to protect their families' well-being.[19] High perceived threat to one's family was associated with parental stress; children experienced fear, sadness, and depression as they frequently worried about the threat of deportation or family separation.[20] As this book is being prepared for publication, the children in her study are approaching young adulthood, and some are near the same age as our participants. It is likely that family legal vulnerability creates even more constrained outcomes for such youth when compared to the Californian immigration-impacted students we studied.

The Cascading Consequences of Family Legal Vulnerability

By situating individual college students within their undocumented and mixed-status family context, we are better able to understand how collective experiences of illegality affect their individual outcomes and future mobility. In Part II, we traced the cascading consequences of family legal vulnerability and how they shape immigration-impacted students' mental-health, academic, and political engagement outcomes. We define *cascading consequences* as the repercussions of family legal vulnerability, the channels through which family legal vulnerability shapes individual family members' everyday lives and, ultimately, compromises their outcomes.

Cascading consequences emerge as immigration-impacted students attempt to manage collective constraints and protect their families' collective well-being. They take on family responsibilities, experience strained social relationships, and manage intense worries as they help insulate their family from the worst effects of family legal vulnerability. These tensions set the stage for compromised outcomes.

Family legal vulnerability functions as a chronic stressor that can prompt adverse mental-health outcomes. Interviews revealed that both undocumented and US citizen students with undocumented parents name their parents' deportability and family economic insecurity as strains that have persisted since childhood. These stressors manifest as compromised mental health, as they often worry and feel sad and anxious due to the threat immigration policies pose to their families. For some students, the cascading effects of family legal vulnerability become emotionally debilitating, and they experience trauma responses such as intrusive thoughts and hypervigilance. Yet students are resilient, relying on their social networks and multiple coping strategies to mitigate the effects of family legal vulnerability on their mental health and well-being.

Cascading consequences also shape students' academic life. The physical, financial, and emotional vulnerability of their undocumented parents influences all aspects of students' decision-making, from college choice to whether to live on or off campus. Preoccupation with and efforts to mitigate family economic insecurity and parental deportability disrupt students' attention, resources, and time dedicated to their academics, with adverse consequences on traditional measures of success like GPA and course failure. Yet family legal vulnerability also serves as a source of motivation by strengthening students' commitment to academic success and professional development. However, these forms of positive engagement may also have cascading consequences, as they create increased stress as students spread themselves too thin when they try to (over)compensate for the negative effects of family legal vulnerability.

Family legal vulnerability similarly defines the contours of political engagement among immigration-impacted students. Interviews showed that students are motivated to engage politically in the face of anti-immigrant political rhetoric and policies. However, concerns about deportability and family separation constrain their participation in public-facing forms of political engagement. Many found creative and multi-scalar ways to engage in civic and political processes. This includes voting, campaigning for candidates, and sharing political information online as well as advocacy work at local and state levels. These actions help immigration-impacted students develop and assert a political voice and, collectively, advance inclusionary policies and practices for their families and communities.

The cascading consequences of family legal vulnerability set the stage for disparities to emerge when comparing immigration-impacted students' mental-health, academic, and political engagement outcomes to US citizen peers who have lawfully present parents. Overall, we found significant differences, with immigration-impacted students often reporting worse outcomes than their US citizen peers with lawfully present parents. For some measures—such as failing a class—undocumented students fared worse, and for others—such as having a low GPA—US citizens did. However, there were some outcomes where the immigration-impacted students had similar or even better outcomes than their US citizen peers with lawfully present parents. For instance, there were no differences across the student groups in depression or anxiety, and undocumented students had the highest levels of flourishing. Undocumented students were also more likely to have participated in a professional development opportunity and report more positive academic engagement. They were also more likely to participate in an organization to solve a problem, whereas US citizen students with undocumented parents were more likely to participate in protests. These results complicate prior research that has observed inequities in the mental health, academic performance, and political participation of undocumented and US citizen students.[21] Specifically, these results signal the need to disaggregate US citizen comparison groups to better examine the outcomes of both undocumented students and US citizens with undocumented parents. Doing so allowed us to identify similarly compromised outcomes between undocumented students and US citizens with undocumented parents; the experience of this US citizen subgroup has been obscured by a focus on the individual-level impacts of undocumented immigration status.

Additional survey analysis revealed that perceived threat to family because of restrictive immigration policy profoundly contributes to most of the observed group differences. After accounting for threat to family, undocumented students had lower levels of anxiety and depression and even higher levels of flourishing than their US citizen peers with lawfully present parents. Perceived threat to family also explained the lower GPA and negative academic engagement among US citizen students with undocumented parents and accounted for the higher positive academic engagement among undocumented students. Finally, accounting for perceived threat to family made undocumented students and US citizens students with undocumented parents less likely to participate in protests. These findings affirm that exclusionary immigration policies have a wide-reaching effect on immigration impacted students because they suppress well-being and contribute to poorer academic outcomes while also motivating their academic and political engagement.

Family financial strain explains some of the differences among immigration-impacted students—but not to the same extent as perceived threat to family. It explained the elevated negative academic engagement among US citizen students with undocumented parents and the positive academic engagement among undocumented students. It also contributed to higher levels of protest participation among US citizen students with undocumented parents. Our interviews and prior research have documented that family economic insecurity can push undocumented students to work, compromising their class attendance or ability to complete assignments as they struggle to balance their commitments.[22] US citizens with undocumented parents face similar pressures as their employment authorization propels them to contribute to a household in which they may be the only adult with that privilege.[23] These findings affirm prior research on young children with undocumented parents, showing that parental economic insecurity continues to compromise children's educational opportunities into young adulthood.[24]

Our survey findings also reflect the complicated experience and impact of deportation. Of all our analyses, experiencing the deportation of a family member explained differences in only one outcome: elevated negative academic engagement among US citizen students with undocumented parents. Prior research has established that deportation experiences drastically alter the family context and strain individual family members.[25] Indeed, our interview participants affirmed the upheaval deportations have created in their extended family and friendship networks. Further, fears that they may similarly experience such family separation is a persistent stressor that feeds academic and political disengagement. Yet the limited significance of this form of family legal vulnerability in explaining differences across our three student groups suggests that such experiences are complicated. It is likely not simply if there has ever been a deportation in one's family but also when it happened, if separation persists, and the student's relationship to and (inter)dependence on the deportee. Our interview participants reported few deportations within their immediate family; these were often many years ago, and most separations did not persist beyond a few months. Our participants' hypothesizing alongside other scholarship suggests that the limited significance of this item is also an issue of selection: Those students who had an immediate family member recently deported would likely stop out of school to manage the extreme financial and emotional strain created by the deportation.[26] Thus, those young adults most impacted by deportation are likely not included in our sample of college students.

Collectively, our findings establish the cascading consequences of family legal vulnerability. Perceived threat to family, in particular, explains poorer educational outcomes among immigration-impacted students, motivates their academic and political engagement, and suppresses positive mental-health outcomes. Keeping in mind the inclusive institutional and state context of our study, it is likely that immigration-impacted students in more exclusionary contexts experience even wider gaps in their outcomes. Living in a more restrictive state context or enrolling in a less-resourced educational institution presumably exposes them to more consequential cascading consequences that compromise their overall mobility. However, threat to family and family financial strain conceivably remain key mechanisms in producing unequal outcomes among college students.

Alleviating Family Legal Vulnerability Through Policy and Practice

Universities and colleges offer a range of resources meant to support student success and well-being. Among these are campuswide resources like financial aid and basic needs support, mental health and academic support services, and identity-based centers. The University of California system also hosts some of the most developed undocumented and immigration-impacted student services in the nation, with all campuses providing tailored support to this student population.[27] These university resources are critical for supporting immigrant-impacted students' success as they navigate family legal vulnerability throughout their college careers.

In Part III, we showed that immigration-impacted students use University of California campus resources to help alleviate some of the collective constraints associated with family legal vulnerability and to curb the cascading consequences on their mental health, academics, and political engagement. Students often faced individual financial strains as the result of their family's economic insecurity and students' efforts to help address family financial strain; they accessed university financial aid and campus safety-net resources, like food pantries and basic needs support, to help make ends meet. Some secured free immigration legal services and attended programming to help manage deportation threats and concerns. Students also sought out mental health services, academic support services, and identity-based centers and student organizations, all of which helped shield them from the cascading consequences of family legal vulnerability. Our regression analyses confirmed that family legal vulnerability informed students' use of these various resources.

Our findings affirm that universities are a unique context wherein institutional policy and practice can advance inclusion and justice.[28] To this end, we offered eight recommendations in chapter 5 to guide campuses in strengthening the institutional support available to alleviate the initial and cascading effects of family legal vulnerability on students' success:

- Provide equitable financial aid and establish support for financial aid processes that serve immigration-impacted students.

- Establish, expand, and raise awareness about campus' safety-net resources.
- Provide free immigration legal services to students and their family members and ensure that there are no barriers to accessing these services.
- Offer programming that empowers students' management of deportation threats and concerns.
- Expand access to and types of mental health services available to address family legal vulnerability.
- Strengthen the cultural competency and belonging offered by academic support services when working with immigration-impacted students.
- Dedicate resources to facilitate immigration-impacted students' political empowerment and engagement.
- Invest in undocumented and immigration-impacted student services.

Campus stakeholders at the University of California and beyond can draw on these suggestions to establish or further develop the campus resources available to aid immigration-impacted students.

Although inclusionary policies in all eight areas will help mitigate the effects of family legal vulnerability, stakeholders should assess the institutional and state contexts to prioritize those that may be more impactful for their student populations. For institutions in more exclusionary state contexts, such as those that do not provide undocumented students with access to in-state tuition or state financial aid, changes to financial aid policy and/or scholarship development would have a critical impact on undocumented students' enrollment, retention, and success. Institutions in localities or states where deportation threats are more severe would likely have a greater need to offer programming that empowers students to manage deportation threats and concerns. While these circumstances can guide program implementation, it is critical to consult with local students to assess and meet their unique needs given the varied experiences of immigration-impacted communities across the United States.

We found that undocumented and immigration-impacted student services often created and offered the most innovative resources that directly address family legal vulnerability, demonstrating the critical importance of having an office and/or staff members dedicated to serving this student population. On UC campuses, these offices developed and hosted their own programs, collaborated with other campuswide units to provide tailored services and programming to immigration-impacted students, facilitated referrals to other campus resources, and created spaces of belonging and inclusion. Although undocumented students accessed these at high rates, US citizens with undocumented parents often underused these services because they did not see themselves as the intended recipients. Campuses must invest in the development of these offices to expand their reach to all immigration-impacted students and maximize their impact on student success by alleviating individual *and* family legal vulnerability. On those campuses where such offices already exist, changing their names and/or missions to explicitly welcome US citizens with undocumented family members alongside undocumented students may be helpful, and new offices should keep in mind the challenges of reaching this population. Funding models will also need to consider the staffing and programming costs that come with expanding support to the entire immigration-impacted student population.

University administrators should also dispense with normative assumptions about students as being only tenuously linked to their families. Higher education institutions operate to serve a presumed normative student: a student with a stable family and household economy that is unaffected when one of their own ventures off for four years of learning. As a result, colleges presume financial support from parent to child and assume that students have few family responsibilities. Campus resources, including those designed for immigration-impacted students, thus all too frequently focus on facilitating students' individual success and are only indirectly focused on family legal vulnerability as it relates to mitigating its effect on student outcomes. Our findings challenge the individualistic boundaries of university support by showing how family-level strains pose significant barriers to the educational success and mobility of children of undocumented immigrants. UC Immigrant Legal Services is a unique example of how resources can serve both students and their immediate family members; it can serve as a model nationwide. Programming should also recognize the collective nature of legal vulnerability and aim to support the whole family in order to uplift students. This can be achieved by serving and educating students' family members or, where that proves impractical, guiding students so they can transfer knowledge and information about community-based resources to their families. Such a framework will be particularly useful for federally designated Hispanic-Serving Institutions that are likely serving larger numbers of immigration-impacted students compared to other schools. On these campuses, addressing family legal vulnerability is a critical way to advance Latino student success.

By centering multiply marginalized student populations, such as immigration-impacted students, stakeholders can see to it that institutional policies meet the needs of the broader campus community. The stories of immigration-impacted students shared here provide insight into how a range of marginalized students—underrepresented minorities, low-income students, first-generation college-goers—are negotiating family vulnerabilities that are not sufficiently acknowledged or supported by educational institutions. Students with incarcerated family members similarly contend with the law impinging on family life, with cascading consequences for their educational and mental-health outcomes.[29] Supporting marginalized college students requires actively acknowledging family members' interdependence in managing family-level vulnerabilities, legal or otherwise. Stakeholders need to consider how institutional policies can broadly address family vulnerabilities. For example, financial aid policies could consider students' responsibilities to support family members when making aid awards.

University stakeholders can also engage policymakers to advocate for inclusive local, state, and federal policies that will benefit immigration-impacted students' success by minimizing the salience of undocumented immigration status and alleviating feelings of individual and family legal vulnerability. Inclusive city and county policies can foster feelings of safety and support in the community surrounding campuses as well as where students' families are located. City, county, and state policies that limit deportation and detention practices by local law enforcement officials can decrease perceptions of deportation threats and increase feelings of safety and security when negotiating public space. State laws that provide undocumented immigrants with access to driver's licenses can also lower deportation risks and feelings of social exclusion while facilitating students' ability to get to campus safely. These policies address a range of areas not directly related to immigration but nonetheless lessen the effects of family legal vulnerability in everyday life.

Ultimately, the only way to fully address family legal vulnerability is by creating a pathway to legal status for all undocumented immigrants. In the meantime, inclusive local, state, and federal policies are critical for facilitating family stability and students' potential for mobility after they graduate from college and find themselves suddenly without the support structures provided by the university. For example, economic insecurity can be addressed through education, health care, social-safety-net policies, and programs that aid low-income families by making higher education and food, housing, and health care more affordable. Such programs need to ensure that they maximize eligibility to include undocumented immigrants and their US citizen family members. Such programs must proactively address the potential chilling effects of anti-immigrant rhetoric and threatened exclusionary policy changes.

A Multigenerational Approach: Understanding the Lives of Children of Immigrants

Our findings call on scholars to approach immigrant incorporation as a collective multigenerational process wherein the younger generation experiences, interprets, and builds on prior generations' opportunities and constraints. The incorporation journeys of immigrant parents and their children coincide and overlap, creating opportunities for the multidirectional transmission of resources and collective mobility. The children of immigrants are grounded within families and the complex web of relationships and responsibilities that come with them. It is because of their interconnected lives that family legal vulnerability emerges, producing collective constraints and cascading consequences. We make space for collective processes—like family legal vulnerability—by deploying a multigenerational approach that takes the whole family into account.

Most US immigration scholars draw on assimilation perspectives to understand the mobility prospects of children of immigrants, including undocumented immigrants. This theoretical tradition aims to assess intergenerational mobility on economic and sociocultural characteristics to determine whether immigrants from various racial/ethnic groups converge with the host society as each generation adapts to life in the United States.[30] Such approaches have documented that second-generation Latino children of immigrants have lower educational attainment and poorer well-being outcomes than native-born whites and that exclusion persists well into the third generation.[31] For Mexican Americans, the largest Latino subgroup in the United States, low educational attainment preconditions delayed assimilation on most social dimensions over multiple generations.[32] Scholarship documenting these processes acknowledges families by framing them as actors that transmit knowledge and resources from one generation to the next. This macro-level treatment of family relationships positions them as a source of inherited inequality and misses the everyday processes through which family members of multiple generations confront, experience, and navigate inequality. In other words, the intergenerational lens of assimilation theory misses the multigenerational processes that shape the mobility prospects of Latino children of immigrants.

We contend that research needs to move toward capturing how multiple generations of family members work collectively to create mobility that benefits all family members. Assimilation theory's focus on discrete generations fails to reflect the complexity of family life wherein generations coexist as they support each other's stability and mobility. A multigenerational approach moves away from an individualistic mobility framework to more accurately reflect families' collective operation. For example, we document how the immigration-impacted students who participated in our study aged into adulthood, with some continuing to live at home or temporarily/partially moving out to college dorms or campus-adjacent apartments. Most returned home frequently to participate in family life and support family stability. Many anticipated returning home after graduation and intended to uplift their families with new opportunities arising from their college degree. These decisions were structured by their family's past and current stability as well as future aspirations for family mobility. By nesting individual students within the family context, we highlight the complexities and contradictions of family life to show how generations remain connected over time.

A multigenerational approach is also critical for future studies of higher education. Research has established that low-income students struggle to persist in their higher education aspirations and obtain college degrees.[33] Indeed, a recent study found that the most socioeconomically advantaged students are 38 percentage points more likely to go to college than the most disadvantaged students.[34] Further, financial strain compromises the academic achievement of those that enroll.[35] Immigration-impacted young adults are a subset of this larger marginalized student group. They are a unique case that shows us just how much families matter as students navigate higher education. Thus, education scholars and practitioners must pay particular attention to the range of collective constraints and cascading consequences emerging from students' family contexts.

A multigenerational approach is also increasingly important given the changing dynamics of family household structures. The number of people in the United States living in multigenerational households quadrupled over half a century, with 18 percent of the US population living in a multigenerational family household in 2021.[36] This change has been steepest for young adults aged 25–34, for whom multigenerational living rose from 9 percent in 1971 to 25 percent in 2021.[37] Latinos are the most likely racial/ ethnic group to be living in multigenerational households, with 26 percent doing so compared to 13 percent of whites.[38] Recognizing the coexistence, and often co-residence, of multiple generations is increasingly important, as these realities mean that generations will be intertwined in daily life as they pursue mobility over their lifetimes.

Scholars must account for contemporary family realities when studying immigrant incorporation and their children's experiences and trajectories. For Latino immigrant families, this means accounting for the fact that half of Mexican and Central American immigrants are undocumented.[39] With the rise of increasingly punitive immigration policies and the multigenerational punishment they inflict, it is critical that immigration scholars center and account for family legal vulnerability. This means more than examining or controlling for individual immigration status. It means centering legal vulnerability and investigating the role of one's own and family members' immigration statuses as well as their manifestation in everyday life. Parental immigration status needs to be accounted for as a source of inequality that constrains the resources children have available to them, shapes their experiences, and compromises their outcomes. In practice, this means that future research needs to account for both self and parental immigration status. Researchers need to ask about self and parental immigration status, especially among Latinos and Asian American Pacific Islander groups, among which there are substantial numbers of undocumented immigrants. Self and family members' immigration status need to be taken into account in both quantitative and qualitative analyses to assess how immigration status manifests as legal vulnerability and informs outcomes. Doing so will allow scholars to effectively capture how immigration policy perpetrates legal violence across generations and account for the role of multigenerational family processes and structures.

Entre Familia

Young adult children of immigrants are looking to higher education to carve out a pathway to upward mobility for themselves and their families. Their parents bought into the immigrant bargain, spending a lifetime working hard so that their children could pursue education and upward mobility. As a result, these youth invested in their education, believing that a college degree would be the great equalizer—a pathway to stability on par with their peers. Instead, our investigation of family legal vulnerability foretells a more complicated reality.

Contrary to the meritocratic ideals ingrained in them, students from undocumented and mixed-status families wrestle with the reality that structural inequalities prevent them from achieving the same outcomes as their peers. While their families fuel their hopes and dreams, they are also sources of vulnerability. Students' lives, responsibilities, and opportunities remain linked to their families as they enter young adulthood and embark on their higher education journeys. As a result, the children of undocumented parents share similar family experiences and have similarly compromised outcomes regardless of their own immigration status. They experience US society, the law, and their education *entre familia*—among family.

ACKNOWLEDGMENTS

This book emerged from a collaboration that, at first glance, seemed straightforward: five scholars from different disciplines, united by a shared commitment to understanding how immigration policies affect college students and their families. As it turned out, merging our distinct disciplinary perspectives, methodological approaches, and writing styles proved to be an adventure in academic diplomacy. There were moments when we wondered if we had taken on more than we could handle, but these challenges ultimately strengthened both our analysis and how we approach collaborations—now and in the future. Through countless meetings, revision cycles, and occasional therapeutic venting sessions, we discovered that understanding and accepting our differences could be our greatest asset. This book is a testament not only to our scholarly collaboration but also to the essential role of communication when wrestling with complex ideas as a team. Through this journey, we have gained a deeper appreciation for each scholar's unique contributions, creating space for mutual respect and scholarly growth. This book could not have been written without the collective knowledge that emerged from bringing each other's distinct perspectives and insights together and our shared commitment to the project.

We are grateful for the institutional support that made this research possible. The UC Collaborative to Promote Immigrant and Student Equity (UC PromISE), supported by the University of California Multicampus Research Programs and Initiatives (grant number: MRI-19-601090), funded survey development, data collection, and analysis. The Russell Sage Foundation provided crucial funding for interviews and data analysis.

Our advisory board members were invaluable in project development and policy recommendations, particularly for chapter 5. Their expertise in working with undocumented and immigration-impacted students across the UC system helped ground our analysis in practical reality:

Maria Blanco, Angela Chen, Ana Coria, Alejandro Delgadillo, Valeria Simmons Garcia, Christian Abigail Gonzalez, Liliana Iglesias, Anna Manuel, Oscar Teran, Diana Valdivia, and George Zamora.

This study coincided with a parallel collaboration with colleagues from the California State University system. Their insights expanded our thinking beyond our own campuses and were crucial as we developed our study and data collection instruments: Karina Chavarria, Basia D. Ellis, Melissa J. Hagan, Julián Jefferies, Enrique Murillo Jr., Carly Offidani-Bertrand, Maria Oropeza Fujimoto, William E. Rosales, Heidy Sarabia, Ana K. Soltero López, Mercedes Valadez, and Sharon Velarde Pierce.

We are deeply grateful to our research team. Martha Morales Hernandez provided invaluable project management and data collection support, while also offering crucial feedback on the manuscript. Victoria Rodriguez contributed essential quantitative analysis, while Elisabet Barrios-Dugenia, Daisy Vasquez Vera, Jenniffer C. Perez Lopez, and Carmen Zambrano Torres conducted interviews and qualitative data analysis. The UC PromISE graduate fellows—Monica Cornejo, Josefina Flores Morales, Erin Manalo-Pedro, and Martha Morales Hernandez—enriched our analysis through their thoughtful engagement with our survey data.

We thank Ilene Kalish, Executive Editor and Assistant Editor in Chief at New York University Press, for her support and commitment to this project. Thanks also to Kate Epstein from epsteinwords for her excellent and speedy editorial services.

Our understanding of immigration's impact on families is deeply personal, shaped by our own family histories of migration, sacrifice, and resilience. These lived experiences have informed not only our scholarly perspectives but also our commitment to this work. The stories of determination, hope, and family unity that we witnessed in our own families echo in the narratives we encountered in our research.

We are grateful to our extended network of family, friends, and colleagues who supported us throughout this journey. Their encouragement, patience, and understanding made this work possible.

Laura would like to thank Miguel, Luna, and Maya, whose unyielding love and kindness has deepened her understanding of family and strengthened her commitment to building a more equitable world.

Zulema would like to thank her partner, Andrew Yinger, whose willingness to discuss ideas during long walks with their eager and faithful pups provided clarity and comfort throughout this project.

Annie would like to thank Fernando, Calvin, Audrey, and her extended family, who remind her again and again that family ties are what sustain us.

Cecilia would like to thank her parents, Salvador and Graciela Ayón, for being unwavering examples of the resilience and strength that define immigrants. Their perseverance not only shaped her own values but also serves as a powerful reminder of the grit it takes to overcome challenges and create an equitable future.

Jennifer would like to thank her late father, Joe Najera, for carefully laying the foundation for her education and political understanding of the world.

This book is dedicated to the students and families who shared their stories with us, whose experiences remind us why this work matters.

UC PromISE Data Collection Methods

We established the UC Collaborative to Promote Immigrant and Student Equity (UC PromISE) in 2019 with the support of a University of California Multicampus Research Programs and Initiatives award. We aimed to conduct research with the goal of informing policies and practices that would advance equity and inclusion for undocumented and immigrant-origin students. Appendix A details the methods that yielded the data used for this book.

Survey Methods

In spring 2020, we fielded a survey of University of California (UC) students with immigrant parents to assess the extent to which immigration-related policies produce inequalities in the educational and well-being outcomes of undocumented students and US citizen students with undocumented parents. UC respondents were divided into three comparison groups: (1) undocumented students, (2) US citizen students with at least one undocumented parent, and (3) US citizen students with lawfully present parents. In collaboration with the Undocumented Student Equity Project (USEP), California State University (CSU) undocumented students were administered the same survey to explore how institutional context contributes to inequalities among undocumented students attending California's public four-year universities; this data is not included in this book but has been published elsewhere.[1] All project activities received approval from the Institutional Review Board at the University of California, Irvine.

Instrument Development
Potential survey items were gathered from the USEP 2016 survey of UC undocumented students, the UndocuScholars Project national survey

of undocumented students, the UC Undergraduate Experience Survey, and existing validated scales used in nationally representative surveys to facilitate comparative analyses. Multiple rounds of revisions were conducted in consultation with CSU faculty collaborators and a community advisory board consisting mostly of UC undocumented student services professionals. An initial pilot phase administered the full survey one-on-one with 10 current and recently graduated UC students who fit the criteria for the three comparison groups. They were encouraged to voice their internal monologue while taking the survey and identify points of confusion. A research team member and respondent then discussed their experience taking the survey, including how certain questions made them feel and specific suggested edits. A second pilot phase administered the near-final online version of the survey to one UC and one CSU undergraduate class. Students completed supplementary handouts and participated in a discussion that solicited feedback about their feelings while taking the survey as well as comments on specific survey items and wording.

The COVID-19 pandemic and the implementation of shelter-in-place policies in California began shortly after we launched our survey. We temporarily paused recruitment during the second half of March 2020 to adjust our recruitment plans and revise our survey instrument. Responses begun after March 30 were instructed to answer the questions based on what was typical before the COVID-19 crisis occurred. They were also asked four additional questions about the impact of the COVID-19 pandemic.

Data Collection Procedures

A 418-item survey was administered online from March to June 2020. The survey closed with the conclusion of the spring term; this was in mid-May for campuses on the semester system and in early June for those on the quarter system. The survey included questions about academic performance, educational experiences, health and well-being, political engagement, the immigration policy context, institutional context and resource use, and self and family demographics.

Participants were recruited at all nine UC undergraduate campuses. Recruitment announcements were distributed widely. Here we list those that yielded increased response rates after we implemented them. Undocumented student services staff circulated a dedicated undocumented student recruitment flyer to their listservs multiple times and/or posted to social media; at several campuses these listservs reached all enrolled undocumented students. We also worked with staff to approach higher-level administrators to circulate the recruitment materials widely via student affairs office newsletters, listservs, and campuswide emails. We individually emailed faculty asking them to forward a recruitment email message to their classes; we targeted faculty known to us as well as those who were listed in the current term's course schedule as teaching large general education classes and courses in ethnic studies, race/ethnicity, or immigration-related topics. We also contacted administrative staff and undergraduate advisers of ethnic studies departments as well as the top 10–15 campus majors to have the recruitment materials distributed to undergraduate majors. Finally, we asked undocumented and racial/ethnic student organizations to circulate the materials to their memberships. For most of these strategies, the initial requests used a general UC recruitment flyer that called for students who had an immigrant parent. Upon recruiting enough US citizen students with lawfully present parents, we used requests with language that recruited students who had an undocumented parent.

The survey was administered via Qualtrics with an estimated completion time of 25 to 35 minutes. Participants had to self-identify as being over 18, having at least one immigrant parent, and being a currently enrolled undergraduate student at a UC campus. Self and parental immigration status was used to ensure that the respondent fell into one of the three comparison groups. The undocumented group had to identify as being born outside the United States and having no permanent legal status (e.g., no lawful status, DACA, Temporary Protected Status, or some other status considered to be undocumented). The other two groups had to identify as being born in the United States. If they had one or more undocumented parent, they were classified as a US citizen with undocumented parents. They were classified as having lawfully present immigrant parents if all reported parents had lawful presence, including lawful permanent residency, naturalized US citizenship, and US-born citizenship. Respondents were emailed a $10 electronic Amazon gift card after completing the survey.

Response Validation Procedures

All responses were reviewed to identify ones that were invalid due to the following criteria: (1) completion time under 12 minutes, which captures those terminated by Qualtrics due to ineligibility and who took the survey too quickly to have reliable data (n = 1,563); (2) location outside of California and no valid university email address (n = 246); (3) email address determined to be falsified based on email address and email service (n = 248); and (4) took longer than 12 minutes but was terminated by Qualtrics due to responses on the initial eligibility questions (n = 119). Reason (5): Responses in progress when the survey closed were recorded and marked invalid if they were less than 90 percent complete (n = 996). Reason (6): Repeated IP addresses were flagged and responses were reviewed to determine whether it was more likely they were the same person, rather than siblings, roommates, or romantic partners (n = 929). And reason (7): Repeated email addresses and names were flagged and reviewed by two team members to confirm they were likely the same person (n = 31). For reasons 6 and 7, most often the first response was preserved and subsequent ones were marked invalid.

Second, for all remaining responses, a research team member applied a protocol that reviewed 17 to 20 survey items to identify unlikely responses that may indicate falsified or careless responses; criteria included specific responses for items such as age, race, countries of origin for respondents and their parent(s); immigration status for respondents, their parent(s), and their family members; and several more including deportation concerns, household size, year in school and transfer status, course units, hours worked, wage, and source of health insurance. If there were less than two unlikely responses and they were logically possible (e.g., non–traditionally aged students working more hours), the response was considered valid. If there were three or more unlikely responses that were not logically possible, the full survey response was reviewed for internal consistency. Those that had more than two inexplicable inconsistencies were marked as invalid as a falsified response (n = 176). At this stage, we also identified respondents that had completed the survey but were deemed ineligible based on their answers to survey items such as self/parental immigration status and country of origin, as well as year in school (n = 17).

Survey Sample

The full UC survey sample consists of 2,746 respondents: 667 undocumented students, 645 US citizen students with at least one undocumented parent, and 1,434 US citizen students with lawfully present immigrant parents. For our analyses in this book, we restricted the sample to those who identified as Latina/o/x.

Interview Methods

In summer 2021, we conducted interviews with a subset of survey participants from two of the comparison groups: (1) undocumented students, and (2) US citizens with at least one undocumented parent. The goal of the interviews was to shed light on the survey responses through further interrogation of legal vulnerability in the lives of students and their families and how these experiences shape their educational, mental-health, and political engagement outcomes.

Instrument Guide Development and Training

The interview guide was developed collaboratively by our project team over several months. The first third of the interview explored self and family members' immigration status and their experiences of legal vulnerability including deportation concerns, past deportation experiences, financial strain, access to resources, and discrimination and how these are shared among family members. The second third assessed multiple outcomes including educational pathways, academic performance and engagement, mental health and well-being, and political engagement. The final set of questions explored the use of campus resources and perceptions of campus climate, particularly as these relate to helping students manage their own or family members' legal vulnerability.

We hired four graduate students to conduct interviews. Interviewers were selected for their experiential and academic knowledge of undocumented and mixed-status families. They received one week of intensive training in June 2021, including panel discussions about interviewing undocumented and mixed-status immigrant populations; detailed review of the project goals and the purpose and meaning of each interview guide question; practice interviews; and reflection discussions.

We reviewed initial interviews to provide feedback on how to improve follow-up and probing questions. Weekly team meetings offered opportunities to obtain feedback on how to improve questions and identify areas to explore more deeply in future interviews.

Data Collection Procedures

We interviewed 63 students split between 31 undocumented students and 32 US citizens with at least one undocumented parent; two-thirds of the undocumented students were DACA recipients (n = 21). The sampling pool comprised Latina/o/x-identified survey respondents who consented to be contacted about future research opportunities. Eligible survey participants were divided into rosters for the three groups: undocumented students with no lawful status, DACA recipients, and US citizens with undocumented parents. Given the limited representation of some demographic groups in the survey data, all individuals who fell into the following categories were sent recruitment information: participants who identified as men, undocumented students who had no lawful status, and US citizens who had used undocumented student services. Recruitment then proceeded in waves by contacting every fifth person on an alphabetized list of the remaining eligible survey participants (i.e., women who were DACA recipients or US citizens who had never used undocumented student services) at three UC campuses. After this list was exhausted, recruitment was expanded to two additional campuses. Eligible participants who were selected for recruitment were sent an email message and up to three follow-up text messages.

Interested participants could submit an interest survey or respond directly to a research team member via email or text. To be eligible to participate in an interview, individuals must have been 18 years of age or older, currently living in the US without permanent legal status or a US born citizen with at least one undocumented parent, and enrolled as a junior or higher at a University of California campus during the 2020–2021 academic year.

Interviews were conducted on Zoom due to the COVID-19 pandemic and averaged 1.5 hours long. Most participants enabled their video, but some elected to turn it off for part or the entirety of the interview. Zoom sessions were recorded, and the audio file was stripped from the recording and the video file was deleted within 24 hours of the interview.

Respondents received a $40 electronic gift card as compensation for their time.

Data Analysis

Interviews were transcribed and uploaded to HyperResearch. Each case was index-coded with demographic attributes and 10 index codes related to broad areas covered by the interview guide: introduction, self and family immigration status, legal vulnerability, educational journey, academic, mental health, political engagement, campus resources, campus climate, and life after college. Index coding was completed in two rounds by four research assistants to confirm that all relevant text was captured. The faculty lead for each chapter then worked with one or two research assistants to develop an analytic codebook associated with the research questions for each chapter.

APPENDIX B

Survey Measures and Descriptive Data

Appendix B includes descriptions of all survey measures used in the book. This is followed by descriptive data for all items.

Self and Parental Immigration Status

Immigration Status—Self
Participants self-identified their country of birth. Respondents born in the United States were classified as US citizens. Respondents born elsewhere were asked to identify their current immigration status. Those who identified as having no permanent legal status were categorized as undocumented; this included no legal status, DACA recipients, U visa holders, and asylum seekers.

Immigration Status—Parents
Participants were asked to identify the current immigration status of up to two parents/guardians. Response categories included: no current legal status, DACA recipient, Temporary Protected Status (TPS) recipient, permanent resident/green card holder, US citizen, does not live in the United States, deceased, I don't know, and other. Parents/guardians were categorized as undocumented if they had no legal status, DACA, TPS, or identified another form of liminal legal status in the "other" response category.

Student Comparison Groups
We compare students across three self/parental immigration status groups: undocumented students, US citizen students with undocumented parents, and US citizen students with lawfully present parents. Self and parental immigration status items were used to place respondents in each category.

Family Legal Vulnerability

Threat to Family Due to Restrictive Immigration Policy

Perceived threat to family due to restrictive immigration policy was measured by the threat to family subscale of the Perceived Immigration Policy Effects Scale (PIPES).[1] PIPES asks respondents how frequently they experienced actions or felt certain ways due to the immigration policy context. This subscale includes three items: "Do you worry about the impact immigration policies have on you or your family?"; "Do you fear that you or a family member will be reported to immigration officials?"; and "Do you worry about family separation due to deportation." Response categories included: never (1), rarely (2), sometimes (3), often (4), and always (5). Items were added up for a score that ranged from 3 to 15. Cronbach's alpha = 0.90.

Deported Family Member

Having a deported family member is a dichotomous variable. Participants were asked: "Have you or any of your family or friends been in deportation proceedings, detained, or deported?" Response categories included: yes, no, I don't know, and decline to state. "I don't know" responses were treated as "no" and "decline to state" as missing data. Respondents who selected "yes" were asked which relations had been deported: parent(s)/guardian(s), sibling(s), extended family member(s) who live in your permanent household, and extended family member(s) who do not live in your permanent household. Participants who selected any of the groups were identified as having a deported family member.

Family Financial Strain

Family financial strain was measured with two validated items.[2] Participants were prompted: "Thinking about your family's current economic situation, indicate how often you expect that your family will face the following circumstances in the next three months." Two statements were provided: "Your family will experience bad times such as poor housing or not having enough food" and "Your family will have to do without the basic things that your family needs." Response categories included: almost never or never (0), once in a while (1), sometimes (2), a lot of the time (3), and almost always or always (4). Responses were summed, resulting in a family financial strain score that ranged from 0 to 8. Cronbach's alpha = 0.86.

Mental-Health Outcomes

Anxiety
Anxiety symptomatology was measured using the General Anxiety Disorder (GAD-7) scale, a seven-item validated scale that asks respondents to indicate how often they have been bothered by various problems over the previous two weeks.[3] Examples include "feeling nervous, anxious, or on edge," "trouble relaxing," and "becoming easily annoyed or irritable." Respondents rated the frequency of each feeling from not at all (0), several days (1), more than half the days (2), and nearly every day (3). Responses were summed across all scale items, resulting in a score that ranged from 0 to 21. Cronbach's alpha = 0.92.

Depression
We measured depression symptomatology using the Patient Health Questionnaire (PHQ-9), a nine-item validated scale that asks respondents to indicate how often they have been bothered by various problems over the previous two weeks.[4] Examples include "little interest or pleasure in doing things," "feeling down, depressed, or hopeless," and "feeling tired or having little energy." Respondents rated the frequency of each feeling from not at all (0), several days (1), more than half the days (2), and nearly every day (3). Responses were summed across all scale items, resulting in a depression score that ranged from 0 to 27. Cronbach's alpha = 0.89.

Flourishing
Psychological resources and strengths were measured using the Flourishing Scale, which asks respondents to indicate their level of agreement with eight statements.[5] Examples include "I lead a purposeful and meaningful life," "I am a good person and live a good life," and "I am optimistic about my future." Response options included strongly disagree (1), disagree (2), slightly disagree (3), neither agree nor disagree (4), slightly agree (5), agree (6), and strongly agree (7). Responses were summed across all scale items, resulting in a score that ranged from 8 to 56. Cronbach's alpha = 0.92.

Academic Outcomes

Failed a Course
We measured whether participants had ever failed a course with one dichotomous item. Participants were asked: "Have you ever failed a course at [campus]?" Response options included: no, yes, and I don't know. Responses of "I don't know" were treated as missing data.

Low Grade Point Average (GPA)
Low GPA was measured with one item. Participants were asked: "What is your overall GPA at [campus]?" Response options were in 0.25-point categories extending from 0.00–0.24 to 3.75–3.99, and 4.0. Responses were dichotomized into "2.5 GPA and above" and "Below 2.5 GPA."

Negative Academic Engagement
Negative academic engagement was measured with three items. Participants were asked how frequently they had done the following in the current academic year: "failed to turn in a course assignment," "gone to class unprepared," and "skipped class." Response categories included: never (0), rarely (1), sometimes (2), often (3), and not applicable, which was recorded as missing data. Responses were averaged across the three items resulting in a score that ranged from 0 to 3. Cronbach's alpha = 0.73.

Positive Academic Engagement
Positive academic engagement was measured with four items. Participants were asked how frequently they had done the following in the current academic year: "sought academic help from instructor or tutor when needed," "studied with a group of classmates outside of class," "contributed to a class discussion," and "communicated with the instructor outside of class about issues and concepts derived from a course." Response categories included: never (0), rarely (1), sometimes (2), often (3), and not applicable, which was recorded as missing data. Responses were averaged across the four items resulting in a score that ranged from 0 to 3. Cronbach's alpha = 0.70.

Professional Development Opportunity
Participation in a professional development opportunity was measured by asking participants to select various opportunities that they had

participated in while at their university. Opportunities included an unpaid internship, paid internship, credit-based internship/practicum/field experience, and career-relevant job. Responses for these four opportunities were combined to create a dichotomous variable to represent whether the participant had one or more professional development experiences versus none.

Political Engagement Outcomes

Organization Participation

Participants were asked: "Have you ever participated in any organization that tried to solve a problem at your school, in the community, or in the broader society?" Response options included: No, I have not done it; Yes, I have done it in the past but not this academic year; Yes, I have done it this academic year; and I don't know. Responses were dichotomized into "no" and "yes" categories. Responses of "I don't know" were treated as "no."

Protest Participation

Participation in a protest was a dichotomous variable. Participants were asked: "Below is a list of things that some people do to express their views. For each one, identify how often you do it." Two of the actions were: "Take part in a protest, march, demonstration, or rally on campus" and "take part in a protest, march, demonstration, or rally off campus." Response options included never, rarely, sometimes, often, and I don't know. Responses were dichotomized with affirmative participation including "sometimes" and "often" responses and nonparticipation including "never," "rarely," and "I don't know" responses. The responses for both actions were combined and used to generate a binary variable that captured whether they had participated in a protest either on or off campus.

Talk About Voting

We measured whether participants talked about voting with others. Participants were asked: "Do you talk to people and try to show them why they should vote for or against one of the parties or candidates?" Response options included: never, rarely, sometimes, often, always, and I don't know. Responses were then dichotomized into "never or rarely" and "sometimes or more." Responses of "I don't know" were treated as "never or rarely."

Campus Resource Use Outcomes

Frequency Visited: Campus Resource Offices
Participants were asked to identify how frequently they visited six campus resource offices on their campus during the current academic year: (1) "academic support services (e.g., writing center, EOP, tutoring center)," (2) "basic needs/food pantry," (3) "identity-based center (e.g., women's center, LGBTQ center, multicultural center)," (4) "immigration-related legal services," (5) "mental health counseling center," and (6) "undocumented student program office/center." They were instructed to answer with what was typical before campuses closed for the COVID-19 pandemic. Response options included: never, a few times a year, about once a month, about once a week, more than once a week, and I don't think this exists on my campus. Responses were collapsed into four categories with increasing frequency: "never" (including "I don't think this exists on my campus" (0)), "a few times a week" (1), "about once a month" (2), and "once a week or more" (3).

Other Items

Deportability Concerns—Parents
Deportability concerns for parents was measured with one continuous item. Participants were asked: "Please rate how frequently you think about your parent(s)/guardian(s) deportation." Response options included: never (0), a few times a year (1), about once a month (2), about once a week (3), and daily (4). The responses ranged from 0 to 4, representing the frequency of deportability concerns.

Deported Immediate Family Member
Having an immediate family member deported was a dichotomous variable. Participants were asked: "Have you or any of your family or friends been in deportation proceedings, detained, or deported?" Response categories included: yes, no, I don't know, and decline to state; "I don't know" responses were treated as "no" and "decline to state" as missing

data. Respondents who answered "yes" were asked which types of relations had been deported, including parent(s)/guardian(s) and sibling(s). Participants who selected "yes" for either group were identified as having experienced the deportation of an immediate family member.

Food Security
Food security was measured using the five-item US Household Food Security Survey Module, which asks respondents about the food eaten in their household in the previous 12 months and whether they were able to afford the food they needed within the previous year.[6] Sample items included not being able to afford to eat balanced meals, cutting the size or skipping meals because of money, and eating less than you felt you should because of money. Responses were scored as directed by the module with affirmative responses summed together for a raw food security score ranging from 0 to 6. Scores were then categorized as directed into three groups to represent food security status. Raw scores ranging from 0 to 1 indicate high or marginal food security, 2–4 indicate low food security, and 5–6 indicate very low food security.

Did Not Use Undocumented Student Services Office
We measured reasons why participants reported not using undocumented student services offices. First, participants were asked: "Have you ever been to an office or met with a staff person at [campus] who focuses on supporting undocumented students and/or students with undocumented family members?" If participants selected "no," they were asked: "To what extent do the following reasons explain why you have not visited this office?" and provided two statements to evaluate: "These resources are not for students like me" and "I did not know it exists." Response options included not at all, somewhat, and a lot. Responses were dichotomized with the affirmative category including responses of "somewhat" and "a lot."

Undocumented Student Services: Campus Partners
Referral to campus partners from undocumented student services and speaking with a campus partner at the office are both dichotomous variables. Participants were asked: "Have you ever been to an office or met with a staff person at [campus] who focuses on supporting

undocumented students and/or students with undocumented family members?" Response options included: no, yes, decline to state, and I don't know. If participants selected "yes," they were asked: "Have undocumented student program staff connected you to another person on campus who could provide support, services, or resources?" and "Have you ever been to an office or met with a staff person at [campus] who focuses on supporting undocumented students and/or students with undocumented family members?" Response options included: no never, yes one other person, yes more than one other person, and I don't know. Responses of "never" and "I don't know" were collapsed into "no." Responses of "yes one other person" and "yes more than one other person" were collapsed into "yes."

Demographic Controls

Campus
Participants were asked: "What campus are you currently enrolled at?" This included a dropdown menu of all nine University of California undergraduate campuses.

First-Generation College Student
Participants were asked: "What category best describes the highest level of education parent/guardian 1/2 has completed?" for two parents/guardians. Response categories included: none, 6th grade or lower, 7th to 8th grade, 9th to 12th grade, high-school diploma or GED, some college (including vocational or technical program), bachelor's degree, postgraduate degree, I don't know, and other (please specify). Responses were dichotomized into "bachelor's degree or higher" and "lower than bachelor's degree" for each parent/guardian. Next, these two variables were combined into a dichotomous variable with the categories "one or more parents have a bachelor's degree or higher" and "no parents have a bachelor's degree or higher."

Gender
Participants were asked: "What is your gender identity?" Responses options included: female/woman; male/man; gender queer, gender nonconforming, nonbinary gender, and a free response for those who

preferred to self-describe. Responses were categorized into three groups: women, men, and alternative gender identification.

Major
Participants were asked: "In what area is your primary major?" There were fourteen options including a free response of "other (please specify)." Responses were then categorized into four groups: arts and humanities, social science, STEM, and other/undecided.

Transfer Student
Participants were asked: "Did you begin attending [campus] as a first-year student or transfer student?" Response options included: first-year student, transfer student, and other (please specify). Responses of "other" were treated as missing data.

Year in College
Participants were asked: "What year are you?" Response options included: first year undergraduate, second year undergraduate, third year undergraduate, fourth year undergraduate, fifth year or more undergraduate, other (please specify), and I don't know. Responses were then categorized into three groups: first- and second-years, third-years, and fourth-years and higher.

Additional Demographic Characteristics

Age
Participants were asked: "How old are you?" Responses were categorized into eight groups: 18, 19, 20, 21, 22, 23, 24, and 25 and older.

Age of First Arrival to the United States
Participants were asked: "How old were you when you first arrived to the United States?" Responses were categorized into three groups: 0–5 years, 6–10 years, and 11+ years.

Mother's and Father's Immigration Status
Participants were asked to identify their relationship for up to two parents/guardians with response options of: Mother (biological or

adoptive), Father (biological or adoptive), Stepmother, Stepfather, and other (please specify). For each they were asked: "Is Parent/Guardian 1/2 a US citizen, permanent resident, or have some other immigration status?" Response options included: no current legal status, DACA recipient, TPS recipient, permanent resident, US citizen, does not live in the United States, deceased, I don't know, and other (please specify). Those who did not identify a mother or stepmother were treated as missing data for mother's immigration status, and those who did not identify a father or stepfather were treated as missing data for father's immigration status. Those who selected "I don't know" for either parent/ guardian's immigration status were also treated as missing data.

Mother's and Father's Highest Level of Education
Participants were asked to identify their relationship for up to two parents/guardians with response options of: Mother (biological or adoptive), Father (biological or adoptive), Stepmother, Stepfather, and other (please specify). For each they were asked: "What category best describes the highest level of education Parent/Guardian 1/2 has completed?" Response options included: none, 6th grade or lower, 7th to 8th grade, 9th to 12th grade, high-school diploma or GED, some college (including vocational or technical program), bachelor's degree, postgraduate degree (e.g., MA, PhD, professional degree), I don't know, and other (please specify). Responses were re-categorized into five groups: 6th grade or lower, some middle or high school, high-school diploma or GED, some college, and bachelor's degree or higher. Those who did not have a mother or stepmother were treated as missing data for mother's level of education, and those who did not identify a father or stepfather were treated as missing data for father's level of education. Those who selected "I don't know" for either parent/guardian's education level were also treated as missing data.

Mother's and Father's Employment
Participants were asked to identify their relationship for up to two parents/guardians with response options of: Mother (biological or adoptive), Father (biological or adoptive), Stepmother, Stepfather, and other (please specify). For each they were asked: "What category best describes Parent/Guardian 1/2's employment?" Response options included:

employee who works for wages or salary, self-employed; temporary/
seasonal worker (e.g., seasonal agriculture, day labor), unemployed
and looking for work, not working (e.g., retired, stay-at-home parent,
disabled), I don't know, and other (please specify). Those who did not
have a mother or stepmother were treated as missing data for mother's
employment, and those who did not identify a father or stepfather were
treated as missing data for father's employment. Those who selected "I
don't know" for either parent/guardian's employment were also treated
as missing data.

Household Income
Participants were asked: "What was your estimated total household
income in 2019?" Participants were directed to estimate their total
household income by including everyone who lives in their permanent home, including themselves, and helps pay for shared expenses.
Response options included the following categories: $0; $1–$10,000;
$10,001–$20,000; $20,001–$30,000; $30,001–$40,000; $40,001–$50,000;
$50,001–$75,000; $75,001–$100,000; $100,001–$125,000; $125,001–
$150,000; $150,001–$175,000; $175,001–$200,000; $200,001 or more; and I
don't know. Responses were re-categorized into seven groups: $0–$20,000;
$20,001–$30,000; $30,001–$40,000; $40,001–$50,000; $50,001–$75,000;
$75,001–$100,000; and $100,001 or more.

Has at Least One Undocumented Sibling
Participants were asked to identify the current immigration status of
their sibling(s) and to check multiple boxes if they had multiple siblings
with different immigration statuses. Responses of no current legal status,
DACA, TPS, U visa, and pending asylum were considered "undocumented." Responses of permanent resident, US citizen, does not live in
the United States, and deceased were considered "not undocumented."
Responses were then dichotomized into having an undocumented sibling or not.

Has at Least One Undocumented Extended Family Member
Participants were asked to select the current immigration status of
two groups: "extended family member(s) who live in your permanent
household (e.g., grandparents, aunts, uncles, cousins, in-laws, etc.)" and

"extended family member(s) who do not live in your permanent household." They were instructed to check multiple boxes if they had extended family members with different immigration statuses. Responses of no current legal status, DACA, TPS, U visa, and pending asylum were considered "undocumented." Responses of permanent resident, US citizen, does not live in the United States, and deceased were considered "not undocumented." These two variables were then combined into one dichotomized variable of either "has undocumented extended family member" or "does not have undocumented extended family member."

Table B.1. Descriptive statistics for measures.

	Undocumented Students (n=548)	U.S. Citizen Students with Undocumented Parents (n=615)	U.S. Citizen Students with Lawfully Present Parents (n=633)
	n (%) or Mean (SD)	n (%) or Mean (SD)	n (%) or Mean (SD)
Family Legal Vulnerability Predictors			
Threat to Family	12.47 (2.64)	12.34 (2.92)	7.87 (3.46)
Missing	5	5	9
Deported Family Member			
No	360 (70.3)	336 (57.0)	414 (68.1)
Yes	152 (29.7)	254 (43.1)	194 (31.9)
Missing	36	25	25
Family Financial Strain	2.51 (2.18)	2.40 (2.21)	1.58 (1.97)
Missing	1	4	1
Mental Health Outcomes			
Anxiety	9.32 (5.88)	9.23 (5.95)	8.68 (5.75)
Missing	10	12	23
Depression	10.53 (6.53)	10.54 (6.63)	9.79 (6.25)
Missing	14	15	23
Flourishing	44.12 (7.60)	42.96 (7.76)	43.35 (8.27)
Missing	6	6	8
Academic Outcomes			
Failed a Course			
No	290 (53.2)	354 (58.0)	385 (61.8)
Yes	255 (46.8)	256 (42.0)	238 (38.2)
Missing	3	5	10
Low GPA			
Above 2.5	480 (89.4)	531 (87.5)	577 (92.8)
Below 2.5	57 (10.6)	76 (12.5)	45 (7.2)
Missing	11	8	11
Negative Academic Engagement	1.29 (.76)	1.29 (.74)	1.20 (.77)
Missing	5	10	7
Positive Academic Engagement	1.60 (.72)	1.54 (.72)	1.53 (.75)
Missing	9	9	10
Professional Development Opportunity			
No	300 (54.7)	398 (64.7)	390 (61.6)
Yes	248 (45.3)	217 (35.3)	243 (38.4)
Missing	0	0	0

(Continued)

	Undocumented Students (n=548)	U.S. Citizen Students with Undocumented Parents (n=615)	U.S. Citizen Students with Lawfully Present Parents (n=633)
	n (%) or Mean (SD)	n (%) or Mean (SD)	n (%) or Mean (SD)
Political Participation Outcomes			
Organization Participation			
No	245 (44.7)	341 (55.4)	346 (54.8)
Yes	303 (55.3)	274 (44.6)	286 (45.3)
Missing	0	0	1
Protest Participation			
No	296 (54.0)	306 (49.8)	333 (52.9)
Yes	252 (46.0)	308 (50.2)	297 (47.1)
Missing	0	1	3
Talk about Voting			
Never or rarely	186 (34.3)	211 (34.4)	227 (36.0)
Sometimes or more	356 (65.7)	403 (65.6)	403 (64.0)
Missing	6	1	3
Campus Resource Use Outcomes			
Visited Academic Support Services			
Never	204 (37.4)	253 (41.1)	295 (46.8)
Once a week or more	65 (11.9)	72 (11.7)	58 (9.2)
About once a month	66 (12.1)	78 (12.7)	64 (10.2)
A few times a year	211 (38.6)	212 (34.5)	213 (33.8)
Missing	2	0	3
Visited Basic Needs Center			
Never	180 (33.0)	243 (39.5)	300 (47.5)
Once a week or more	129 (23.6)	120 (19.5)	90 (14.3)
About once a month	81 (14.8)	93 (15.1)	80 (12.7)
A few times a year	156 (28.6)	159 (25.9)	161 (25.5)
Missing	2	0	2
Visited Identity-Based Centers			
Never	293 (53.7)	412 (67.1)	415 (65.9)
Once a week or more	90 (16.5)	58 (9.5)	50 (7.9)
About once a month	49 (9.0)	48 (7.8)	45 (7.1)
A few times a year	114 (20.9)	96 (15.6)	120 (19.1)
Missing	2	1	3
Visited Immigration-Related Legal Services			
Never	169 (31.0)	536 (87.2)	598 (94.9)

Once a week or more	28 (5.1)	4 (0.7)	5 (0.8)
About once a month	71 (13.0)	23 (3.7)	8 (1.3)
A few times a year	278 (50.9)	52 (8.5)	19 (3.0)
Missing	2	0	3
Visited Mental Health Services			
Never	370 (67.9)	470 (76.4)	472 (74.9)
Once a week or more	25 (4.6)	29 (4.7)	29 (4.6)
About once a month	46 (8.4)	33 (5.4)	35 (5.6)
A few times a year	104 (19.1)	83 (13.5)	94 (14.9)
Missing	3	0	3
Visited Undocumented Student Services			
Never	163 (29.8)	548 (89.1)	598 (95.2)
Once a week or more	94 (17.2)	11 (1.8)	4 (0.6)
About once a month	86 (15.7)	8 (1.3)	2 (0.3)
A few times a year	204 (37.3)	48 (7.8)	24 (3.8)
Missing	1	0	5
Other Items			
Deportability Concerns - Parents			
Never	31 (5.7)	18 (2.9)	444 (71.3)
A few times a year	114 (21.0)	129 (21.0)	138 (22.2)
About once a month	122 (22.5)	149 (24.3)	28 (4.5)
About once a week	130 (23.9)	133 (21.7)	6 (1.0)
Daily	146 (26.9)	184 (30.0)	7 (1.1)
Missing	5	2	10
Deported Immediate Family Member			
No	459 (89.3)	484 (82.6)	564 (93.1)
Yes	55 (10.7)	102 (17.4)	42 (6.9)
Missing	34	29	27
Food Security			
High/marginal food security	209 (38.5)	244 (39.8)	263 (42.0)
Low food security	105 (19.3)	146 (23.8)	164 (26.2)
Very low food security	229 (42.2)	223 (36.4)	200 (31.9)
Missing	5	2	6
Did Not Use Undocumented Student Services: Is Not for Students Like Me			
Not at all	111 (82.2)	265 (51.5)	176 (31.5)
Somewhat	20 (14.8)	173 (33.6)	181 (32.4)
A lot	4 (3.0)	77 (15.0)	202 (36.1)

(Continued)

	Undocumented Students (n=548)	U.S. Citizen Students with Undocumented Parents (n=615)	U.S. Citizen Students with Lawfully Present Parents (n=633)
	n (%) or Mean (SD)	n (%) or Mean (SD)	n (%) or Mean (SD)
Used undoc. student services	413	95	68
Missing	0	5	6
Did Not Use Undocumented Student Services: Did Not Know It Existed			
Not at all	70 (51.9)	159 (30.8)	214 (38.3)
Somewhat	46 (34.1)	132 (25.6)	129 (23.1)
A lot	19 (14.1)	225 (43.6)	216 (38.6)
Used undoc. student services	413	95	68
Missing	0	4	6
Undocumented Student Services Referred to Campus Partner			
No	103 (24.2)	100 (65.4)	105 (77.2)
Yes	1	53 (34.6)	31 (22.8)
Did not use undoc. student services	115	462	491
Missing	8	0	6
Undocumented Student Services Spoke with Campus Partner			
No	217 (50.4)	112 (73.2)	106 (77.9)
Yes	214 (49.7)	41 (26.8)	30 (22.1)
Did not use undoc. student services	115	462	491
Missing	2	0	6

APPENDIX C

Multivariate Regression Analyses and Results

Appendix C includes information about each of the multivariate regressions presented in chapters 2–5. We present details about the analytic approach and provide the full tabular regression results for each model.

MODELING APPROACH

The regression models tested group differences in mental health, academic success, political engagement, and campus resource use among three student groups in our survey: undocumented students, US citizen students with undocumented parents, and US citizens students with lawfully present parents. Each chapter followed the same model sequence. In Model 1, we first determined baseline differences across the three groups in the outcomes when controlling for gender, first-generation student status, year in school, major, and UC campus. US citizens with lawfully present parents were the reference category. In Model 2, we included the measure of perceived threat to family due to restrictive immigration policy to examine how the initial differences among the three student groups changed after we accounted for this measure of family legal vulnerability. Models 3 and 4 were the same as Model 2, except we replaced perceived threats to family with measures for having a deported family member and family financial strain, respectively. This sequential modeling approach allowed us to determine whether initial group differences were explained by varying exposure to the three aspects of family legal vulnerability measured in our survey. The models were either linear or logistic regression models based on the coding of the outcome variable. We conducted likelihood ratio tests to compare the overall fit of the baseline model to subsequent models. We also conducted Wald tests to compare the equivalence of the student group coefficients after each model.

The figures presented in the chapters are the predicted probability (for binary outcomes) or adjusted means (for continuous outcomes) from each of the models described above. We used Stata 17's margins command, which calculates average marginal effects as the default. This approach calculates each observation's predicted probability or adjusted mean at the different self and parental immigration categories while using the observation's own values for the covariates. The predicted probabilities are averaged across self and parental immigration categories to produce the average predicted probability or adjusted mean.

Mental-Health Outcomes

We examined three outcomes related to mental health: depression, anxiety, and flourishing. Depression was measured using the major depressive disorder module of the Patient Health Questionnaire (PHQ-9). Anxiety was assessed using the Generalized Anxiety Disorder (GAD-7) questionnaire. Flourishing was measured using the Flourishing Scale, an eight-item scale of the respondent's self-perceived success in important areas such as relationships, self-esteem, purpose, and optimism. We conducted listwise deletion for participants who were missing any of our mental-health outcome variables or covariates, leaving us with a final analytic sample of 1,583 for chapter 2.

Academic Outcomes

We examined five academic outcomes: positive academic engagement, negative academic engagement, failing a course, low GPA, and participating in a professional development opportunity. The measures represented long- and short-term academic performance (low GPA, failing a class) as well as participation in academic engagement (e.g., professional development opportunities, class participation). We conducted listwise deletion for participants who were missing any of our academic outcome variables or covariates, leaving us with a final analytic sample of 1,580 for chapter 3.

Political Engagement Outcomes

We examined three measures of political engagement: talking to others about voting, participating in a protest, and participating in an organization to solve a problem. These measures captured a range of activities that come with different levels of risk for encountering deportation threats or anti-immigrant sentiment. Further, some were more public in nature (e.g., protest), while others could be private or semiprivate. We conducted listwise deletion for participants who were missing any of our political engagement outcome variables or covariates, leaving us with a final analytic sample of 1,645 for chapter 4.

Campus Resource Use Outcomes
We examined five measures of campus resource use: visiting the basic needs center, visiting campus mental health services, visiting academic support services, visiting identity-based centers, and visiting the undocumented student services office. These measures represented a range of campus resources that students can tap into to support their educational success. We conducted listwise deletion for participants who were missing any of our outcome variables or covariates, leaving us with a final analytic sample of 1,639 for chapter 5.

Table C.1. Linear regression results for depression by self/parental immigration status.

	Model 1			Model 2			Model 3			Model 4		
	β	95% CI	p	β	95% CI	p	β	95% CI	p	β	95% CI	p
Self/ Parental Immigration Status												
US citizen with lawfully present parents	Ref.	-	-	-	Ref.	-	-	-	Ref.	-	-	-	Ref.	-	-	-
Undocu- mented stu- dents	0.46	-0.35	1.26		-1.77	-2.68	-0.86	**	0.51	-0.29	1.31		-0.32	-1.10	0.46	
US citizen with un- documented parents	0.61	-0.17	1.39		-1.51	-2.40	-0.63	*	0.49	-0.29	1.27		-0.15	-0.91	0.61	
Family Legal Vulnerability												
Threat to family					0.50	0.39	0.60	**								
Deported family member																
No									Ref.	-	-	-				
Yes									1.30	0.63	1.97	**				
Family finan- cial strain													0.89	0.75	1.04	**
Controls												
Gender																
Men	Ref.	-	-	-	Ref.	-	-	-	Ref.	-	-	-	Ref.	-	-	-
Women	1.62	0.82	2.42	**	0.97	0.18	1.77	*	1.61	0.81	2.41	**	1.50	0.73	2.27	**
Alterna- tive gender identification	6.08	3.76	8.40	**	4.77	2.49	7.04	**	5.77	3.46	8.09	**	4.95	2.72	7.18	**
First-gen student																
No	Ref.	-	-	-	Ref.	-	-	-	Ref.	-	-	-	Ref.	-	-	-
Yes	1.18	-0.06	2.41		0.46	-0.75	1.68		0.99	-0.24	2.23		0.59	-0.60	1.78	
Year in school																
1st and 2nd years	Ref.	-	-	-	Ref.	-	-	-	Ref.	-	-	-	Ref.	-	-	-
3rd years	0.10	-0.75	0.94		0.15	-0.67	0.97		0.02	-0.82	0.87		-0.08	-0.89	0.73	
4th years and higher	-0.31	-1.13	0.51		-0.21	-1.01	0.59		-0.37	-1.19	0.45		-0.54	-1.33	0.25	

	M1				M2				M3				M4			
Transfer student																
No	Ref.	-	-	-	Ref.	-	-	-	Ref.	-	-	-	Ref.	-	-	-
Yes	0.71	-0.21	1.63		0.75	-0.14	1.64		0.74	-0.18	1.65		0.38	-0.50	1.26	
Major																
Arts and humanities	Ref.	-	-	-	Ref.	-	-	-	Ref.	-	-	-	Ref.	-	-	-
Social science	-0.52	-1.48	0.45		-0.50	-1.44	0.44		-0.50	-1.46	0.46		-0.41	-1.34	0.51	
STEM	-0.42	-1.49	0.65		-0.33	-1.37	0.71		-0.43	-1.49	0.64		-0.56	-1.58	0.46	
Other and undeclared	-0.69	-1.89	0.52		-0.57	-1.74	0.61		-0.72	-1.92	0.48		-0.98	-2.13	0.18	
Campus																
UC Berkeley	Ref.	-	-	-	Ref.	-	-	-	Ref.	-	-	-	Ref.	-	-	-
UC Davis	-0.41	-2.09	1.28		-0.40	-2.04	1.24		-0.44	-2.11	1.24		-0.41	-2.02	1.20	
UC Irvine	-0.87	-2.40	0.66		-0.67	-2.16	0.82		-0.92	-2.44	0.60		-0.65	-2.12	0.81	
UC Los Angeles	0.16	-1.44	1.77		0.38	-1.19	1.94		0.13	-1.47	1.73		0.31	-1.23	1.85	
UC Merced	-0.66	-2.31	0.99		-0.39	-1.99	1.22		-0.71	-2.35	0.93		-0.44	-2.02	1.14	
UC Riverside	-0.98	-2.49	0.54		-0.67	-2.15	0.80		-1.09	-2.60	0.42		-0.63	-2.09	0.82	
UC Santa Barbara	-1.28	-2.97	0.42		-1.16	-2.80	0.49		-1.42	-3.11	0.27		-0.94	-2.57	0.68	
UC Santa Cruz	-0.82	-2.44	0.80		-0.70	-2.28	0.88		-0.88	-2.50	0.73		-0.88	-2.42	0.67	
UC San Diego	0.28	-1.72	2.29		0.36	-1.60	2.31		0.27	-1.73	2.27		0.39	-1.53	2.31	
Constant	8.40	6.29	10.52	**	5.35	3.19	7.50	**	8.26	6.16	10.36	**	7.73	5.70	9.75	**

$*p<.05, **p<.01$

Model 1 Wald test: $F=1.25$, $p=0.28$; Model 2 Wald test: $F=8.06$, $p<.05$; Model 3 Wald test: 1.03, $p=0.35$; Model 4 Wald test: 0.32, $p=0.72$

LR Test Model 1 v Model 2: $\chi2=8.1$, $p<.05$; LR Test Model 1 v Model 3: $\chi2=14.5$, $p<.05$; LR Test Model 1 v Model 4: $\chi2=140.1$, $p<.05$

Table C.2. Linear regression results for anxiety by self/parental immigration status.

	Model 1			Model 2			Model 3			Model 4		
	β	95% CI	p	β	95% CI	p	β	95% CI	p	β	95% CI	p
Self/Parental Immigration Status												
US citizen with lawfully present parents	Ref.	-	-	-	Ref.	-	-	-	Ref.	-	-	-	Ref.	-	-	-
Undocumented students	0.45	-0.27	1.18		-1.83	-2.65	-1.02	**	0.48	-0.25	1.20		-0.25	-0.95	0.45	
US citizen with undocumented parents	0.46	-0.24	1.17		-1.72	-2.51	-0.94	**	0.41	-0.29	1.12		-0.23	-0.91	0.46	
Family Legal Vulnerability												
Threat to family					0.51	0.42	0.60	**								
Deported family member																
No									Ref.	-	-	-				
Yes									0.57	-0.04	1.17					
Family financial strain													0.81	0.68	0.94	**
Controls												
Gender												
Men	Ref.	-	-	-	Ref.	-	-	-	Ref.	-	-	-	Ref.	-	-	-
Women	2.42	1.70	3.15	**	1.76	1.05	2.47	**	2.42	1.70	3.14	**	2.31	1.62	3.00	**
Alternative gender identification	5.63	3.54	7.72	**	4.27	2.24	6.30	**	5.49	3.40	7.59	**	4.60	2.59	6.60	**
First-gen student												
No	Ref.	-	-	-	Ref.	-	-	-	Ref.	-	-	-	Ref.	-	-	-
Yes	0.69	-0.42	1.80		-0.04	-1.13	1.04		0.61	-0.51	1.72		0.15	-0.91	1.22	
Year in school												
1st and 2nd years	Ref.	-	-	-	Ref.	-	-	-	Ref.	-	-	-	Ref.	-	-	-
3rd years	0.18	-0.58	0.94		0.23	-0.50	0.97		0.15	-0.61	0.91		0.02	-0.71	0.75	
4th years and higher	0.30	-0.44	1.04		0.41	-0.31	1.12		0.28	-0.46	1.02		0.10	-0.61	0.81	
Transfer student												
No	Ref.	-	-	-	Ref.	-	-	-	Ref.	-	-	-	Ref.	-	-	-

Yes	0.40	-0.42	1.22		0.44	-0.36	1.23		0.41	-0.41	1.23		0.10	-0.69	0.89	
Major																
Arts and humanities	Ref.	-	-	-	Ref.	-	-	-	Ref.	-	-	-	Ref.	-	-	-
Social science	0.23	-0.64	1.10		0.25	-0.59	1.09		0.24	-0.63	1.11		0.32	-0.51	1.16	
STEM	0.55	-0.41	1.51		0.64	-0.29	1.57		0.55	-0.42	1.51		0.42	-0.50	1.34	
Other and undeclared	0.30	-0.79	1.38		0.42	-0.62	1.47		0.29	-0.80	1.37		0.04	-1.00	1.08	
Campus																
UC Berkeley	Ref.	-	-	-	Ref.	-	-	-	Ref.	-	-	-	Ref.	-	-	-
UC Davis	-0.39	-1.91	1.12		-0.38	-1.84	1.08		-0.40	-1.92	1.11		-0.39	-1.84	1.06	
UC Irvine	-0.35	-1.72	1.03		-0.14	-1.47	1.19		-0.37	-1.74	1.01		-0.15	-1.47	1.16	
UC Los Angeles	0.59	-0.86	2.03		0.80	-0.59	2.20		0.57	-0.87	2.01		0.72	-0.66	2.10	
UC Merced	0.00	-1.49	1.48		0.28	-1.16	1.71		-0.02	-1.51	1.46		0.19	-1.22	1.61	
UC Riverside	0.16	-1.21	1.52		0.47	-0.85	1.79		0.11	-1.26	1.47		0.47	-0.84	1.78	
UC Santa Barbara	-0.37	-1.90	1.15		-0.25	-1.72	1.23		-0.44	-1.96	1.09		-0.07	-1.53	1.39	
UC Santa Cruz	0.23	-1.22	1.69		0.36	-1.05	1.76		0.21	-1.25	1.66		0.18	-1.21	1.57	
UC San Diego	0.41	-1.39	2.22		0.49	-1.25	2.24		0.41	-1.40	2.21		0.51	-1.22	2.24	
Constant	5.55	3.65	7.45	**	2.41	0.49	4.33	*	5.49	3.59	7.39	**	4.94	3.12	6.76	**

*p<.05, **p<.01

Model 1 Wald test: F=1.07, p=0.34; Model 2 Wald test: F=11.75, p<.05; Model 3 Wald test: 1.01, p=0.36; Model 4 Wald test: 1.26, p=0.28

LR Test Model 1 v Model 2: χ2=114.26, p<.05; LR Test Model 1 v Model 3: χ2=3.41, p=0.06; LR Test Model 1 v Model 4: χ2=142.25, p<.05

Table C.3. Linear regression results for flourishing by self/parental immigration status.

	Model 1			Model 2			Model 3			Model 4		
	β	95% CI	p	β	95% CI	p	β	95% CI	p	β	95% CI	p
Self/Parental Immigration Status												
US citizen with lawfully present parents	Ref.	-	-	-	Ref.	-	-	-	Ref.	-	-	-	Ref.	-	-	-
Undocumented students	1.52	0.52	2.52	*	2.21	1.05	3.37	**	1.50	0.50	2.50	*	2.01	1.01	3.01	**
US citizen with undocumented parents	0.02	-0.95	0.99		0.68	-0.45	1.80		0.06	-0.91	1.03		0.50	-0.48	1.47	
Family Legal Vulnerability												
Threat to family					-0.15	-0.29	-0.02	*								
Deported family member																
No									Ref.	-	-	-				
Yes									-0.45	-1.29	0.38					
Family financial strain													-0.56	-0.75	-0.38	**
Controls												
Gender																
Men	Ref.	-	-	-	Ref.	-	-	-	Ref.	-	-	-	Ref.	-	-	-
Women	-0.94	-1.94	0.06		-0.74	-1.75	0.27		-0.94	-1.93	0.06		-0.86	-1.85	0.12	
Alternative gender identification	-3.59	-6.48	-0.71	*	-3.19	-6.09	-0.29	*	-3.49	-6.38	-0.60	*	-2.88	-5.74	-0.02	*
First-gen student																
No	Ref.	-	-	-	Ref.	-	-	-	Ref.	-	-	-	Ref.	-	-	-
Yes	-1.37	-2.91	0.16		-1.15	-2.70	0.39		-1.31	-2.85	0.23		-1.00	-2.53	0.52	
Year in school																
1st and 2nd years	Ref.	-	-	-	Ref.	-	-	-	Ref.	-	-	-	Ref.	-	-	-
3rd years	-0.07	-1.12	0.98		-0.09	-1.14	0.96		-0.05	-1.10	1.00		0.04	-1.00	1.08	

4th years and higher	0.72	-0.30	1.74		0.69	-0.33	1.71		0.74	-0.28	1.76		0.86	-0.15	1.88
Transfer student															
No	Ref.	-	-	-	Ref.	-	-	-	Ref.	-	-	-	Ref.	-	-
Yes	-0.53	-1.66	0.61		-0.54	-1.67	0.60		-0.53	-1.67	0.60		-0.32	-1.45	0.81
Major															
Arts and humanities	Ref.	-	-	-	Ref.	-	-	-	Ref.	-	-	-	Ref.	-	-
Social science	0.49	-0.71	1.69		0.49	-0.71	1.68		0.48	-0.71	1.68		0.43	-0.76	1.61
STEM	0.10	-1.22	1.43		0.08	-1.25	1.40		0.11	-1.22	1.43		0.19	-1.12	1.51
Other and undeclared	0.71	-0.79	2.21		0.67	-0.82	2.17		0.72	-0.78	2.22		0.89	-0.59	2.38
Campus															
UC Berkeley	Ref.	-	-	-	Ref.	-	-	-	Ref.	-	-	-	Ref.	-	-
UC Davis	1.52	-0.57	3.61		1.52	-0.57	3.61		1.53	-0.56	3.62		1.52	-0.54	3.59
UC Irvine	0.32	-1.57	2.22		0.26	-1.63	2.16		0.34	-1.56	2.24		0.19	-1.69	2.07
UC Los Angeles	0.30	-1.69	2.29		0.24	-1.75	2.23		0.32	-1.68	2.31		0.21	-1.76	2.18
UC Merced	1.54	-0.51	3.58		1.45	-0.59	3.50		1.56	-0.49	3.60		1.40	-0.62	3.43
UC Riverside	1.06	-0.83	2.94		0.96	-0.92	2.85		1.10	-0.79	2.98		0.84	-1.02	2.70
UC Santa Barbara	1.09	-1.01	3.19		1.05	-1.05	3.15		1.14	-0.97	3.25		0.88	-1.20	2.96
UC Santa Cruz	2.39	0.38	4.40	*	2.36	0.35	4.36	*	2.42	0.41	4.43	*	2.43	0.44	4.42
UC San Diego	0.90	-1.60	3.39		0.87	-1.62	3.36		0.90	-1.59	3.39		0.83	-1.64	3.30
Constant	43.65	41.02	46.27	**	44.59	41.85	47.33	**	43.70	41.07	46.32	**	44.07	41.47	46.67

*p<.05, **p<.01

Model 1 Wald test: F=5.78, p<0.05; Model 2 Wald test: F=8.01, p<0.05; Model 3 Wald test: 5.47, p<0.05; Model 4 Wald test: 8.37, p<0.05

LR Test Model 1 v Model 2: $\chi2$=127.67, p<.05; LR Test Model 1 v Model 3: $\chi2$=1.15, p=0.28; LR Test Model 1 v Model 4: $\chi2$=35.03, p<.05

Table C.4. Logistic regression results for low GPA by self/parental immigration status.

	Model 1			Model 2			Model 3			Model 4		
	OR	95% CI	p	OR	95% CI	p	OR	95% CI	p	OR	95% CI	p
Self/Parental Immigration Status												
US citizen with lawfully present parents	Ref.	-	-	-	Ref.	-	-	-	Ref.	-	-	-	Ref.	-	-	-
Undocumented students	1.46	0.94	2.28		1.20	0.72	1.99		1.49	0.95	2.32		1.41	0.90	2.21	
US citizen with undocumented parents	1.63	1.07	2.48	*	1.35	0.83	2.19		1.59	1.04	2.43	*	1.58	1.03	2.41	*
Family Legal Vulnerability												
Threat to family					1.05	0.99	1.11									
Deported family member																
No									Ref.	-	-	-				
Yes									1.26	0.89	1.77					
Family financial strain													1.05	0.97	1.13	
Controls												
Gender																
Men	Ref.	-	-	-	Ref.	-	-	-	Ref.	-	-	-	Ref.	-	-	-
Women	1.03	0.68	1.57		0.97	0.63	1.48		1.03	0.67	1.56		1.02	0.67	1.56	
Alternative gender identification	1.16	0.32	4.18		1.05	0.29	3.79		1.11	0.31	3.99		1.11	0.31	3.99	
First-gen student																
No	Ref.	-	-	-	Ref.	-	-	-	Ref.	-	-	-	Ref.	-	-	-
Yes	1.16	0.56	2.40		1.10	0.53	2.29		1.12	0.54	2.32		1.13	0.55	2.34	
Year in school																
1st and 2nd years	Ref.	-	-	-	Ref.	-	-	-	Ref.	-	-	-	Ref.	-	-	-
3rd years	0.75	0.48	1.16		0.75	0.48	1.17		0.73	0.47	1.15		0.73	0.47	1.15	
4th years and higher	0.66	0.42	1.03		0.66	0.42	1.03		0.65	0.42	1.02		0.65	0.42	1.02	
Transfer student																
No	Ref.	-	-	-	Ref.	-	-	-	Ref.	-	-	-	Ref.	-	-	-
Yes	1.14	0.67	1.95		1.15	0.68	1.96		1.15	0.67	1.95		1.14	0.67	1.93	

Major																
Arts and humanities	Ref.	-	-	-	Ref.	-	-	-	Ref.	-	-	-	Ref.	-	-	-
Social science	0.62	0.37	1.02		0.61	0.37	1.02		0.62	0.38	1.03		0.62	0.37	1.03	
STEM	0.90	0.53	1.53		0.90	0.53	1.53		0.90	0.53	1.54		0.90	0.53	1.52	
Other and undeclared	1.01	0.56	1.80		1.02	0.57	1.82		1.01	0.57	1.81		1.00	0.56	1.79	
Campus																
UC Berkeley	Ref.	-	-	-	Ref.	-	-	-	Ref.	-	-	-	Ref.	-	-	-
UC Davis	0.76	0.30	1.92		0.76	0.30	1.93		0.75	0.30	1.90		0.77	0.30	1.94	
UC Irvine	1.28	0.58	2.82		1.31	0.60	2.89		1.27	0.58	2.79		1.31	0.59	2.87	
UC Los Angeles	0.26	0.08	0.81	*	0.26	0.09	0.82	*	0.26	0.08	0.80	*	0.26	0.08	0.82	*
UC Merced	1.39	0.61	3.16		1.44	0.63	3.28		1.39	0.61	3.15		1.41	0.62	3.21	
UC Riverside	1.24	0.56	2.73		1.28	0.58	2.82		1.21	0.55	2.68		1.27	0.58	2.81	
UC Santa Barbara	1.55	0.65	3.65		1.57	0.66	3.71		1.50	0.64	3.56		1.58	0.67	3.74	
UC Santa Cruz	0.87	0.36	2.09		0.89	0.37	2.15		0.86	0.36	2.07		0.87	0.36	2.09	
UC San Diego	1.32	0.49	3.55		1.34	0.50	3.60		1.31	0.49	3.53		1.33	0.50	3.59	
Constant	0.10	0.03	0.31	**	0.07	0.02	0.25	**	0.09	0.03	0.30	**	0.09	0.03	0.30	**

*p<.05, **p<.01

Model 1 Wald test: $\chi2$=5.37, p=0.09; Model 2 Wald test: $\chi2$=1.48, p=0.48; Model 3 Wald test: $\chi2$=5.03, p=0.08; Model 4 Wald test: $\chi2$=4.52, p=0.10

LR Test Model 1 v Model 2: $\chi2$=2.40, p=0.12; LR Test Model 1 v Model 3: $\chi2$=5.03, p=0.08; LR Test Model 1 v Model 4: $\chi2$=4.52, p=0.10

Table C.5. Logistic regression results for course failure by self/parental immigration status.

	Model 1			Model 2			Model 3			Model 4		
	OR	95% CI	p	OR	95% CI	p	OR	95% CI	p	OR	95% CI	p
Self/Parental Immigration Status												
US citizen with lawfully present parents	Ref.	-	-	-	Ref.	-	-	-	Ref.	-	-	-	Ref.	-	-	-
Undocumented students	1.44	1.10	1.89	*	1.25	0.91	1.71		1.44	1.10	1.90	*	1.37	1.04	1.81	*
US citizen with undocumented parents	1.20	0.92	1.56		1.04	0.77	1.42		1.19	0.91	1.55		1.15	0.88	1.50	
Family Legal Vulnerability												
Threat to family					1.03	1.00	1.07									
Deported family member																
No								Ref.	-	-	-				
Yes								1.11	0.88	1.39					
Family financial strain												1.06	1.00	1.11	*
Controls												
Gender												
Men	Ref.	-	-	-	Ref.	-	-	-	Ref.	-	-	-	Ref.	-	-	-
Women	1.03	0.79	1.36		0.99	0.75	1.31		1.03	0.79	1.36		1.03	0.78	1.35	
Alternative gender identification	1.47	0.66	3.30		1.36	0.60	3.07		1.44	0.64	3.23		1.38	0.61	3.12	
First-gen student												
No	Ref.	-	-	-	Ref.	-	-	-	Ref.	-	-	-	Ref.	-	-	-
Yes	1.28	0.82	1.98		1.22	0.79	1.90		1.26	0.81	1.95		1.23	0.79	1.91	
Year in school												
1st and 2nd years	Ref.	-	-	-	Ref.	-	-	-	Ref.	-	-	-	Ref.	-	-	-
3rd years	2.65	2.00	3.51	**	2.66	2.00	3.53	**	2.64	1.99	3.50	**	2.62	1.97	3.48	**
4th years and higher	4.04	3.05	5.36	**	4.06	3.07	5.39	**	4.03	3.04	5.33	**	4.00	3.02	5.30	**
Transfer student												
No	Ref.	-	-	-	Ref.	-	-	-	Ref.	-	-	-	Ref.	-	-	-
Yes	0.29	0.21	0.40	**	0.29	0.21	0.40	**	0.29	0.21	0.40	**	0.29	0.21	0.39	**
Major												
Arts and humanities	Ref.	-	-	-	Ref.	-	-	-	Ref.	-	-	-	Ref.	-	-	-

		Model 1				Model 2				Model 3				Model 4		
Social science	0.68	0.49	0.95	*	0.68	0.49	0.95	*	0.68	0.49	0.96	*	0.69	0.49	0.96	*
STEM	1.00	0.70	1.44		1.00	0.70	1.44		1.01	0.70	1.45		1.00	0.69	1.43	
Other and undeclared	1.10	0.73	1.65		1.10	0.73	1.65		1.09	0.73	1.65		1.08	0.72	1.63	
Campus																
UC Berkeley	Ref.	-	-	-	Ref.	-	-	-	Ref.	-	-	-	Ref.	-	-	-
UC Davis	1.34	0.77	2.33		1.35	0.77	2.35		1.33	0.77	2.32		1.36	0.78	2.37	
UC Irvine	0.80	0.48	1.34		0.82	0.49	1.36		0.80	0.48	1.33		0.82	0.49	1.37	
UC Los Angeles	0.43	0.25	0.76	*	0.44	0.25	0.77	*	0.43	0.25	0.75	*	0.44	0.25	0.77	*
UC Merced	0.97	0.57	1.67		1.00	0.58	1.72		0.97	0.56	1.67		0.99	0.57	1.71	
UC Riverside	0.74	0.45	1.24		0.76	0.46	1.26		0.73	0.44	1.22		0.76	0.46	1.27	
UC Santa Barbara	2.15	1.22	3.81	*	2.18	1.23	3.86	*	2.13	1.20	3.77	*	2.22	1.25	3.94	*
UC Santa Cruz	1.26	0.74	2.14		1.28	0.75	2.18		1.25	0.73	2.13		1.25	0.73	2.14	
UC San Diego	0.80	0.41	1.54		0.81	0.42	1.57		0.79	0.41	1.54		0.81	0.42	1.57	
Constant	0.34	0.17	0.71	*	0.28	0.13	0.60	*	0.34	0.16	0.70	*	0.33	0.16	0.68	*

*p<.05, **p<.01
Model 1 Wald test: $\chi2$=6.89, p<0.05; Model 2 Wald test: $\chi2$=2.42, p=0.30; Model 3 Wald test: $\chi2$=7.00, p<0.05; Model 4 Wald test: $\chi2$=5.10, p=0.07
LR Test Model 1 v Model 2: $\chi2$=3.07, p=0.08; LR Test Model 1 v Model 3: $\chi2$=0.79, p=0.38; LR Test Model 1 v Model 4: $\chi2$=4.24, p<0.05

Table C.6. Linear regression results for negative academic engagement by self/parental immigration status.

	Model 1			Model 2			Model 3			Model 4		
	β	95% CI	p	β	95% CI	p	β	95% CI	p	β	95% CI	p
Self/ Parental Immigra- tion Status												
US citizen with lawfully present parents	Ref.	-	-	-	Ref.	-	-	-	Ref.	-	-	-	Ref.	-	-	-
Undocu- mented students	0.06	-0.03	0.15		-0.08	-0.18	0.03		0.06	-0.03	0.16		0.01	-0.08	0.11	
US citizen with un- documented parents	0.10	0.01	0.19	*	-0.03	-0.14	0.07		0.08	-0.01	0.17		0.05	-0.04	0.14	
Family Legal Vul- nerability												
Threat to family					0.03	0.02	0.04	**								
Deported family member																
No									Ref.	-	-	-				
Yes									0.14	0.06	0.21	*				
Family finan- cial strain													0.06	0.04	0.07	**
Controls												
Gender												
Men	Ref.	-	-	-	Ref.	-	-	-	Ref.	-	-	-	Ref.	-	-	-
Women	0.02	-0.07	0.11		-0.02	-0.11	0.07		0.02	-0.07	0.11		0.01	-0.08	0.10	
Alternative gender identifica- tion	0.61	0.34	0.89	**	0.54	0.26	0.81	**	0.58	0.31	0.85	**	0.54	0.27	0.81	**
First-gen student												
No	Ref.	-	-	-	Ref.	-	-	-	Ref.	-	-	-	Ref.	-	-	-
Yes	0.07	-0.08	0.21		0.02	-0.12	0.16		0.05	-0.10	0.19		0.03	-0.12	0.17	
Year in school												
1st and 2nd years	Ref.	-	-	-	Ref.	-	-	-	Ref.	-	-	-	Ref.	-	-	-
3rd years	0.14	0.05	0.24	*	0.14	0.05	0.24	*	0.13	0.04	0.23	*	0.13	0.03	0.22	*

4th years and higher	0.22	0.13	0.32	**	0.22	0.13	0.32	**	0.21	0.12	0.31	**	0.21	0.11	0.30	**
Transfer student																
No	Ref.	-	-	-	Ref.	-	-	-	Ref.	-	-	-	Ref.	-	-	-
Yes	-0.13	-0.23	-0.02	*	-0.12	-0.22	-0.01	*	-0.12	-0.23	-0.02	*	-0.15	-0.25	-0.04	*
Major																
Arts and humanities	Ref.	-	-	-	Ref.	-	-	-	Ref.	-	-	-	Ref.	-	-	-
Social science	-0.19	-0.30	-0.07	*	-0.19	-0.30	-0.08	*	-0.18	-0.30	-0.07	*	-0.18	-0.29	-0.07	*
STEM	-0.11	-0.23	0.01		-0.11	-0.23	0.01		-0.11	-0.23	0.02		-0.12	-0.24	0.01	
Other and undeclared	-0.19	-0.33	-0.05	*	-0.18	-0.32	-0.05	*	-0.19	-0.33	-0.05	*	-0.20	-0.34	-0.07	*
Campus																
UC Berkeley	Ref.	-	-	-	Ref.	-	-	-	Ref.	-	-	-	Ref.	-	-	-
UC Davis	-0.38	-0.58	-0.19	**	-0.38	-0.57	-0.19	**	-0.39	-0.58	-0.20	**	-0.37	-0.56	-0.18	**
UC Irvine	-0.30	-0.47	-0.12	*	-0.28	-0.45	-0.10	*	-0.30	-0.48	-0.13	*	-0.27	-0.45	-0.10	*
UC Los Angeles	-0.30	-0.49	-0.12	*	-0.29	-0.47	-0.11	*	-0.31	-0.49	-0.12	*	-0.29	-0.47	-0.10	*
UC Merced	-0.50	-0.68	-0.31	**	-0.47	-0.66	-0.29	**	-0.50	-0.69	-0.32	**	-0.48	-0.67	-0.29	**
UC Riverside	-0.39	-0.56	-0.21	**	-0.37	-0.54	-0.20	**	-0.40	-0.58	-0.23	**	-0.36	-0.53	-0.19	**
UC Santa Barbara	-0.28	-0.47	-0.08	*	-0.27	-0.46	-0.07	*	-0.30	-0.49	-0.10	*	-0.25	-0.44	-0.06	*
UC Santa Cruz	-0.29	-0.47	-0.10	*	-0.28	-0.46	-0.09	*	-0.30	-0.48	-0.11	*	-0.29	-0.48	-0.11	*
UC San Diego	-0.13	-0.35	0.10		-0.11	-0.34	0.11		-0.13	-0.36	0.09		-0.11	-0.34	0.11	
Constant	1.49	1.24	1.73	**	1.30	1.05	1.55	**	1.47	1.23	1.72	**	1.44	1.20	1.68	**

*p<.05, **p<.01

Model 1 Wald test: F=2.34, p=0.10; Model 2 Wald test: F=1.00, p=0.37; Model 3 Wald test: F=1.83, p=0.16; Model 4 Wald test: F=0.76, p=0.47

LR Test Model 1 v Model 2: $\chi2$=23.94, p<0.05; LR Test Model 1 v Model 3: $\chi2$=11.89, p<0.05; LR Test Model 1 v Model 4: $\chi2$=39.89, p<0.05

Table C.7. Linear regression results for positive academic engagement by self/parental immigration status.

	Model 1				Model 2				Model 3				Model 4			
	β	95% CI		p	β	95% CI		p	β	95% CI		p	β	95% CI		p
Self/Parental Immigration Status																
US citizen with lawfully present parents	Ref.	-	-	-	Ref.	-	-	-	Ref.	-	-	-	Ref.	-	-	-
Undocumented students	0.09	0.00	0.18	*	-0.02	-0.12	0.09		0.09	0.00	0.18	*	0.07	-0.02	0.16	
US citizen with undocumented parents	0.07	-0.02	0.15		-0.04	-0.14	0.06		0.07	-0.02	0.15		0.05	-0.04	0.14	
Family Legal Vulnerability																
Threat to family					0.02	0.01	0.04	**								
Deported family member																
No									Ref.	-	-	-				
Yes									0.00	-0.07	0.08					
Family financial strain													0.02	0.01	0.04	*
Controls																
Gender																
Men	Ref.	-	-	-	Ref.	-	-	-	Ref.	-	-	-	Ref.	-	-	-
Women	-0.02	-0.11	0.07		-0.05	-0.15	0.04		-0.02	-0.11	0.07		-0.03	-0.12	0.07	
Alternative gender identification	-0.11	-0.37	0.16		-0.17	-0.44	0.10		-0.11	-0.37	0.16		-0.14	-0.40	0.13	
First-gen student																
No	Ref.	-	-	-	Ref.	-	-	-	Ref.	-	-	-	Ref.	-	-	-
Yes	-0.20	-0.34	-0.06	*	-0.23	-0.37	-0.09	*	-0.20	-0.34	-0.06	*	-0.21	-0.36	-0.07	*
Year in school																
1st and 2nd years	Ref.	-	-	-	Ref.	-	-	-	Ref.	-	-	-	Ref.	-	-	-
3rd years	-0.01	-0.11	0.08		-0.01	-0.11	0.08		-0.01	-0.11	0.08		-0.02	-0.11	0.08	
4th years and higher	-0.01	-0.10	0.08		-0.01	-0.10	0.09		-0.01	-0.10	0.08		-0.01	-0.11	0.08	
Transfer student																
No	Ref.	-	-	-	Ref.	-	-	-	Ref.	-	-	-	Ref.	-	-	-
Yes	0.01	-0.09	0.12		0.02	-0.08	0.12		0.01	-0.09	0.12		0.01	-0.10	0.11	

Major																
Arts and humanities	Ref.	-	-	-	Ref.	-	-	-	Ref.	-	-	-	Ref.	-	-	-
Social science	-0.07	-0.19	0.04		-0.08	-0.19	0.03		-0.07	-0.19	0.04		-0.07	-0.18	0.04	
STEM	0.06	-0.06	0.18		0.06	-0.06	0.18		0.06	-0.06	0.18		0.06	-0.06	0.18	
Other and undeclared	-0.04	-0.18	0.09		-0.04	-0.18	0.10		-0.04	-0.18	0.09		-0.05	-0.19	0.09	
Campus																
UC Berkeley	Ref.	-	-	-	Ref.	-	-	-	Ref.	-	-	-	Ref.	-	-	-
UC Davis	-0.01	-0.20	0.18		0.00	-0.19	0.18		-0.01	-0.20	0.18		0.00	-0.19	0.19	
UC Irvine	-0.18	-0.35	-0.01	*	-0.16	-0.34	0.01		-0.18	-0.35	-0.01	*	-0.17	-0.34	0.00	
UC Los Angeles	-0.08	-0.26	0.10		-0.07	-0.25	0.11		-0.08	-0.26	0.10		-0.07	-0.25	0.11	
UC Merced	-0.02	-0.21	0.16		-0.01	-0.19	0.18		-0.02	-0.21	0.16		-0.02	-0.20	0.17	
UC Riverside	-0.03	-0.20	0.14		-0.01	-0.18	0.16		-0.03	-0.20	0.14		-0.02	-0.19	0.16	
UC Santa Barbara	-0.13	-0.32	0.06		-0.12	-0.31	0.07		-0.13	-0.32	0.06		-0.12	-0.31	0.07	
UC Santa Cruz	0.07	-0.11	0.25		0.08	-0.10	0.26		0.07	-0.11	0.25		0.07	-0.11	0.25	
UC San Diego	-0.06	-0.28	0.16		-0.05	-0.27	0.17		-0.06	-0.28	0.16		-0.05	-0.27	0.17	
Constant	1.78	1.54	2.02	**	1.63	1.38	1.88	**	1.78	1.54	2.02	**	1.76	1.52	2.00	**

*p<.05, **p<.01
Model 1 Wald test: F=2.14, p=0.12; Model 2 Wald test: F=0.30, p=0.74; Model 3 Wald test: F=2.14, p=0.12; Model 4 Wald test: F=1.24, p=0.29
LR Test Model 1 v Model 2: χ2=15.54, p<0.05; LR Test Model 1 v Model 3: χ2=0.01, p=0.94; LR Test Model 1 v Model 4: χ2=7.13, p<0.05

Table C.8. Logistic regression results for professional development participation by self/parental immigration status.

	Model 1				Model 2				Model 3				Model 4			
	OR	95% CI		p	OR	95% CI		p	OR	95% CI		p	OR	95% CI		p
Self/Parental Immigration Status																
US citizen with lawfully present parents	Ref.	-	-	-	Ref.	-	-	-	Ref.	-	-	-	Ref.	-	-	-
Undocumented students	1.39	1.05	1.83	*	1.48	1.06	2.05	*	1.38	1.05	1.83	*	1.37	1.03	1.82	*
US citizen with undocumented parents	0.97	0.73	1.28		1.03	0.74	1.42		0.98	0.74	1.29		0.96	0.72	1.27	
Family Legal Vulnerability																
Threat to family					0.99	0.95	1.02									
Deported family member																
No									Ref.	-	-	-				
Yes									0.89	0.70	1.13					
Family financial strain													1.01	0.96	1.07	
Controls																
Gender																
Men	Ref.	-	-	-	Ref.	-	-	-	Ref.	-	-	-	Ref.	-	-	-
Women	1.13	0.84	1.51		1.15	0.86	1.54		1.13	0.84	1.51		1.13	0.84	1.50	
Alternative gender identification	1.92	0.83	4.46		1.99	0.86	4.63		1.98	0.85	4.60		1.89	0.82	4.40	
First-gen student																
No	Ref.	-	-	-	Ref.	-	-	-	Ref.	-	-	-	Ref.	-	-	-
Yes	0.64	0.42	0.98	*	0.65	0.42	1.01		0.65	0.42	1.00		0.63	0.41	0.98	*
Year in school																
1st and 2nd years	Ref.	-	-	-	Ref.	-	-	-	Ref.	-	-	-	Ref.	-	-	-
3rd years	2.65	1.97	3.56	**	2.65	1.98	3.56	**	2.67	1.99	3.59	**	2.64	1.97	3.55	**
4th years and higher	6.71	5.00	9.02	**	6.72	5.00	9.02	**	6.76	5.03	9.09	**	6.69	4.98	8.99	**
Transfer student																
No	Ref.	-	-	-	Ref.	-	-	-	Ref.	-	-	-	Ref.	-	-	-
Yes	0.52	0.38	0.70	**	0.51	0.38	0.70	**	0.51	0.38	0.70	**	0.51	0.38	0.70	**

APPENDIX C: REGRESSION ANALYSES | 279

Major																
Arts and humanities	Ref.	-	-	-	Ref.	-	-	-	Ref.	-	-	-	Ref.	-	-	-
Social science	1.00	0.72	1.41		1.00	0.72	1.41		1.00	0.71	1.40		1.01	0.72	1.41	
STEM	0.58	0.40	0.86	*	0.58	0.40	0.86	*	0.58	0.40	0.85	*	0.58	0.40	0.85	*
Other and undeclared	0.69	0.45	1.06		0.69	0.45	1.06		0.69	0.45	1.07		0.69	0.45	1.06	
Campus																
UC Berkeley	Ref.	-	-	-	Ref.	-	-	-	Ref.	-	-	-	Ref.	-	-	-
UC Davis	0.65	0.37	1.13		0.64	0.37	1.13		0.65	0.37	1.14		0.65	0.37	1.14	
UC Irvine	0.51	0.30	0.85	*	0.50	0.30	0.84	*	0.51	0.30	0.85	*	0.51	0.30	0.85	*
UC Los Angeles	0.72	0.42	1.23		0.71	0.42	1.22		0.72	0.42	1.24		0.72	0.42	1.23	
UC Merced	0.21	0.11	0.37	**	0.20	0.11	0.37	**	0.21	0.11	0.38	**	0.21	0.11	0.38	**
UC Riverside	0.23	0.13	0.38	**	0.22	0.13	0.38	**	0.23	0.13	0.39	**	0.23	0.13	0.38	**
UC Santa Barbara	0.33	0.18	0.59	**	0.33	0.18	0.58	**	0.33	0.19	0.60	**	0.33	0.19	0.59	**
UC Santa Cruz	0.82	0.48	1.41		0.82	0.48	1.40		0.83	0.48	1.42		0.82	0.48	1.40	
UC San Diego	0.55	0.28	1.07		0.55	0.28	1.07		0.55	0.28	1.08		0.55	0.28	1.08	
Constant	0.98	0.47	2.02		1.06	0.49	2.28		0.99	0.48	2.05		0.97	0.47	2.01	

*p<.05, **p<.01

Model 1 Wald test: $\chi2$=7.63, p<0.05; Model 2 Wald test: $\chi2$=8.10, p<0.05; Model 3 Wald test: $\chi2$=0.98, p=0.32; Model 4 Wald test: $\chi2$=7.36, p<0.05

LR Test Model 1 v Model 2: $\chi2$=0.50, p=0.48; LR Test Model 1 v Model 3: $\chi2$=0.98, p=0.32; LR Test Model 1 v Model 4: $\chi2$=0.21, p=0.65

Table C.9. Logistic regression results for talking to others about voting by self/parental immigration status.

	Model 1			Model 2			Model 3			Model 4		
	OR	95% CI	p	OR	95% CI	p	OR	95% CI	p	OR	95% CI	p
Self/Parental Immigration Status												
US citizen with lawfully present parents	Ref.	-	-	-	Ref.	-	-	-	Ref.	-	-	-	Ref.	-	-	-
Undocumented students	1.18	0.91	1.54		0.68	0.50	0.93	*	1.20	0.92	1.57		1.13	0.87	1.48	
US citizen with undocumented parents	1.16	0.90	1.49		0.69	0.51	0.93	*	1.12	0.86	1.44		1.12	0.86	1.44	
Family Legal Vulnerability												
Threat to family					1.13	1.09	1.17	**								
Deported family member																
No									Ref.	-	-	-				
Yes									1.51	1.21	1.89	**				
Family financial strain													1.05	1.00	1.10	
Controls												
Gender																
Men	Ref.	-	-	-	Ref.	-	-	-	Ref.	-	-	-	Ref.	-	-	-
Women	1.42	1.10	1.83	*	1.22	0.94	1.59		1.42	1.10	1.83	*	1.41	1.10	1.82	*
Alternative gender identification	2.46	1.02	5.92	*	1.78	0.73	4.34		2.26	0.93	5.48		2.32	0.96	5.59	
First-gen student																
No	Ref.	-	-	-	Ref.	-	-	-	Ref.	-	-	-	Ref.	-	-	-
Yes	0.92	0.61	1.38		0.77	0.50	1.17		0.87	0.57	1.31		0.89	0.59	1.34	
Year in school																
1st and 2nd years	Ref.	-	-	-	Ref.	-	-	-	Ref.	-	-	-	Ref.	-	-	-
3rd years	1.06	0.80	1.39		1.07	0.81	1.41		1.03	0.78	1.36		1.05	0.80	1.38	
4th years and higher	1.08	0.82	1.42		1.10	0.83	1.44		1.06	0.81	1.39		1.07	0.82	1.40	
Transfer student																
No	Ref.	-	-	-	Ref.	-	-	-	Ref.	-	-	-	Ref.	-	-	-
Yes	0.88	0.65	1.19		0.90	0.66	1.22		0.88	0.65	1.20		0.87	0.64	1.17	

Major																
Arts and humanities	Ref.	-	-	-	Ref.	-	-	-	Ref.	-	-	-	Ref.	-	-	-
Social science	0.87	0.63	1.22		0.87	0.62	1.22		0.88	0.63	1.23		0.88	0.63	1.22	
STEM	0.61	0.43	0.87	*	0.61	0.43	0.88	*	0.61	0.43	0.87	*	0.61	0.42	0.87	*
Other and undeclared	0.61	0.41	0.90		0.61	0.41	0.92		0.60	0.40	0.89	*	0.60	0.40	0.89	*
Campus																
UC Berkeley	Ref.	-	-	-	Ref.	-	-	-	Ref.	-	-	-	Ref.	-	-	-
UC Davis	0.53	0.30	0.94	*	0.52	0.29	0.93	*	0.52	0.29	0.93	*	0.53	0.30	0.94	*
UC Irvine	0.43	0.26	0.74	*	0.45	0.26	0.77	*	0.42	0.25	0.72	*	0.44	0.26	0.75	*
UC Los Angeles	0.77	0.44	1.36		0.79	0.45	1.41		0.76	0.43	1.34		0.78	0.44	1.38	
UC Merced	0.39	0.22	0.68	*	0.41	0.23	0.72	*	0.38	0.22	0.66	*	0.39	0.22	0.69	*
UC Riverside	0.48	0.28	0.82	*	0.51	0.30	0.87	*	0.46	0.27	0.78	*	0.49	0.29	0.84	*
UC Santa Barbara	0.68	0.37	1.24		0.69	0.37	1.26		0.65	0.35	1.18		0.69	0.38	1.26	
UC Santa Cruz	0.61	0.35	1.08		0.63	0.36	1.11		0.60	0.34	1.05		0.61	0.35	1.07	
UC San Diego	0.78	0.39	1.54		0.80	0.40	1.59		0.76	0.38	1.51		0.78	0.39	1.55	
Constant	3.19	1.55	6.55	*	1.60	0.75	3.40		3.07	1.49	6.33	*	3.08	1.50	6.32	*

*p<.05, **p<.01

Model 1 Wald test: χ2=1.90, p=0.39; Model 2 Wald test: χ2=7.27, p<0.05; Model 3 Wald test: χ2=5.42, p=0.07; Model 4 Wald test: χ2=1.05, p=0.59

LR Test Model 1 v Model 2: χ2=45.57, p<0.05; LR Test Model 1 v Model 3: χ2=6.11, p<0.05; LR Test Model 1 v Model 4: χ2=3.40, p=0.07

Table C.10. Logistic regression results for protest participation by self/parental immigration status.

	Model 1			Model 2			Model 3			Model 4		
	OR	95% CI	p	OR	95% CI	p	OR	95% CI	p	OR	95% CI	p
Self/Parental Immigration Status												
US citizen with lawfully present parents	Ref.	-	-	-	Ref.	-	-	-	Ref.	-	-	-	Ref.	-	-	-
Undocumented students	1.11	0.85	1.44		0.58	0.42	0.79	*	1.12	0.86	1.46		1.01	0.78	1.32	
US citizen with undocumented parents	1.35	1.04	1.73	*	0.73	0.54	0.99	*	1.31	1.02	1.69	*	1.24	0.96	1.60	
Family Legal Vulnerability												
Threat to family					1.16	1.11	1.20	**								
Deported family member																
No									Ref.	-	-	-				
Yes									1.32	1.06	1.64	*				
Family financial strain													1.12	1.06	1.17	**
Controls												
Gender																
Men	Ref.	-	-	-	Ref.	-	-	-	Ref.	-	-	-	Ref.	-	-	-
Women	1.99	1.52	2.60	**	1.69	1.28	2.23	**	1.99	1.52	2.60	**	1.98	1.51	2.59	**
Alternative gender identification	18.12	5.28	62.26	**	12.99	3.75	45.05	**	17.26	5.01	59.46	**	16.12	4.67	55.66	**
First-gen student																
No	Ref.	-	-	-	Ref.	-	-	-	Ref.	-	-	-	Ref.	-	-	-
Yes	0.83	0.55	1.25		0.66	0.44	1.01		0.80	0.53	1.21		0.77	0.51	1.16	
Year in school																
1st and 2nd years	Ref.	-	-	-	Ref.	-	-	-	Ref.	-	-	-	Ref.	-	-	-
3rd years	1.21	0.92	1.59		1.24	0.94	1.63		1.19	0.91	1.56		1.19	0.91	1.57	
4th years and higher	0.97	0.74	1.26		0.99	0.75	1.30		0.96	0.73	1.25		0.94	0.72	1.23	
Transfer student																
No	Ref.	-	-	-	Ref.	-	-	-	Ref.	-	-	-	Ref.	-	-	-
Yes	0.89	0.66	1.20		0.92	0.68	1.24		0.90	0.67	1.21		0.86	0.64	1.16	
Major																
Arts and humanities	Ref.	-	-	-	Ref.	-	-	-	Ref.	-	-	-	Ref.	-	-	-

Social science	1.10	0.81	1.51		1.12	0.81	1.54		1.11	0.81	1.52		1.11	0.81	1.53	
STEM	0.59	0.42	0.84	*	0.60	0.42	0.85	*	0.59	0.42	0.84	*	0.57	0.40	0.82	*
Other and undeclared	1.09	0.74	1.60		1.13	0.76	1.68		1.08	0.73	1.59		1.05	0.71	1.55	
Campus																
UC Berkeley	Ref.	-	-	-	Ref.	-	-	-	Ref.	-	-	-	Ref.	-	-	-
UC Davis	0.32	0.19	0.57	**	0.31	0.18	0.55	**	0.32	0.18	0.56	**	0.32	0.18	0.57	**
UC Irvine	0.21	0.12	0.35	**	0.21	0.12	0.35	**	0.20	0.12	0.34	**	0.21	0.12	0.36	**
UC Los Angeles	0.28	0.16	0.48	**	0.28	0.16	0.48	**	0.28	0.16	0.47	**	0.29	0.17	0.49	**
UC Merced	0.20	0.12	0.36	**	0.21	0.12	0.37	**	0.20	0.11	0.35	**	0.21	0.12	0.36	**
UC Riverside	0.26	0.16	0.43	**	0.27	0.16	0.45	**	0.25	0.15	0.42	**	0.27	0.16	0.45	**
UC Santa Barbara	0.64	0.36	1.14		0.64	0.36	1.16		0.62	0.35	1.10		0.67	0.38	1.20	
UC Santa Cruz	0.76	0.44	1.32		0.80	0.45	1.40		0.75	0.43	1.30		0.76	0.44	1.32	
UC San Diego	0.35	0.18	0.66	*	0.35	0.18	0.68	*	0.34	0.18	0.65	*	0.35	0.18	0.68	*
Constant	1.67	0.83	3.36		0.71	0.33	1.49		1.62	0.80	3.27		1.53	0.76	3.09	

*p<.05, **p<.01

Model 1 Wald test: $\chi2=5.42$, p=0.07; Model 2 Wald test: $\chi2=11.64$, p<0.05; Model 3 Wald test: $\chi2=4.39$, p=0.11; Model 4 Wald test: $\chi2=3.26$, p=0.20

LR Test Model 1 v Model 2: $\chi2=63.25$, p<0.05; LR Test Model 1 v Model 3: $\chi2=6.11$, p<0.05; LR Test Model 1 v Model 4: $\chi2=18.35$, p<0.05

Table C.11. Logistic regression results for organizational participation by self/parental immigration status.

	Model 1			Model 2			Model 3			Model 4		
	OR	95% CI	p	OR	95% CI	p	OR	95% CI	p	OR	95% CI	p
Self/Parental Immigration Status												
US citizen with lawfully present parents	Ref.	-	-	-	Ref.	-	-	-	Ref.	-	-	-	Ref.	-	-	-
Undocumented students	1.62	1.25	2.08	**	1.31	0.97	1.76		1.63	1.26	2.10	**	1.54	1.19	1.99	*
US citizen with undocumented parents	1.07	0.83	1.36		0.87	0.65	1.16		1.05	0.82	1.34		1.02	0.79	1.30	
Family Legal Vulnerability												
Threat to family					1.05	1.01	1.08	*								
Deported family member																
No									Ref.	-	-	-				
Yes									1.20	0.97	1.49					
Family financial strain													1.06	1.01	1.11	*
Controls												
Gender																
Men	Ref.	-	-	-	Ref.	-	-	-	Ref.	-	-	-	Ref.	-	-	-
Women	1.01	0.78	1.29		0.95	0.73	1.22		1.00	0.78	1.29		1.00	0.77	1.28	
Alternative gender identification	2.80	1.20	6.52	*	2.47	1.06	5.76	*	2.69	1.15	6.27	*	2.61	1.12	6.09	*
First-gen student																
No	Ref.	-	-	-	Ref.	-	-	-	Ref.	-	-	-	Ref.	-	-	-
Yes	0.75	0.50	1.11		0.70	0.47	1.04		0.73	0.49	1.08		0.72	0.48	1.07	
Year in school																
1st and 2nd years	Ref.	-	-	-	Ref.	-	-	-	Ref.	-	-	-	Ref.	-	-	-
3rd years	1.58	1.21	2.06	*	1.59	1.22	2.07	*	1.56	1.20	2.03	*	1.57	1.20	2.04	*
4th years and higher	1.82	1.41	2.36	**	1.84	1.42	2.38	**	1.81	1.40	2.35	**	1.80	1.39	2.33	**
Transfer student																
No	Ref.	-	-	-	Ref.	-	-	-	Ref.	-	-	-	Ref.	-	-	-
Yes	0.66	0.49	0.88	*	0.66	0.50	0.89	*	0.66	0.50	0.88	*	0.65	0.48	0.86	*

Major																
Arts and humanities	Ref.	-	-	-	Ref.	-	-	-	Ref.	-	-	-	Ref.	-	-	-
Social science	1.02	0.75	1.39		1.02	0.75	1.39		1.03	0.76	1.39		1.03	0.76	1.40	
STEM	0.93	0.66	1.31		0.94	0.67	1.31		0.93	0.66	1.31		0.92	0.65	1.29	
Other and undeclared	1.08	0.74	1.58		1.09	0.75	1.60		1.08	0.74	1.57		1.06	0.72	1.55	
Campus																
UC Berkeley	Ref.	-	-	-	Ref.	-	-	-	Ref.	-	-	-	Ref.	-	-	-
UC Davis	0.52	0.30	0.88	*	0.52	0.30	0.88	*	0.52	0.30	0.88	*	0.52	0.30	0.89	*
UC Irvine	0.40	0.25	0.66	**	0.41	0.25	0.67	**	0.40	0.24	0.65	**	0.41	0.25	0.67	**
UC Los Angeles	0.68	0.40	1.13		0.68	0.41	1.14		0.67	0.40	1.12		0.69	0.41	1.15	
UC Merced	0.29	0.17	0.49	**	0.29	0.17	0.50	**	0.28	0.17	0.48	**	0.29	0.17	0.50	**
UC Riverside	0.38	0.23	0.61	**	0.39	0.24	0.63	**	0.37	0.23	0.60	**	0.39	0.24	0.63	**
UC Santa Barbara	0.68	0.39	1.17		0.68	0.40	1.18		0.66	0.38	1.14		0.69	0.40	1.20	
UC Santa Cruz	0.56	0.34	0.94	*	0.57	0.34	0.95	*	0.55	0.33	0.93	*	0.56	0.33	0.94	*
UC San Diego	0.55	0.29	1.02		0.55	0.30	1.04		0.54	0.29	1.01		0.55	0.30	1.03	
Constant	1.62	0.83	3.17		1.23	0.61	2.47		1.59	0.81	3.12		1.55	0.79	3.04	

*p<.05, **p<.01

Model 1 Wald test: $\chi 2=15.87$, p<0.05; Model 2 Wald test: $\chi 2=9.95$, p<0.05; Model 3 Wald test: $\chi 2=16.70$, p<0.05; Model 4 Wald test: $\chi 2=13.76$, p<0.05

LR Test Model 1 v Model 2: $\chi 2=7.46$, p<0.05; LR Test Model 1 v Model 3: $\chi 2=2.87$, p=0.09; LR Test Model 1 v Model 4: $\chi 2=5.84$, p<0.05

Table C.12. Logistic regression results for visiting the basic needs center by self/parental immigration status.

	Model 1			Model 2			Model 3			Model 4		
	OR	95% CI	p	OR	95% CI	p	OR	95% CI	p	OR	95% CI	p
Self/Parental Immigration Status												
US citizen with lawfully present parents	Ref.	-	-	-	Ref.	-	-	-	Ref.	-	-	-	Ref.	-	-	-
Undocumented students	1.61	1.23	2.11	*	1.07	0.78	1.47		1.62	1.23	2.12	*	1.38	1.04	1.82	*
US citizen with undocumented parents	1.43	1.09	1.87	*	0.96	0.70	1.32		1.40	1.07	1.84	*	1.22	0.93	1.61	
Family Legal Vulnerability												
Threat to family					1.10	1.06	1.14	**								
Deported family member																
No									Ref.	-	-	-				
Yes									1.20	0.96	1.50					
Family financial strain													1.21	1.15	1.28	**
Controls												
Gender																
Men	Ref.	-	-	-	Ref.	-	-	-	Ref.	-	-	-	Ref.	-	-	-
Women	1.43	1.08	1.89	*	1.27	0.95	1.69		1.42	1.07	1.88	*	1.40	1.05	1.86	*
Alternative gender identification	3.76	1.73	8.14	*	3.00	1.37	6.58	*	3.61	1.66	7.85	*	3.13	1.42	6.89	*
First-gen student																
No	Ref.	-	-	-	Ref.	-	-	-	Ref.	-	-	-	Ref.	-	-	-
Yes	1.43	0.91	2.26		1.25	0.79	1.99		1.39	0.88	2.20		1.26	0.79	2.01	
Year in school																
1st and 2nd years	Ref.	-	-	-	Ref.	-	-	-	Ref.	-	-	-	Ref.	-	-	-
3rd years	1.43	1.08	1.90	*	1.45	1.09	1.93	*	1.41	1.06	1.88	*	1.39	1.04	1.86	*
4th years and higher	1.51	1.14	1.99	*	1.53	1.15	2.02	*	1.49	1.13	1.97	*	1.44	1.08	1.91	*
Transfer student																
No	Ref.	-	-	-	Ref.	-	-	-	Ref.	-	-	-	Ref.	-	-	-
Yes	1.15	0.85	1.55		1.16	0.86	1.58		1.16	0.86	1.56		1.08	0.79	1.47	

Major															
Arts and humanities	Ref.	-	-	-	Ref.	-	-	-	Ref.	-	-	-	Ref.	-	-	-
Social science	1.08	0.78	1.51		1.08	0.77	1.50		1.09	0.78	1.51		1.12	0.80	1.57	
STEM	1.13	0.79	1.64		1.14	0.79	1.64		1.14	0.79	1.64		1.10	0.76	1.60	
Other and undeclared	1.50	1.00	2.26	*	1.53	1.02	2.29	*	1.50	1.00	2.25	*	1.43	0.95	2.16	
Campus																
UC Berkeley	Ref.	-	-	-	Ref.	-	-	-	Ref.	-	-	-	Ref.	-	-	-
UC Davis	2.56	1.47	4.45	*	2.57	1.48	4.48	*	2.55	1.47	4.43	*	2.75	1.56	4.85	**
UC Irvine	1.01	0.60	1.70		1.04	0.62	1.76		1.00	0.59	1.69		1.10	0.65	1.88	
UC Los Angeles	1.17	0.68	2.02		1.19	0.69	2.07		1.16	0.67	2.01		1.26	0.72	2.20	
UC Merced	1.47	0.84	2.55		1.54	0.88	2.69		1.46	0.84	2.53		1.61	0.91	2.84	
UC Riverside	0.84	0.50	1.42		0.87	0.51	1.47		0.82	0.49	1.39		0.94	0.55	1.61	
UC Santa Barbara	2.46	1.40	4.31	*	2.52	1.43	4.44	*	2.41	1.37	4.23	*	2.83	1.59	5.05	**
UC Santa Cruz	1.63	0.95	2.80		1.67	0.97	2.87		1.61	0.94	2.77		1.68	0.96	2.92	
UC San Diego	0.87	0.43	1.77		0.88	0.43	1.80		0.87	0.42	1.76		0.94	0.46	1.94	
Constant	0.10	0.05	0.21	**	0.06	0.03	0.12	**	0.10	0.05	0.21	**	0.08	0.04	0.17	**

*p<.05, **p<.01

Model 1 Wald test: $\chi 2$=12.66, p<0.05; Model 2 Wald test: $\chi 2$=0.61, p=0.74; Model 3 Wald test: $\chi 2$=12.63, p<0.05; Model 4 Wald test: $\chi 2$=5.14, p=0.08

LR Test Model 1 v Model 2: $\chi 2$=23.35, p<0.05; LR Test Model 1 v Model 3: $\chi 2$=12.63, p<0.05; LR Test Model 1 v Model 4: $\chi 2$=54.39, p<0.05

Table C.13. Logistic regression results for visiting campus mental health services by self/parental immigration status.

	Model 1			Model 2			Model 3			Model 4		
	OR	95% CI	p	OR	95% CI	p	OR	95% CI	p	OR	95% CI	p
Self/Parental Immigration Status												
US citizen with lawfully present parents	Ref.	-	-	-	Ref.	-	-	-	Ref.	-	-	-	Ref.	-	-	-
Undocumented students	1.21	0.82	1.78		0.90	0.57	1.43		1.21	0.82	1.78		1.03	0.69	1.53	
US citizen with undocumented parents	1.00	0.67	1.50		0.75	0.47	1.20		1.00	0.67	1.50		0.85	0.56	1.29	
Family Legal Vulnerability												
Threat to family					1.07	1.01	1.13	*								
Deported family member																
No									Ref.	-	-	-				
Yes									1.02	0.73	1.43					
Family financial strain													1.18	1.10	1.26	**
Controls												
Gender																
Men	Ref.	-	-	-	Ref.	-	-	-	Ref.	-	-	-	Ref.	-	-	-
Women	1.15	0.75	1.76		1.06	0.69	1.63		1.15	0.75	1.76		1.11	0.73	1.70	
Alternative gender identification	2.41	0.96	6.04		2.05	0.81	5.20		2.39	0.95	6.03		1.97	0.77	5.03	
First-gen student																
No	Ref.	-	-	-	Ref.	-	-	-	Ref.	-	-	-	Ref.	-	-	-
Yes	1.39	0.70	2.76		1.26	0.63	2.52		1.38	0.69	2.76		1.24	0.62	2.48	
Year in school																
1st and 2nd years	Ref.	-	-	-	Ref.	-	-	-	Ref.	-	-	-	Ref.	-	-	-
3rd years	1.83	1.17	2.85	*	1.84	1.18	2.88	*	1.82	1.17	2.85	*	1.76	1.13	2.77	*
4th years and higher	2.24	1.46	3.42	**	2.25	1.47	3.44	**	2.23	1.46	3.41	**	2.12	1.38	3.25	*
Transfer student																
No	Ref.	-	-	-	Ref.	-	-	-	Ref.	-	-	-	Ref.	-	-	-
Yes	1.07	0.71	1.61		1.08	0.72	1.63		1.07	0.71	1.61		1.02	0.67	1.54	
Major																
Arts and humanities	Ref.	-	-	-	Ref.	-	-	-	Ref.	-	-	-	Ref.	-	-	-

Social science	0.81	0.51	1.28		0.81	0.51	1.29		0.81	0.51	1.28		0.83	0.52	1.32	
STEM	0.68	0.40	1.17		0.68	0.40	1.17		0.68	0.40	1.17		0.64	0.37	1.11	
Other and undeclared	1.25	0.71	2.18		1.25	0.72	2.20		1.24	0.71	2.17		1.17	0.66	2.05	
Campus																
UC Berkeley	Ref.	-	-	-	Ref.	-	-	-	Ref.	-	-	-	Ref.	-	-	-
UC Davis	0.66	0.34	1.30		0.66	0.34	1.29		0.66	0.34	1.29		0.69	0.35	1.36	
UC Irvine	0.31	0.16	0.60	*	0.31	0.16	0.61	*	0.31	0.16	0.60	*	0.33	0.16	0.65	*
UC Los Angeles	0.56	0.29	1.07		0.57	0.30	1.08		0.56	0.29	1.07		0.58	0.30	1.12	
UC Merced	0.21	0.09	0.50	**	0.22	0.09	0.52	*	0.21	0.09	0.50	**	0.22	0.09	0.53	*
UC Riverside	0.37	0.20	0.70	*	0.38	0.20	0.72	*	0.37	0.20	0.70	*	0.41	0.21	0.78	*
UC Santa Barbara	0.51	0.25	1.04		0.51	0.25	1.04		0.51	0.25	1.03		0.55	0.27	1.13	
UC Santa Cruz	0.43	0.22	0.84	*	0.43	0.22	0.84	*	0.42	0.22	0.84	*	0.42	0.21	0.83	*
UC San Diego	0.65	0.28	1.50		0.66	0.28	1.52		0.65	0.28	1.50		0.70	0.30	1.64	
Constant	0.12	0.04	0.32	**	0.08	0.03	0.23	**	0.11	0.04	0.32	**	0.10	0.04	0.28	**

*p<.05, **p<.01
Model 1 Wald test: $\chi 2$=1.16, p=0.56; Model 2 Wald test: $\chi 2$=1.60, p=0.45; Model 3 Wald test: $\chi 2$=1.17, p=0.58; Model 4 Wald test: $\chi 2$=0.94, p=0.62
LR Test Model 1 v Model 2: $\chi 2$=5.34, p<0.05; LR Test Model 1 v Model 3: $\chi 2$=0.02, p=0.89; LR Test Model 1 v Model 4: $\chi 2$=20.00, p<0.05

Table C.14. Logistic regression results for visiting academic support services by self/parental immigration status.

	Model 1			Model 2			Model 3			Model 4		
	OR	95% CI	p	OR	95% CI	p	OR	95% CI	p	OR	95% CI	p
Self/Parental Immigration Status												
US citizen with lawfully present parents	Ref.	-	-	-	Ref.	-	-	-	Ref.	-	-	-	Ref.	-	-	-
Undocumented students	1.40	1.03	1.90	*	0.90	0.63	1.28		1.40	1.03	1.91	*	1.24	0.91	1.70	
US citizen with undocumented parents	1.33	0.99	1.80		0.86	0.61	1.22		1.33	0.98	1.80		1.20	0.88	1.63	
Family Legal Vulnerability												
Threat to family					1.11	1.06	1.16	**								
Deported family member																
No									Ref.	-	-	-				
Yes									1.04	0.80	1.34					
Family financial strain													1.14	1.08	1.21	**
Controls												
Gender																
Men	Ref.	-	-	-	Ref.	-	-	-	Ref.	-	-	-	Ref.	-	-	-
Women	0.79	0.59	1.05		0.69	0.51	0.93	*	0.79	0.59	1.05		0.77	0.57	1.03	
Alternative gender identification	0.68	0.26	1.75		0.52	0.20	1.36		0.67	0.26	1.74		0.59	0.23	1.54	
First-gen student																
No	Ref.	-	-	-	Ref.	-	-	-	Ref.	-	-	-	Ref.	-	-	-
Yes	1.41	0.84	2.39		1.25	0.73	2.14		1.41	0.83	2.38		1.30	0.77	2.20	
Year in school																
1st and 2nd years	Ref.	-	-	-	Ref.	-	-	-	Ref.	-	-	-	Ref.	-	-	-
3rd years	0.55	0.40	0.76	**	0.54	0.39	0.75	**	0.55	0.40	0.76	**	0.53	0.38	0.73	**
4th years and higher	0.43	0.31	0.59	**	0.42	0.30	0.59	**	0.42	0.31	0.59	**	0.40	0.29	0.56	**
Transfer student																
No	Ref.	-	-	-	Ref.	-	-	-	Ref.	-	-	-	Ref.	-	-	-
Yes	1.23	0.85	1.77		1.25	0.86	1.80		1.23	0.85	1.77		1.17	0.81	1.69	

Major																
Arts and humanities	Ref.	-	-	-	Ref.	-	-	-	Ref.	-	-	-	Ref.	-	-	-
Social science	1.02	0.69	1.50		1.00	0.68	1.49		1.02	0.69	1.51		1.04	0.70	1.55	
STEM	1.85	1.24	2.78	*	1.88	1.25	2.83	*	1.86	1.24	2.78	*	1.83	1.22	2.76	*
Other and undeclared	1.53	0.97	2.42		1.57	0.99	2.48		1.53	0.97	2.42		1.47	0.93	2.33	
Campus																
UC Berkeley	Ref.	-	-	-	Ref.	-	-	-	Ref.	-	-	-	Ref.	-	-	-
UC Davis	0.97	0.55	1.71		0.96	0.55	1.71		0.97	0.55	1.71		0.99	0.56	1.74	
UC Irvine	0.37	0.21	0.64	**	0.38	0.22	0.67	*	0.37	0.21	0.64	**	0.38	0.22	0.67	*
UC Los Angeles	0.77	0.44	1.34		0.78	0.45	1.38		0.77	0.44	1.34		0.79	0.45	1.39	
UC Merced	0.44	0.25	0.79	*	0.46	0.26	0.83	*	0.44	0.25	0.79	*	0.45	0.25	0.82	*
UC Riverside	0.61	0.36	1.03		0.64	0.37	1.09		0.60	0.36	1.03		0.65	0.38	1.12	
UC Santa Barbara	0.76	0.42	1.40		0.78	0.42	1.44		0.76	0.41	1.40		0.81	0.44	1.49	
UC Santa Cruz	1.47	0.86	2.53		1.54	0.89	2.65		1.47	0.86	2.52		1.48	0.86	2.55	
UC San Diego	0.41	0.19	0.89	*	0.40	0.19	0.88	*	0.41	0.19	0.88	*	0.41	0.19	0.89	*
Constant	0.33	0.15	0.74	*	0.17	0.07	0.40	**	0.33	0.15	0.74	*	0.29	0.13	0.66	*

*p<.05, **p<.01
Model 1 Wald test: χ2=5.32, p=0.07; Model 2 Wald test: χ2=0.69, p=0.71; Model 3 Wald test: χ2=5.31, p=0.07; Model 4 Wald test: χ2=2.10, p=0.35
LR Test Model 1 v Model 2: χ2=23.24, p<0.05; LR Test Model 1 v Model 3: χ2=0.08, p=0.78; LR Test Model 1 v Model 4: χ2=21.92, p<0.05

Table C.15. Logistic regression results for visiting identity-based centers by self/parental immigration status.

	Model 1			Model 2			Model 3			Model 4		
	OR	95% CI	p	OR	95% CI	p	OR	95% CI	p	OR	95% CI	p
Self/Parental Immigration Status												
US citizen with lawfully present parents	Ref.	-	-	-	Ref.	-	-	-	Ref.	-	-	-	Ref.	-	-	-
Undocumented students	2.31	1.66	3.20	**	1.49	1.02	2.17	*	2.31	1.67	3.21	**	2.01	1.44	2.81	**
US citizen with undocumented parents	1.29	0.92	1.82		0.84	0.56	1.24		1.27	0.90	1.79		1.11	0.78	1.58	
Family Legal Vulnerability												
Threat to family					1.11	1.06	1.16	**								
Deported family member																
No									Ref.	-	-	-				
Yes									1.20	0.91	1.57					
Family financial strain													1.18	1.11	1.25	**
Controls												
Gender																
Men	Ref.	-	-	-	Ref.	-	-	-	Ref.	-	-	-	Ref.	-	-	-
Women	1.40	0.98	2.01		1.24	0.86	1.79		1.40	0.98	2.01		1.37	0.96	1.97	
Alternative gender identification	8.40	3.70	19.07	**	6.66	2.91	15.27	**	8.10	3.56	18.43	**	7.26	3.17	16.63	**
First-gen student																
No	Ref.	-	-	-	Ref.	-	-	-	Ref.	-	-	-	Ref.	-	-	-
Yes	0.99	0.59	1.68		0.87	0.51	1.48		0.97	0.57	1.64		0.89	0.52	1.52	
Year in school																
1st and 2nd years	Ref.	-	-	-	Ref.	-	-	-	Ref.	-	-	-	Ref.	-	-	-

3rd years	1.00	0.70	1.43		1.01	0.71	1.45		0.99	0.69	1.41		0.96	0.67	1.38	
4th years and higher	1.28	0.91	1.78		1.29	0.92	1.80		1.26	0.90	1.76		1.21	0.87	1.70	
Transfer student																
No	Ref.	-	-	-	Ref.	-	-	-	Ref.	-	-	-	Ref.	-	-	-
Yes	1.04	0.72	1.50		1.06	0.73	1.52		1.05	0.73	1.51		1.00	0.69	1.45	
Major																
Arts and humanities	Ref.	-	-	-	Ref.	-	-	-	Ref.	-	-	-	Ref.	-	-	-
Social science	0.76	0.52	1.10		0.76	0.53	1.11		0.76	0.52	1.10		0.77	0.53	1.12	
STEM	0.54	0.35	0.83	*	0.54	0.35	0.84	*	0.54	0.35	0.83	*	0.51	0.33	0.80	*
Other and undeclared	0.91	0.57	1.44		0.93	0.58	1.48		0.90	0.57	1.43		0.85	0.53	1.35	
Campus																
UC Berkeley	Ref.	-	-	-	Ref.	-	-	-	Ref.	-	-	-	Ref.	-	-	-
UC Davis	1.91	1.06	3.42	*	1.91	1.06	3.43	*	1.90	1.06	3.42	*	2.00	1.10	3.62	*
UC Irvine	0.37	0.20	0.67	*	0.37	0.20	0.69	*	0.36	0.20	0.67	*	0.39	0.21	0.72	*
UC Los Angeles	0.57	0.31	1.05		0.57	0.31	1.07		0.56	0.30	1.04		0.58	0.31	1.09	
UC Merced	0.34	0.17	0.69	*	0.35	0.17	0.72	*	0.34	0.17	0.69	*	0.36	0.17	0.74	*
UC Riverside	0.94	0.54	1.63		0.98	0.56	1.70		0.93	0.53	1.61		1.04	0.59	1.83	
UC Santa Barbara	0.65	0.34	1.24		0.66	0.34	1.25		0.64	0.33	1.22		0.71	0.37	1.37	
UC Santa Cruz	0.52	0.28	0.98	*	0.53	0.28	1.00	*	0.51	0.27	0.97	*	0.52	0.27	0.99	*
UC San Diego	1.22	0.59	2.51		1.24	0.60	2.58		1.21	0.59	2.51		1.31	0.63	2.73	
Constant	0.20	0.08	0.46	**	0.10	0.04	0.25	**	0.19	0.08	0.45	**	0.16	0.07	0.39	**

*p<.05, **p<.01

Model 1 Wald test: $\chi2$=27.61, p<0.05; Model 2 Wald test: $\chi2$=13.25, p<0.05; Model 3 Wald test: $\chi2$=28.16, p<0.05; Model 4 Wald test: $\chi2$=21.21, p<0.05

LR Test Model 1 v Model 2: $\chi2$=19.43, p<0.05; LR Test Model 1 v Model 3: $\chi2$=1.65, p=0.20; LR Test Model 1 v Model 4: $\chi2$=28.00, p<0.05

Table C.16. Logistic regression results for visiting undocumented student services by self/ parental immigration status.

	Model 1			Model 2			Model 3			Model 4		
	OR	95% CI	p	OR	95% CI	p	OR	95% CI	p	OR	95% CI	p
Self/Parental Immigration Status												
US citizen with lawfully present parents	Ref.	-	-	-	Ref.	-	-	-	Ref.	-	-	-	Ref.	-	-	-
Undocumented students	48.76	21.07	112.87	**	33.89	14.04	81.83	**	48.70	21.03	112.73	**	45.45	19.60	105.42	**
US citizen with undocumented parents	3.25	1.28	8.26	*	2.23	0.84	5.93		3.28	1.29	8.37	*	3.00	1.17	7.67	*
Family Legal Vulnerability												
Threat to family					1.09	1.02	1.17	*								
Deported family member																
No									Ref.	-	-	-				
Yes									0.88	0.60	1.30					
Family financial strain													1.09	1.00	1.18	*
Controls												
Gender												
Men	Ref.	-	-	-	Ref.	-	-	-	Ref.	-	-	-	Ref.	-	-	-
Women	0.95	0.61	1.48		0.86	0.54	1.35		0.95	0.61	1.48		0.94	0.60	1.47	
Alternative gender identification	1.17	0.34	4.02		0.97	0.28	3.35		1.22	0.35	4.20		1.10	0.32	3.80	
First-gen student												
No	Ref.	-	-	-	Ref.	-	-	-	Ref.	-	-	-	Ref.	-	-	-
Yes	2.11	0.83	5.37		1.97	0.77	5.03		2.16	0.85	5.52		2.04	0.80	5.23	
Year in school												
1st and 2nd years	Ref.	-	-	-	Ref.	-	-	-	Ref.	-	-	-	Ref.	-	-	-
3rd years	1.95	1.23	3.11	*	1.95	1.22	3.11	*	1.98	1.24	3.16	*	1.92	1.20	3.06	*
4th years and higher	1.29	0.80	2.06		1.29	0.80	2.07		1.30	0.81	2.09		1.27	0.79	2.04	

		Model 1				Model 2				Model 3				Model 4	
Transfer student															
No	Ref.	-	-	-	Ref.	-	-	-	Ref.	-	-	-	Ref.	-	-	-
Yes	0.96	0.60	1.55		0.94	0.59	1.52		0.96	0.60	1.54		0.95	0.59	1.53	
Major															
Arts and humanities	Ref.	-	-	-	Ref.	-	-	-	Ref.	-	-	-	Ref.	-	-	-
Social science	1.01	0.59	1.70		1.00	0.59	1.70		1.01	0.59	1.70		1.03	0.61	1.74	
STEM	1.08	0.61	1.91		1.07	0.60	1.89		1.08	0.61	1.91		1.07	0.61	1.90	
Other and undeclared	0.73	0.36	1.46		0.73	0.36	1.47		0.72	0.36	1.46		0.71	0.35	1.43	
Campus															
UC Berkeley	Ref.	-	-	-	Ref.	-	-	-	Ref.	-	-	-	Ref.	-	-	-
UC Davis	4.15	1.78	9.67	*	4.12	1.76	9.65	*	4.16	1.79	9.71	*	4.40	1.87	10.34	*
UC Irvine	1.09	0.49	2.45		1.13	0.50	2.55		1.10	0.49	2.46		1.18	0.52	2.68	
UC Los Angeles	1.34	0.57	3.17		1.33	0.56	3.15		1.36	0.57	3.20		1.40	0.59	3.33	
UC Merced	0.96	0.38	2.43		0.97	0.38	2.46		0.95	0.37	2.41		1.06	0.41	2.71	
UC Riverside	0.84	0.36	1.96		0.87	0.38	2.03		0.85	0.37	1.97		0.94	0.40	2.21	
UC Santa Barbara	1.51	0.63	3.65		1.50	0.62	3.64		1.51	0.63	3.65		1.65	0.68	4.03	
UC Santa Cruz	0.78	0.31	1.98		0.82	0.32	2.09		0.78	0.31	1.99		0.82	0.32	2.10	
UC San Diego	2.70	0.94	7.71		2.83	0.99	8.13		2.66	0.93	7.63		2.93	1.02	8.42	*
Constant	0.00	0.00	0.01	**	0.00	0.00	0.01	**	0.00	0.00	0.01	**	0.00	0.00	0.01	**

*p<.05, **p<.01

Model 1 Wald test: $\chi2$=171.67, p<0.05; Model 2 Wald test: $\chi2$=155.91, p<0.05; Model 3 Wald test: $\chi2$=170.09, p<0.05; Model 4 Wald test: $\chi2$=169.34, p<0.05

LR Test Model 1 v Model 2: $\chi2$=5.91, p<0.05; LR Test Model 1 v Model 3: $\chi2$=0.42, p=0.51; LR Test Model 1 v Model 4: $\chi2$=4.06, p<0.05

NOTES

INTRODUCTION

1   Menjívar and Kanstroom (2014).
2   Dreby (2015); Enriquez (2020); Gleeson (2016); Gonzales (2016); Waters and Gerstein Pineau (2015).
3   Menjívar and Abrego (2012, 1383).
4   Menjívar and Abrego (2012, 1384).
5   De León (2015); Hagan (2012).
6   Boehm (2016); Enriquez and Millán (2021); Martinez-Aranda (2020) Talavera et al. (2010).
7   Ayón (2018); Becerra (2016); Maldonado et al. (2016).
8   Canizales (2021); Gleeson (2016); Rosales (2020).
9   Ballerini and Feldblum (2021); Gonzales (2016).
10   Abrego (2011).
11   Rodriguez (2023).
12   Brabeck et al. (2016a); Ha et al. (2017); Hainmueller et al. (2017); Yoshikawa (2012).
13   Bean et al. (2015).
14   Enriquez (2020); Yoshikawa (2012).
15   Abrego (2018); Enriquez (2020); Rodriguez (2019).
16   Flores Morales et al. (2024).
17   Rubio-Hernandez and Ayón (2016); Dreby (2015); Enriquez (2015); Schmalzbauer and Andrés (2019).
18   Enriquez (2015, 2020).
19   Enriquez (2020).
20   Bronfenbrenner and Morris (2006). See also Suárez-Orozco et al. (2011).
21   Bump (2018).
22   Chavez (2008, 2017).
23   Elder (1994).
24   Carr (2018).
25   We use "Latino" to refer broadly to populations of Latin American origin and do not mean this to be exclusive by gender. We do not use "Latinx," a gender-neutral version, because most participants used "Latino" when referring to their communities.
26   Jiménez (2010); Kasinitz et al. (2008); Portes and Rumbaut (2001); Telles and Ortiz (2008); Vasquez (2011); Vega et al. (2009).

27 In 2019, there were 10.9 million Mexican immigrants in the United States and 3.8 million Central American immigrants (Babich and Batalova 2021; Israel and Batalova 2020). An estimated 5.3 million undocumented immigrants are from Mexico and 2.1 million are Central American (Migration Policy Institute n.d).

28 Migration Policy Institute (2020).

29 Estimates from multiple data sets suggest that 25–28 percent of the 18 million Latino children living in the United States have an undocumented parent (Clarke et al. 2017).

30 Bustamante (2002, 341).

31 De Genova (2002).

32 Abrego (2011); Asad (2023); Enriquez and Millán (2021); García (2019).

33 Velarde Pierce et al. (2021).

34 Brabeck et al. (2016b); Brabeck and Xu (2010).

35 Siegel et al. (2021).

36 De Genova (2002).

37 Boehm (2016); Golash-Boza (2015); Lopez et al. (2022); Lovato (2019); Valdivia (2021); Zayas (2015).

38 Armenta (2017).

39 Asad (2020).

40 DHS (2022). For discussions of E-Verify see, Goldstein and Alonso-Bejarano (2017) and Orrenius and Zavodny (2015).

41 Passel and Cohn (2015).

42 Bernhardt et al. (2013); Gleeson (2016).

43 Enriquez (2020); Morales Hernandez and Enriquez (2021).

44 Enriquez (2020).

45 Cort et al. (2014).

46 USDA (2022).

47 Asad and Rosen (2019); Stuesse and Coleman (2014).

48 Simmons et al. (2021).

49 Enriquez (2020).

50 Gomez and Perez Huber (2019).

51 Chavez (2008, 2017).

52 García (2017); Rodriguez et al. (2023).

53 Abrego (2011); Dreby (2015).

54 Lipson et al. (2022).

55 Enriquez et al. (2018); Hainmueller et al. (2017); Suárez-Orozco and López Hernández (2020); Velarde Pierce et al. (2021).

56 We are grateful to UC PromISE research assistant and graduate fellow Martha Morales Hernandez, whose research has informed and advanced our thinking in this area.

57 Contreras (2009); Gámez et al. (2017).

58 Kam et al. (2018); Vaquera et al. (2017).

59 Diener et al. (2010).

60 Barry (2009).
61 Ha et al. (2017); Hsin and Reed (2020); Kreisberg and Hsin (2021).
62 Suárez-Orozco et al. (2010).
63 Fredricks et al. (2004).
64 Kuh (2008, 2009).
65 Knouse et al. (1999); Nunley et al. (2016).
66 Morales Hernandez and Enriquez (2021).
67 Perrin and Gillis (2019).
68 Galston (2001); Perrin and Gillis (2019).
69 Enriquez (2014); Nájera (2024); Rosales et al. (2021); Street et al. (2017).
70 Golash-Boza and Valdez (2018).
71 Amuedo-Dorantes and Antman (2017); Gonzales et al. (2019); Morales Hernandez and Enriquez (2021); Patler et al. (2021); Patler and Laster Pirtle (2018).
72 Cebulko and Silver (2016); Enriquez et al. (2019); Rodríguez (2008).
73 Aranda et al. (2023); Burciaga and Malone (2021); Kidder and Johnson (2025); Mallet and Garcia Bedolla (2019).
74 Colbern and Ramakrishnan (2021); Pastor (2018).
75 Armbruster et al. (1995); Ono and Sloop (2002).
76 Seif (2004).
77 Flores and Chapa (2009); Ngo and Astudillo (2019).
78 Immigrants Rising (2023).
79 Cheong (2021); Cho (2022).
80 Colbern and Ramakrishnan (2021); Pastor (2018).
81 Sanchez and So (2015).
82 UCOP (2013).
83 UCOP (2016).
84 Chen and Rhoads (2016); Cisneros et al. (2021); Cisneros and Valdivia (2020); Sanchez and So (2015).
85 University of California Immigrant Legal Services Center (n.d.).
86 Enriquez et al. (2019); Golash-Boza and Valdez (2018).
87 UCOP (2007).
88 The Campaign for College Opportunity (2018).
89 The Campaign for College Opportunity (2018).
90 Cebulko and Silver (2016); Flores et al. (2019).
91 We did not recruit at the tenth campus, UC San Francisco, because it does not have an undergraduate student population.
92 Deterding and Waters (2021).

CHAPTER 1. "WE ARE ALL IN THIS TOGETHER"

1 Enriquez (2020).
2 Dreby (2012).
3 De Genova (2002).
4 Enriquez and Millán (2021).

5 For examples see Aizeki (2017) and Heim (2017).

6 Lopez et al. (2022); Lovato (2019); Zayas (2015).

7 Valdivia (2021).

8 Undocumented immigrants are not eligible for federally funded supplemental nutrition benefits, commonly known as food stamps (NILC 2007). Alonzo's family may have received such support because they had at least one US citizen member, or he may have been referring to a nutrition program that serves undocumented immigrants.

9 NILC (2007).

10 Asad (2023).

11 Kaiser Family Foundation (2019).

12 Gomez and Perez Huber (2019, 1).

13 Rodriguez et al. (2023).

14 Silver (2018).

15 See also Aranda et al. (2023); Burciaga and Malone (2021).

16 Gonzales (2016); Morales Hernandez and Enriquez (2021).

17 Goldrick-Rab (2016).

18 Castañeda (2019).

19 Getrich (2019); Rodriguez (2023).

20 American Immigration Council (2024).

21 USCIS (2020).

22 Castañeda (2019); Getrich (2019); Rodriguez (2023).

23 Getrich (2019).

24 Aries and Seider (2005); Armstrong and Hamilton (2013); Lee (2016).

25 Estrada and Ruth (2021); Ruth and Estrada (2019). DACA recipients are eligible to apply for advance parole, a travel document that allows them to travel abroad for education, employment, or humanitarian purposes and reenter the United States. Applications are costly and take time, and applicants face the risk being denied reentry. For more information, see Enriquez and Perez Lopez (2024), and Higher Ed Immigration Portal (n.d.)

CHAPTER 2. "IT BEGINS TO TAKE ITS TOLL"

1 Grant et al. (2004).

2 Enriquez and Millán (2021, p. 2097).

3 Morales Hernandez (2023).

4 American Psychiatric Association (2000).

5 Levers and Hyatt-Burkhart (2012).

6 Levers and Hyatt-Burkhart (2012, p. 73).

7 Likewise, Luz Garcini and colleagues suggest that raising awareness about how the structural context shapes mental health and well-being helps to "avoid pathologizing the immigrant experience" and reduce stigmatization; see Garcini et al. (2021, p. 10).

8 Dougall et al. (1999).
9 American Psychological Association (n.d.).
10 Capps et al. (2020); Rubio-Hernandez and Ayón (2016).
11 Sangalang et al. (2019).
12 Velarde Pierce et al. (2021).
13 Pearlin and Bierman (2013).
14 Lazarus and Folkman (1984).
15 Chen and Miller (2012).
16 Chen and Miller (2012); Christophe et al. (2019).
17 Frankenhuis and Nettle (2020).
18 Cohen and Wills (1985).
19 Chu et al. (2010).
20 Ciarrochi et al. (2017).
21 Lee et al. (2018).
22 Ayón and Naddy (2013); Finch et al. (2000); Finch and Vega (2003); Vaquera et al. (2017).
23 Thoits (2011).
24 Ayón (2016); Philbin and Ayón (2016); Valdez et al. (2021).
25 Thoits (2011, 152).
26 Thoits (2011, 152).
27 Druckenmiller (2022).
28 Andrews (2023); Boehm (2016); Brabeck and Xu (2010); Lovato (2019); Macías and Collet (2016); Rojas-Flores et al. (2016); Valdivia (2021); Ybarra and Peña (2016); Zayas (2015).
29 Diener et al. (2010).
30 Diener et al. (2010).
31 Hsin and Reed (2020).
32 Hsin and Ortega (2018). See also Enriquez (2017b); Gonzales (2016).

CHAPTER 3. "I PUSH AWAY FROM SCHOOL"

1 Brabeck et al. (2016a); Dreby (2015); Enriquez (2020); Ha et al. (2017); Yoshikawa (2012).
2 National Center for Education Statistics (2018).
3 Cox (2016).
4 See also García (2019).
5 Krogstad (2016).
6 Chavarria et al. (2021).
7 See Elder (1994).
8 Goldrick-Rab (2016).
9 Goldrick-Rab (2016); Martinez et al. (2018).
10 Sallie Mae (2022).
11 Gurantz and Obadan (2022); Terriquez (2015); Terriquez and Gurantz (2015).

12 See also Enriquez et al. (2019).
13 Rendón (2019).
14 Jackson (1968).
15 Kuh (2008, 2009).
16 Morales Hernandez and Enriquez (2021).
17 National Association of Colleges and Employers (2019).
18 Hsin and Reed (2020).
19 Valadez et al. (2021).
20 Valadez et al. (2021).
21 Lara and Nava (2018); Morales Hernandez and Enriquez (2021); Ortiz and Hinojosa (2010); Salazar et al. (2024).

CHAPTER 4. "WE'RE TRYING FOR PEOPLE THAT CAN'T"
1 Washington Post Staff (2015).
2 Menjívar and Abrego (2012).
3 See also Dreby (2015).
4 Cornejo et al. (2023).
5 Cohen et al. (2012).
6 CHIRLA (n.d.).
7 USCIS (2018).
8 Zepeda-Millán (2017).
9 LAPD (2007).
10 Terriquez and Milkman (2021).
11 USCIS (2018).
12 Saguy and Enriquez (2020).
13 CIRCLE (2018).
14 Holbein et al. (2021).
15 CIRCLE (2018).
16 Terriquez and Kwon (2015).

CHAPTER 5. WHAT CAN UNIVERSITIES DO?
1 Enriquez et al. (2019); Golash-Boza and Valdez (2018).
2 Chen and Rhoads (2016); Cisneros and Valdivia (2020); Sanchez and So (2015).
3 Federal Student Aid (n.d.).
4 California AB 540 (passed in 2001) required three years of high-school attendance and a high-school diploma or equivalent; AB 2000 (passed in 2014), SB 68 (passed in 2017), and SB 1141 (passed in 2022) expanded the length-of-time requirement to include three years of attendance at any combination of California high schools, adult schools, or community colleges or three years of high-school coursework and three years of total attendance in a California elementary school and/or secondary school. It also extended benefits to those who received an associate's degree from a California community college or ful-

filled minimum transfer requirements for the UC or CSU systems (Immigrants Rising 2023).

5 University of California (n.d.-a).

6 University of California (n.d.-b).

7 See Goldrick-Rab (2016) and Hamilton and Nielsen (2021).

8 The mission of the Presidents' Alliance on Higher Education and Immigration is to facilitate higher education institutions' efforts to advocate for inclusive policies by educating the public and policymakers, sharing best practices, and support-ing the adoption of inclusive federal and state policies and the reconsideration of exclusionary policies (Presidents' Alliance on Higher Education and Immigration n.d.-a). They also maintain the higher ed immigration portal that documents and classifies state policies that impact undocumented students' educational opportu-nities (www.higheredimmigrationportal.org/).

9 For example, Rhode Island's Board of Governors for Higher Education amended the state's residency policy in 2011 to allow eligible undocumented students to access in-state tuition (Presidents' Alliance on Higher Education and Immigration n.d.-b). Effective in 2013, the University of Hawai'i's Board of Regents similarly expanded access to in-state tuition (University of Hawai'i 2014).

10 USDA (2022).

11 Pearson chi2(4) = 15.2369; Pr = 0.004.

12 Maroto et al. (2015); Silva et al. (2017).

13 See Appendix C for full details on the regression models contained in this chapter.

14 Maroto et al. (2015); Silva et al. (2017).

15 Thank you to Dr. Angela Chuan-Ru Chen for bringing this to our attention.

16 University of California Immigrant Legal Services Center (n.d.).

17 Ryo (2018); Ryo and Peacock (2021).

18 Brabeck and Xu (2010); Lovato (2019); Lovato et al. (2018); Valdivia (2021).

19 Pearson chi2(2) = 384.2232; Pr = 0.000.

20 For more details see Enriquez (2020) and Gomberg-Muñoz (2017).

21 California State University (n.d.).

22 Guidelines for "know your rights" workshops are available in multiple languages from trusted sources including the American Civil Liberties Union and the National Immigration Law Center (ACLU n.d.; NILC n.d.).

23 Kivlighan et al. (2021).

24 Shuford (2011).

25 Cha et al. (2019).

26 Ayón et al. (2022); Cha et al. (2019).

27 Means and Pyne (2017). For a general discussion of the importance of belonging for education success, see Strayhorn (2018).

28 Patton (2010); Reyes (2015, 2018).

29 Chen and Rhoads (2016); Cisneros and Valdivia (2020).

30 See Cisneros and Rivarola (2020) for a description of common programming offered by undocumented student services.

31 Pearson chi2(6) = 769.5819; Pr = 0.000.

CONCLUSION

1 Haskins et al. (2008).

2 Armstrong and Hamilton (2013); Rendón (2019); Stuber (2011).

3 Baum and Flores (2011); Rendón (2019).

4 Passel and Cohn (2018).

5 Clarke et al. (2017).

6 Dreby (2015); Enriquez (2020); Lilly Lopez (2021); Rodriguez (2023); Schmalzbauer and Andrés (2019).

7 Carr (2018); Elder (1994).

8 Enriquez (2015, 2020).

9 Rodriguez (2019, 2023).

10 Gonzales (2016). See also Gonzales and Burciaga (2018).

11 Cebulko (2021); Enriquez (2017a, 2017b); Valdez and Golash-Boza (2020).

12 Cebulko and Silver (2016); Enriquez et al. (2019); Flores et al. (2019); Golash-Boza and Valdez (2018); Rodríguez (2008).

13 Colbern and Ramakrishnan (2018); Pastor (2018).

14 University of California (n.d.-c, n.d.-d).

15 Enriquez and Millán (2021).

16 Castañeda (2019); García (2019); Valdivia (2021).

17 Burciaga and Malone (2021); Cebulko and Silver (2016); Enriquez et al. (2021); Suárez-Orozco et al. (2015).

18 Ayón (2018).

19 Ayón (2018).

20 Rubio-Hernandez and Ayón (2016).

21 Enriquez et al. (2021); Enriquez et al. (2018); Hsin and Reed (2020); Kreisberg and Hsin (2021); Rosales et al. (2021); Suárez-Orozco and López Hernández (2020); Terriquez (2015, 2017).

22 Muñoz et al. (2018); Negrón-Gonzales (2017).

23 Rodriguez (2019).

24 Yoshikawa (2012).

25 Boehm (2016); Brabeck et al. (2016b); Brabeck and Xu (2010); Golash-Boza (2015); Lopez et al. (2022); Lovato (2019); Zayas (2015).

26 Valdivia (2021).

27 Cisneros and Valdivia (2020); Sanchez and So (2015); The S.I.N. Collective (2007).

28 See also Enriquez et al. (2019).

29 Miller and Barnes (2015); Turney and Goodsell (2018).

30 Alba and Nee (2003); Kasinitz et al. (2008); Portes and Rumbaut (2001); Portes and Zhou (1993); Telles and Ortiz (2008).

31 Jiménez (2010); Kasinitz et al. (2008); Portes and Rumbaut (2001); Telles and Ortiz (2008); Vasquez (2011); Vega et al. (2009).
32 Telles and Ortiz (2008).
33 Cox (2016); Goldrick-Rab (2016).
34 Reber and Smith (2023).
35 Goldrick-Rab (2016); Martinez et al. (2018).
36 Cohn et al. (2022).
37 Fry (2022).
38 Cohn et al. (2022).
39 In 2019, there were 10.9 million Mexican immigrants in the United States and 3.8 million Central American immigrants (Babich and Batalova 2021; Israel and Batalova 2020). Of these, 5.3 million undocumented immigrants are from Mexico and 2.1 million from Central America (Migration Policy Institute n.d.).

APPENDIX A

1 Ayón et al. (2022); Chavarria et al. (2021); Cornejo et al. (2023); Enriquez et al. (2020); Enriquez et al. (2021); Rosales et al. (2021); Sarabia et al. (2021); Valadez et al. (2021); Velarde Pierce et al. (2021).

APPENDIX B

1 Ayón (2017).
2 Barrera Jr. et al. (2001).
3 Spitzer et al. (2006).
4 Kroenke et al. (2001).
5 Diener et al. (2010).
6 USDA (2012).

REFERENCES

Abrego, Leisy J. 2011. "Legal Consciousness of Undocumented Latinos: Fear and Stigma as Barriers to Claims-Making for First- and 1.5-Generation Immigrants." *Law & Society Review* 45(2):337–70.

Abrego, Leisy J. 2018. "Renewed Optimism and Spatial Mobility: Legal Consciousness of Latino Deferred Action for Childhood Arrivals Recipients and Their Families in Los Angeles." *Ethnicities* 18(2):192–207.

ACLU. n.d. "Know Your Rights: Immigrants' Rights." www.aclu.org/know-your-rights/immigrants-rights.

Aizeki, Mizue. 2017. "Families Fearing Deportation Because of Trump's Immigration Policies Prepare for I.C.E. Raid." *Newsweek.* www.newsweek.com/immigration-immigration-and-customs-enforcement-ice-donald-trump-628896.

Alba, Richard, and Victor Nee. 2003. *Remaking the American Mainstream: Assimilation and Contemporary Immigration.* Harvard University Press.

American Immigration Council. 2024. "How the United States Immigration System Works." www.americanimmigrationcouncil.org/research/how-united-states-immigration-system-works.

American Psychiatric Association. 2000. *Diagnostic and Statistical Manual of Mental Disorders. 4th ed., text rev.* American Psychiatric Association, Washington, DC.

American Psychological Association. n.d. "Hypervigilance." *APA Dictionary of Psychology.* https://dictionary.apa.org/hypervigilance.

Amuedo-Dorantes, Catalina, and Francisca Antman. 2017. "Schooling and Labor Market Effects of Temporary Authorization: Evidence from DACA." *Journal of Population Economics* 30(1):339–73.

Andrews, Abigail. 2023. *Banished Men: How Migrants Endure the Violence of Deportation.* University of California Press.

Aranda, Elizabeth, Elizabeth Vaquera, Heide Castañeda, and Girsea Martinez Rosas. 2023. "Undocumented Again? DACA Rescission, Emotions, and Incorporation Outcomes Among Young Adults." *Social Forces* 101(3):1321–42.

Aries, Elizabeth, and Maynard Seider. 2005. "The Interactive Relationship between Class Identity and the College Experience: The Case of Lower Income Students." *Qualitative Sociology* 28(4):419–43.

Armbruster, Ralph, Kim Geron, and Edna Bonacich. 1995. "The Assault on California's Latino Immigrants: The Politics of Proposition 187." *International Journal of Urban & Regional Research* 19(4):655–63.

Armenta, Amada. 2017. *Protect, Serve, and Deport: The Rise of Policing as Immigration Enforcement.* University of California Press.

Armstrong, Elizabeth A., and Laura T. Hamilton. 2013. *Paying for the Party: How College Maintains Inequality.* Harvard University Press.

Asad, Asad L. 2020. "Latinos' Deportation Fears by Citizenship and Legal Status, 2007 to 2018." *Proceedings of the National Academy of Sciences* 117(16):8836–44.

Asad, Asad L. 2023. *Engage and Evade: How Latino Immigrant Families Manage Surveillance in Everyday Life.* Princeton University Press.

Asad, Asad L., and Eva Rosen. 2019. "Hiding within Racial Hierarchies: How Undocumented Immigrants Make Residential Decisions in an American City." *Journal of Ethnic and Migration Studies* 45(11):1857–82.

Ayón, Cecilia. 2016. "Talking to Latino Children About Race, Inequality, and Discrimination: Raising Families in an Anti-Immigrant Political Environment." *Journal of the Society for Social Work and Research* 7(3):449–77.

Ayón, Cecilia. 2017. "Perceived Immigration Policy Effects Scale: Development and Validation of a Scale on the Impact of State-Level Immigration Policies on Latino Immigrant Families." *Hispanic Journal of Behavioral Sciences* 39(1):19–33.

Ayón, Cecilia. 2018. ""Vivimos en Jaula de Oro": The Impact of State-Level Legislation on Immigrant Latino Families." *Journal of Immigrant & Refugee Studies* 16(4):351–71.

Ayón, Cecilia, Basia D. Ellis, Melissa J. Hagan, Laura E. Enriquez, and Carly Offidani-Bertrand. 2022. "Mental Health Help-Seeking Among Latina/o/x Undocumented College Students." *Cultural Diversity and Ethnic Minority Psychology* 30(3):434–46.

Ayón, Cecilia, and Michela Bou Ghosn Naddy. 2013. "Latino Immigrant Families' Social Support Networks: Strengths and Limitations During a Time of Stringent Immigration Legislation and Economic Insecurity." *Journal of Community Psychology* 41(3):359–77.

Babich, Erin, and Jeanne Batalova. 2021. "Central American Immigrants in the United States." Migration Policy Institute, Washington, DC. www.migrationpolicy.org/article/central-american-immigrants-united-states#:~:text=The%203.8%20million%20Central%20American%20immigrants%20present%20in%202019%20accounted,million%20(see%20Figure%201).&text=Sources%3A%20Data%20from%20U.S.%20Census,ACS)%2C%20and%20Campbell%20J.

Ballerini, Victoria, and Miriam Feldblum. 2021. "Immigration Status and Postsecondary Opportunity: Barriers to Affordability, Access, and Success for Undocumented Students, and Policy Solutions." *American Journal of Economics and Sociology* 80(1):161–86.

Barrera Jr., Manuel, Heather Caples, and Jenn-Yun Tein. 2001. "The Psychological Sense of Economic Hardship: Measurement Models, Validity, and Cross-Ethnic Equivalence for Urban Families." *American Journal of Community Psychology* 29(3):493–517.

Barry, Margaret M. 2009. "Addressing the Determinants of Positive Mental Health: Concepts, Evidence and Practice." *International Journal of Mental Health Promotion* 11(3):4–17.

Baum, Sandy, and Stella M. Flores. 2011. "Higher Education and Children in Immigrant Families." *Future of Children* 21(1):171–93.

Bean, Frank D., Susan K. Brown, and James D. Bachmeier. 2015. *Parents without Papers: The Progress and Pitfalls of Mexican-American Integration*. Russell Sage Foundation.

Becerra, David. 2016. "Anti-Immigration Policies and Fear of Deportation: A Human Rights Issue." *Journal of Human Rights and Social Work* 1(3):109–19.

Bernhardt, Annette, Michael W. Spiller, and Diana Polson. 2013. "All Work and No Pay: Violations of Employment and Labor Laws in Chicago, Los Angeles and New York City." *Social Forces* 91(3):725–46.

Boehm, Deborah A. 2016. *Returned: Going and Coming in an Age of Deportation*. University of California Press.

Brabeck, Kalina M., Erin Sibley, Patricia Taubin, and Angela Murcia. 2016a. "The Influence of Immigrant Parent Legal Status on U.S.-Born Children's Academic Abilities: The Moderating Effects of Social Service Use." *Applied Developmental Science* 20(4):237–49.

Brabeck, Kalina M., and Qingwen Xu. 2010. "The Impact of Detention and Deportation on Latino Immigrant Children and Families: A Quantitative Exploration." *Hispanic Journal of Behavioral Sciences* 32(3):341–61.

Brabeck, Kalina M., Erin Sibley, and M. Brinton Lykes. 2016b. "Authorized and Unauthorized Immigrant Parents: The Impact of Legal Vulnerability on Family Contexts." *Hispanic Journal of Behavioral Sciences* 38(1):3–30.

Bronfenbrenner, Urie, and Pamela A. Morris. 2006. "The Bioecological Model of Human Development." Pp. 793–828 in *Handbook of Child Development: Theoretical Models of Human Development*. Volume 1, edited by R. Lerner. Wiley.

Bump, Philip. 2018. "Here Are the Administration Officials Who Have Said That Family Separation Is Meant as a Deterrent." *Washington Post*. June 19. www.washingtonpost.com/news/politics/wp/2018/06/19/here-are-the-administration-officials-who-have-said-that-family-separation-is-meant-as-a-deterrent/?utm_term=.cc9fe57e8991.

Burciaga, Edelina M., and Aaron Malone. 2021. "Intensified Liminal Legality: The Impact of the DACA Rescission for Undocumented Young Adults in Colorado." *Law & Social Inquiry* 46(4):1092–1114.

Bustamante, Jorge A. 2002. "Immigrants' Vulnerability as Subjects of Human Rights." *International Migration Review* 36(2):333–54.

California State University. n.d. "Legal Support Services." www.calstate.edu/student-services/resources-for-undocumented-students/pages/legal-support-services.aspx.

The Campaign for College Opportunity. 2018. "Higher Education Affordability for Undocumented Students in California." The Campaign for College Opportunity, Los Angeles, CA. https://collegecampaign.org/wp-content/uploads/2019/10/CCO_Undoc.pdf.

Canizales, Stephanie L. 2021. "Work Primacy and the Social Incorporation of Unaccompanied, Undocumented Latinx Youth in the United States." *Social Forces* 101(3):1372–95.

Capps, Randy, Jodi Berger Cardoso, Kalina Brabeck, Michael Fix, and Ariel G. Ruiz Soto. 2020. "Immigration Enforcement and the Mental Health of Latino High School Students." Migration Policy Institute, Washington, DC. www.migrationpol icy.org/sites/default/files/publications/immigration-enforcement-mental-health -latino-students_final.pdf.

Carr, Deborah. 2018. "The Linked Lives Principle in Life Course Studies: Classic Approaches and Contemporary Advances." Pp. 41–63 in *Social Networks and the Life Course: Integrating the Development of Human Lives and Social Relational Networks*, edited by D. F. Alwin, D. H. Felmlee, and D. A. Kreager. Springer.

Castañeda, Heide. 2019. *Borders of Belonging: Struggle and Solidarity in Mixed-Status Immigrant Families*. Stanford University Press.

Cebulko, Kara. 2021. "Becoming White in a White Supremacist State: The Public and Psychological Wages of Whiteness for Undocumented 1.5-Generation Brazilians." *Social Sciences* 10(5):1–20.

Cebulko, Kara, and Alexis Silver. 2016. "Navigating DACA in Hospitable and Hostile States: State Responses and Access to Membership in the Wake of Deferred Action for Childhood Arrivals." *American Behavioral Scientist* 60(13):1553–74.

Cha, Biblia, Laura E. Enriquez, and Annie Ro. 2019. "Beyond Access: Psychosocial Barriers to Undocumented Students' Use of Mental Health Services." *Social Science & Medicine* 233:193–200.

Chavarria, Karina, Monica Cornejo, Cecilia Ayón, and Laura E. Enriquez. 2021. "Disrupted Education? A Latent Profile Analysis of Immigration-Related Distractions and Academic Engagement Among Among Undocumented College Students." *Journal of Latinos and Education* 20(3):232–45.

Chavez, Leo. 2008. *The Latino Threat: Constructing Immigrants, Citizens, and the Nation*. Stanford University Press.

Chavez, Leo. 2017. *Anchor Babies and the Challenge of Birthright Citizenship*. Stanford University Press.

Chen, Angela Chuan-Ru, and Robert A. Rhoads. 2016. "Undocumented Student Allies and Transformative Resistance: An Ethnographic Case Study." *Review of Higher Education* 39(4):515–42.

Chen, Edith, and Gregory E. Miller. 2012. ""Shift-and-Persist" Strategies: Why Low Socioeconomic Status Isn't Always Bad for Health." *Perspectives on Psychological Science* 7(2):135–58.

Cheong, Amanda R. 2021. "How Driver's Licenses Matter for Undocumented Immigrants." *Contexts* 20(3):22–7.

CHIRLA [Coalition for Humane Immigrant Rights in Los Angeles]. n.d. "Wise Up!" www.chirla.org/what-we-do/programs-initiatives/organizing-leadership-develop ment/wise-up/.

Cho, Heepyung. 2022. "Driver's License Reforms and Job Accessibility Among Undocumented Immigrants." *Labour Economics* 76:1–20.

Christophe, N. Keita, Gabriela Livas Stein, Michelle Y. Martin Romero, Michele Chan,
Michaeline Jensen, Laura M. Gonzalez, and Lisa Kiang. 2019. "Coping and Culture:
The Protective Effects of Shift-&-Persist and Ethnic-Racial Identity on Depressive
Symptoms in Latinx Youth." *Journal of Youth and Adolescence* 48(8):1592–604.

Chu, Po Sen, Donald A. Saucier, and Eric Hafner. 2010. "Meta-Analysis of the Relationships between Social Support and Well-Being in Children and Adolescents."
Journal of Social and Clinical Psychology 29(6):624–45.

Ciarrochi, Joseph, Alexandre J. S. Morin, Baljinder K. Sahdra, David Litalien, and
Philip D. Parker. 2017. "A Longitudinal Person-Centered Perspective on Youth
Social Support: Relations with Psychological Wellbeing." *Developmental Psychology*
53(6):1154–69.

CIRCLE. 2018. "Ahead of the 2018 Midterms, a New Generation Finds Its Political
Voice." Center for Information & Research on Civic Learning and Engagement,
Medford, MA. https://circle.tufts.edu/latest-research/ahead-2018-midterms-new
-generation-finds-its-political-voice.

Cisneros, Jesus, and Alonso R. Reyna Rivarola. 2020. "Undocumented Student Resource Centers." *Journal of College Student Development* 61(5):658–62.

Cisneros, Jesus, and Diana Valdivia. 2020. ""We Are Legit Now": Establishing Undocumented Student Resource Centers on Campus." *Journal of College Student Development* 61(1):51–66.

Cisneros, Jesus, Diana Valdivia, Alonso R. Reyna Rivarola, and Felecia Russell. 2021.
""I'm Here to Fight Along with You": Undocumented Student Resource Centers
Creating Possibilities." *Journal of Diversity in Higher Education* 15(5):607–16.

Clarke, Wyatt, Kimberly Turner, and Lina Guzman. 2017. "One Quarter of Hispanic
Children in the United States Have an Unauthorized Immigrant Parent." National
Research Center on Hispanic Children and Families, Bethesda, MD. www.hispa
nicresearchcenter.org/wp-content/uploads/2017/10/Hispanic-Center-Undocu
mented-Brief-FINAL.pdf.

Cohen, Cathy J., Joseph Kahne, Benjamin Bowyer, Ellen Middaugh, and Jon
Rogowski. 2012. "Participatory Politics: New Media and Youth Political Action."
Oakland, CA: Youth and Participatory Politics Research Network. ypp.dmlcen
tral.net/sites/default/files/publications/Participatory_Politics_New_Media_and
_Youth_Political_Action.2012.pdf.

Cohen, Sheldon, and Thomas A. Wills. 1985. "Stress, Social Support, and the Buffering
Hypothesis." *Psychological Bulletin* 98(2):310–57.

Cohn, D'Vera, Juliana Menasce Horowitz, Rachel Minkin, Richard Fry, and Kiley
Hurst. 2022. "Financial Issues Top the List of Reasons U.S. Adults Live in Multigenerational Homes." Pew Research Center, Washington, DC. www.pewresearch
.org/social-trends/2022/03/24/financial-issues-top-the-list-of-reasons-u-s-adults
-live-in-multigenerational-homes/.

Colbern, Allan, and S. Karthick Ramakrishnan. 2021. *Citizenship Reimagined: A New Framework for State Rights in the United States*. Cambridge University Press.

Colbern, Allan, and S. Karthick Ramakrishnan. 2018. "Citizens of California: How the Golden State Went from Worst to First on Immigrant Rights." *New Political Science* 40(2):353–67.

Contreras, Frances. 2009. "Sin Papeles and Rompiendo Barreras: Latino College Students and the Challenges in Persisting in College." *Harvard Educational Review* 79(4):610–32.

Cornejo, Monica, Cecilia Ayón, and Laura E. Enriquez. 2023. "A Latent Profile Analysis of U.S. Undocumented College Students' Advocacy Communication Strategies and Its Relationship with Health." *Journal of Applied Communication Research* 51(3):262–82.

Cort, David A., Ken-Hou Lin, and Gabriela Stevenson. 2014. "Residential Hierarchy in Los Angeles: An Examination of Ethnic and Documentation Status Differences." *Social Science Research* 45:170–83.

Cox, Rebecca D. 2016. "Complicating Conditions: Obstacles and Interruptions to Low-Income Students' College 'Choices.'" *Journal of Higher Education* 87(1):1–26.

De Genova, Nicholas P. 2002. "Migrant "Illegality" and Deportability in Everyday Life." *Annual Review of Anthropology* 31:419–47.

De León, Jason. 2015. *The Land of Open Graves: Living and Dying on the Migrant Trail*. University of California Press.

Deterding, Nicole M., and Mary C. Waters. 2021. "Flexible Coding of In-Depth Interviews: A Twenty-First-Century Approach." *Sociological Methods & Research* 50(2):708–39.

DHS [US Department of Homeland Security]. 2022. "History and Milestones." www.e-verify.gov/about-e-verify/history-and-milestones.

Diener, Ed, Derrick Wirtz, William Tov, Chu Kim-Prieto, Dong-won Choi, Shigehiro Oishi, and Robert Biswas-Diener. 2010. "New Well-Being Measures: Short Scales to Assess Flourishing and Positive and Negative Feelings." *Social Indicators Research* 97(2):143–56.

Dougall, Angela L., Karrie J. Craig, and Andrew Baum. 1999. "Assessment of Characteristics of Intrusive Thoughts and Their Impact on Distress Among Victims of Traumatic Events." *Psychosomatic Medicine* 61(1):38–48.

Dreby, Joanna. 2012. "The Burden of Deportation on Children in Mexican Immigrant Families." *Journal of Marriage and Family* 74(4):829–45.

Dreby, Joanna. 2015. *Everyday Illegal: When Policies Undermine Immigrant Families*. University of California Press.

Druckenmiller, Reese. 2022. "College Students and Depression: A Guide for Parents." Mayo Clinic Health System. www.mayoclinichealthsystem.org/hometown-health/speaking-of-health/college-students-and-depression.

Elder, Glen H. 1994. "Time, Human Agency, and Social Change: Perspectives on the Life Course." *Social Psychology Quarterly* 57(1):4–15.

Enriquez, Laura E. 2014. ""Undocumented and Citizen Students Unite": Building a Cross-Status Coalition through Shared Ideology." *Social Problems* 61(2):155–74.

Enriquez, Laura E. 2015. "Multigenerational Punishment: Shared Experiences of Undocumented Immigration Status within Mixed-Status Families." *Journal of Marriage and Family* 77(4):939–53.

Enriquez, Laura E. 2017a. "Gendering Illegality: Undocumented Young Adults' Negotiation of the Family Formation Process." *American Behavioral Scientist* 61(10):1153–71.

Enriquez, Laura E. 2017b. "A "Master Status" or the "Final Straw"? Assessing the Role of Immigration Status in Latino Undocumented Youths' Pathways Out of School." *Journal of Ethnic and Migration Studies* 43(9):1526–43.

Enriquez, Laura E. 2020. *Of Love and Papers: How Immigration Policy Affects Romance and Family.* University of California Press.

Enriquez, Laura E., Cecilia Ayón, Karina Chavarria, Basia D. Ellis, Melissa J. Hagan, Julián Jefferies, Jannet Lara, Martha Morales Hernandez, Enrique Murillo Jr., Jennifer R. Nájera, Carly Offidani-Bertrand, Maria Oropeza Fujimoto, Annie Ro, Victoria E. Rodriguez, William E. Rosales, Heidy Sarabia, Ana K. Soltero López, Mercedes Valadez, Sharon Velarde Pierce, and Zulema Valdez. 2020. "Persisting Inequalities and Paths Forward: A Report on the State of Undocumented Students in California's Public Universities." UC Collaborative to Promote Immigrant and Student Equity & Undocumented Student Equity Project, Irvine, CA. https://cpb-us -e2.wpmucdn.com/sites.uci.edu/dist/4/3807/files/2020/12/State_Of_Undocumented _Students_2020report.pdf.

Enriquez, Laura E., and Daniel Millán. 2021. "Situational Triggers and Protective Locations: Conceptualising the Salience of Deportability in Everyday Life." *Journal of Ethnic and Migration Studies* 47(9):2089–108.

Enriquez, Laura E., Martha Morales Hernandez, Daniel Millán, and Daisy Vazquez Vera. 2019. "Mediating Illegality: Federal, State, and Institutional Policies in the Educational Experiences of Undocumented College Students." *Law and Social Inquiry* 44(3):679–703.

Enriquez, Laura E., Martha Morales Hernandez, and Annie Ro. 2018. "Deconstructing Immigrant Illegality: A Mixed-Methods Investigation of Stress and Health Among Undocumented College Students." *Race and Social Problems* 10(3):193–208.

Enriquez, Laura E., and Jenniffer C. Perez Lopez. 2024. "(Re)Building Families: Undocumented Young Adults Contest Legal Violence." Pp. 51–72 in *Immigration Policy and Immigrant Families*, edited by J. Van Hook and V. King. Springer.

Enriquez, Laura E., Karina Chavarria, Victoria E. Rodriguez, Cecilia Ayón, Basia D. Ellis, Melissa J. Hagan, Julián Jefferies, Jannet Lara, Martha Morales Hernandez, Enrique Murillo Jr., Jennifer R. Nájera, Carly Offidani-Bertrand, Maria Oropeza Fujimoto, Annie Ro, William E. Rosales, Heidy Sarabia, Ana K. Soltero López, Mercedes Valadez, Zulema Valdez, and Sharon Velarde Pierce. 2021. "Toward a Nuanced and Contextualized Understanding of Undocumented College Students: Lessons from a California Survey." *Journal of Latinos and Education* 20(3):215–31.

Estrada, Emir, and Alissa Ruth. 2021. "Experiential Dual Frame of Reference: Family Consequences After DACA Youth Travel to Mexico Through Advanced Parole." *Qualitative Sociology* 44(2):231–51.

Federal Student Aid. N.d. "Eligibility for Non-U.S. Citizens." https://studentaid.gov /understand-aid/eligibility/requirements/non-us-citizens.

Finch, Brian Karl, Bohdan Kolody, and William A. Vega. 2000. "Perceived Discrimination and Depression Among Mexican-Origin Adults in California." *Journal of Health and Social Behavior* 41(3):295–313.

Finch, Brian Karl, and William A. Vega. 2003. "Acculturation Stress, Social Support, and Self-Rated Health Among Latinos in California." *Journal of Immigrant Health* 5(3):109–17.

Flores, Andrea, Kevin Escudero, and Edelina Burciaga. 2019. "Legal–Spatial Consciousness: A Legal Geography Framework for Examining Migrant Illegality." *Law & Policy* 41(1):12–33.

Flores Morales, Josefina, Laura E. Enriquez, and Cecilia Ayón. 2024. "Do Ties Protect? Examining Economic Insecurity and Mental Health in Mixed-Status Families Among Undocumented Undergraduates." *Family Relations* 73(3):1706–26.

Flores, Stella M., and Jorge Chapa. 2009. "Latino Immigrant Access to Higher Education in a Bipolar Context of Reception." *Journal of Hispanic Higher Education* 8(1):90–109.

Frankenhuis, Willem E., and Daniel Nettle. 2020. "The Strengths of People in Poverty." *Current Directions in Psychological Science* 29(1):16–21.

Fredricks, Jennifer A., Phyllis C. Blumenfeld, and Alison H. Paris. 2004. "School Engagement: Potential of the Concept, State of the Evidence." *Review of Educational Research* 74(1):59–109.

Fry, Richard. 2022. "Young Adults in U.S. Are Much More Likely Than 50 Years Ago to Be Living in a Multigenerational Household." Pew Research Center, Washington, DC. www.pewresearch.org/fact-tank/2022/07/20/young-adults-in-u-s-are-much -more-likely-than-50-years-ago-to-be-living-in-a-multigenerational-household/.

Galston, William A. 2001. "Political Knowledge, Political Engagement, and Civic Education." *Annual Review of Political Science* 4(1):217–34.

Gámez, Raúl, William Lopez, and Betty Overton. 2017. "Mentors, Resiliency, and Ganas: Factors Influencing the Success of DACAmented, Undocumented, and Immigrant Students in Higher Education." *Journal of Hispanic Higher Education* 16(2):144–61.

García, Angela S. 2019. *Legal Passing: Navigating Undocumented Life and Local Immigration Law.* University of California Press.

García, San Juanita. 2017. "Racializing "Illegality": An Intersectional Approach to Understanding How Mexican-Origin Women Navigate an Anti-Immigrant Climate." *Sociology of Race and Ethnicity* 3(4):474–90.

Garcini, Luz M., Ryan Daly, Nellie Chen, Justin Mehl, Tommy Pham, Thuy Phan, Brittany Hansen, and Aishwarya Kothare. 2021. "Undocumented Immigrants and Mental Health: A Systematic Review of Recent Methodology and Findings in the United States." *Journal of Migration and Health* 4:1–13.

Getrich, Christina. 2019. *Border Brokers: Children of Mexican Immigrants Navigating U.S. Society, Laws, and Politics*. University of Arizona Press.

Gleeson, Shannon. 2016. *Precarious Claims: The Promise and Failure of Workplace Protections in the United States*. University of California Press.

Golash-Boza, Tanya. 2015. *Deported: Immigrant Policing, Disposable Labor and Global Capitalism*. New York University Press.

Golash-Boza, Tanya, and Zulema Valdez. 2018. "Nested Contexts of Reception: Undocumented Students at the University of California, Central." *Sociological Perspectives* 61(4):535–52.

Goldrick-Rab, Sara. 2016. *Paying the Price: College Costs, Financial Aid, and the Betrayal of the American Dream*. University of Chicago Press.

Goldstein, Daniel M., and Carolina Alonso-Bejarano. 2017. "E-Terrify: Securitized Immigration and Biometric Surveillance in the Workplace." *Human Organization* 76(1):1–14.

Gomberg-Muñoz, Ruth. 2017. *Becoming Legal: Immigration Law and Mixed-Status Families*. Oxford University Press.

Gomez, Valerie, and Lindsay Perez Huber. 2019. "Examining Racist Nativist Microaggressions on DACAmented College Students in the Trump Era." *California Journal of Politics and Policy* 11(2):1–16.

Gonzales, Roberto G. 2016. *Lives in Limbo: Undocumented and Coming of Age in America*. University of California Press.

Gonzales, Roberto G., and Edelina M. Burciaga. 2018. "Segmented Pathways of Illegality: Reconciling the Coexistence of Master and Auxiliary Statuses in the Experiences of 1.5-Generation Undocumented Young Adults." *Ethnicities* 18(2):178–91.

Gonzales, Roberto G., Sayil Camacho, Kristina Brant, and Carlos Aguilar. 2019. "The Long-Term Impact of DACA: Forging Futures Despite DACA's Uncertainty." Immigration Initiative at Harvard, Cambridge, MA. https://immigrationinitiative.harvard.edu/files/hii/files/final_daca_report.pdf.

Grant, Kathryn E., Bruce E. Compas, Audrey E. Thurm, Susan D. McMahon, and Polly Y. Gipson. 2004. "Stressors and Child and Adolescent Psychopathology: Measurement Issues and Prospective Effects." *Journal of Clinical Child and Adolescent Psychology* 33(2):412–25.

Gurantz, Oded, and Ann Obadan. 2022. "Documenting Their Decisions: How Undocumented Students Enroll and Persist in College." *Educational Researcher* 51(8):524–35.

Ha, Yoonsook, Marci Ybarra, and Anna D. Johnson. 2017. "Variation in Early Cognitive Development by Maternal Immigrant Documentation Status." *Early Childhood Research Quarterly* 41:184–95.

Hagan, Jacqueline Maria. 2012. *Migration Miracle: Faith, Hope, and Meaning on the Undocumented Journey*. Harvard University Press.

Hainmueller, Jens, Duncan Lawrence, Linna Martén, Bernard Black, Lucila Figueroa, Michael Hotard, Tomás R. Jiménez, Fernando Mendoza, Maria I. Rodriguez, Jonas J. Swartz, and David D. Laitin. 2017. "Protecting Unauthorized Immigrant Mothers Improves Their Children's Mental Health." *Science* 357(6355):1041–44.

Hamilton, Laura T. and Kelly Nielsen. 2021. *Broke: The Racial Consequences of Underfunding Public Universities*. University of Chicago Press.

Haskins, Ron, Julia B. Isaacs, and Isabel V. Sawhill. 2008. "Getting Ahead or Losing Ground: Economic Mobility in America." Brookings Institution, Washington, DC.

Heim, Joe. 2017. "Calls for 'Sanctuary' Campuses Multiply as Fears Grow over Trump Immigration Policy." *Washington Post.* Feb 2. www.washingtonpost.com/news/grade-point/wp/2017/02/06/calls-for-sanctuary-campuses-multiply-as-fears-grow-over-trump-immigration-policy/?noredirect=on&utm_term=.742a7bd0ed5c.

Higher Ed Immigration Portal. n.d. "Traveling on Advance Parole: A Guide for DACA Recipients."

Holbein, John, Kei Kawashima-Ginsberg, and Tova Wang. 2021. "Quantifying the Effects of Protests on Voter Registration and Turnout: Study II of 'Protests, Politics, and Power: Exploring the Connections between Youth Voting and Youth Movements.'" CIRCLE, Tufts University, Medford, MA. https://circle.tufts.edu/sites/default/files/2021-09/Youth_Movements_Quant.pdf.

Hsin, Amy, and Francesc Ortega. 2018. "The Effects of Deferred Action for Childhood Arrivals on the Educational Outcomes of Undocumented Students." *Demography* 55(4):1487–1506.

Hsin, Amy, and Holly E. Reed. 2020. "The Academic Performance of Undocumented Students in Higher Education in the United States." *International Migration Review* 54(1):289–315.

Immigrants Rising. 2023. "Quick Guide to AB 540: Expanded In-State Tuition Eligibility in California." https://immigrantsrising.org/wp-content/uploads/Immigrants-Rising_AB-540-Quick-Guide.pdf.

Israel, Emma, and Jeanne Batalova. 2020. "Mexican Immigrants in the United States." Migration Policy Institute, Washington, DC. www.migrationpolicy.org/article/mexican-immigrants-united-states-2019.

Jackson, Philip W. 1968. *Life in Classrooms*. Rinehart and Winston.

Jiménez, Tomás R. 2010. *Replenished Ethnicity: Mexican Americans, Immigration, and Identity*. University of California Press.

Kaiser Family Foundation. 2019. "Changes to "Public Charge" Inadmissibility Rule: Implications for Health and Health Coverage." www.kff.org/racial-equity-and-health-policy/fact-sheet/public-charge-policies-for-immigrants-implications-for-health-coverage/.

Kam, Jennifer A., Debora Pérez Torres, and Keli Steuber Fazio. 2018. "Identifying Individual- and Family-Level Coping Strategies as Sources of Resilience and Thriving for Undocumented Youth of Mexican Origin." *Journal of Applied Communication Research* 46(5):641–64.

Kasinitz, Phillip, John H. Mollenkopf, Mary C. Waters, and Jennifer Holdaway. 2008. *Inheriting the City: The Children of Immigrants Come of Age*. Harvard University Press.

Kidder, William, and Kevin R. Johnson. 2025. "California Dreamin': DACA's Decline and Undocumented College Student Enrollment in the Golden State." *Journal of College and University Law* 50(1):81–1226.

Kivlighan, D. Martin, David Martin, Barry A. Schreier, Chelsey Gates, Jung Eui Hong, Julie M. Corkery, Cari L. Anderson, and Paula M. Keeton. 2021. "The Role of Mental Health Counseling in College Students' Academic Success: An Interrupted Time Series Analysis." *Journal of Counseling Psychology* 68(5):562–70.

Knouse, Stephen B., John R. Tanner, and Elizabeth W. Harris. 1999. "The Relation of College Internships, College Performance, and Subsequent Job Opportunity." *Journal of Employment Counseling* 36(1):35–43.

Kreisberg, A. Nicole, and Amy Hsin. 2021. "The Higher Educational Trajectories of Undocumented Youth in New York City." *Journal of Ethnic and Migration Studies* 47(17):3822–45.

Kroenke, Kurt, Robert L. Spitzer, and Janet B. W. Williams. 2001. "The PHQ-9: Validity of a Brief Depression Severity Measure." *Journal of General Internal Medicine* 16(9):606–13.

Krogstad, Jens Manuel. 2016. "5 Facts About Latinos and Education." Pew Research Center, Washington, DC. www.pewresearch.org/short-reads/2016/07/28/5-facts-about-latinos-and-education/.

Kuh, George D. 2008. "High-Impact Educational Practices: What They Are, Who Has Access to Them, and Why They Matter." Association of American Colleges and Universities, Washington, DC.

Kuh, George D. 2009. "What Student Affairs Professionals Need to Know About Student Engagement." *Journal of College Student Development* 50(6): 683–706.

LAPD [Los Angeles Police Department]. 2007. "Los Angeles Police Department Report to the Board of Police Commissioners: An Examination of May Day 2007." https://static1.squarespace.com/static/5b84cd95e17ba39a889ecaf5/t/5b8fc5804d7a9c8dcd1efc38/1536148881216/May+Day+2007+Final_Report.pdf.

Lara, Argelia, and Pedro E. Nava. 2018. "Achieving the Dream, Uncertain Futures: The Postbaccalaureate Decision-Making Process of Latinx Undocumented Students." *Journal of Hispanic Higher Education* 17(2):112–31.

Lazarus, Richard S., and Susan Folkman. 1984. *Stress, Appraisal, and Coping.* Springer.

Lee, Chih-Yuan Steven, Sara E. Goldstein, and Bryan J. Dik. 2018. "The Relational Context of Social Support in Young Adults: Links with Stress and Well-Being." *Journal of Adult Development* 25(1):25–36.

Lee, Elizabeth. 2016. *Class and Campus Life: Managing and Experiencing Inequality at an Elite College.* Cornell University Press.

Levers, Lisa Lopez, and Debra Hyatt-Burkhart. 2012. "Immigration Reform and the Potential for Psychosocial Trauma: The Missing Link of Lived Human Experience." *Analyses of Social Issues and Public Policy* 12(1):68–77.

Lilly Lopez, Jane. 2021. *Unauthorized Love: Mixed-Citizenship Couples Negotiating Intimacy, Immigration, and the State.* Stanford University Press.

Lipson, Sarah Ketchen, Sasha Zhou, Sara Abelson, Justin Heinze, Matthew Jirsa, Jasmine Morigney, Akilah Patterson, Meghna Singh, and Daniel Eisenberg. 2022. "Trends in College Student Mental Health and Help-Seeking by Race/Ethnicity: Findings from the National Healthy Minds Study, 2013–2021." *Journal of Affective Disorders* 306:138–47.

Lopez, William D., Katherine M. Collins, Guadalupe R. Cervantes, Dalila Reynosa, Julio C. Salazar, and Nicole L. Novak. 2022. "Large-Scale Immigration Worksite Raids and Mixed-Status Families: Separation, Financial Crisis, and Family Role Rearrangement." *Family & Community Health* 45(2):59–66.

Lovato, Kristina. 2019. "Forced Separations: A Qualitative Examination of How Latino/a Adolescents Cope with Parental Deportation." *Children and Youth Services Review* 98:42–50.

Lovato, Kristina, Corina Lopez, Leyla Karimli, and Laura S. Abrams. 2018. "The Impact of Deportation-Related Family Separations on the Well-Being of Latinx Children and Youth: A Review of the Literature." *Children and Youth Services Review* 95:109–16.

Macías, Luis Fernando, and Bruce Anthony Collet. 2016. "Separated by Removal: The Impact of Parental Deportation on Latina/o Children's Postsecondary Educational Goals." *Diaspora, Indigenous, and Minority Education* 10(3):169–81.

Maldonado, Marta María, Adela C. Licona, and Sarah Hendricks. 2016. "Latin@ Immobilities and Altermobilities within the U.S. Deportability Regime." *Annals of the American Association of Geographers* 106:321–29.

Mallet, Marie L., and Lisa Garcia Bedolla. 2019. "Transitory Legality: The Health Implication of Ending DACA." *California Journal of Politics and Policy* 11(2):1–25.

Maroto, Maya E., Anastasia Snelling, and Henry Linck. 2015. "Food Insecurity Among Community College Students: Prevalence and Association with Grade Point Average." *Community College Journal of Research and Practice* 39(6):515–26.

Martinez, Suzanna M., Katie Maynard, and Lorrene D. Ritchie. 2016. "Student Food Access and Security Study." University of California Global Food Initiative, Oakland, CA. www.ucop.edu/global-food-initiative/best-practices/food-access-secu rity/student-food-access-and-security-study.pdf.

Martinez, Suzanna M., Karen Webb, Edward A. Frongillo, and Lorrene D. Ritchie. 2018. "Food Insecurity in California's Public University System: What Are the Risk Factors?" *Journal of Hunger & Environmental Nutrition* 13(1):1–18.

Martinez-Aranda, Mirian G. 2020. "Collective Liminality: The Spillover Effects of Indeterminate Detention on Immigrant Families." *Law & Society Review* 54(4):755–87.

Means, Darris R., and Kimberly B. Pyne. 2017. "Finding My Way: Perceptions of Institutional Support and Belonging in Low-Income, First-Generation, First-Year College Students." *Journal of College Student Development* 58(6):907–24.

Menjívar, Cecilia, and Leisy J. Abrego. 2012. "Legal Violence: Immigration Law and the Lives of Central American Immigrants." *American Journal of Sociology* 117(5):1380–1421.

Menjívar, Cecilia, and Daniel Kanstroom, eds. 2014. *Constructing Immigrant "Illegality": Critiques, Experiences, and Responses.* Cambridge University Press.

Migration Policy Institute. 2020. "Mixed-Status Families Ineligible for CARES Act Federal Pandemic Stimulus Checks." www.migrationpolicy.org/content /mixed-status-families-ineligible-pandemic-stimulus-checks.

Migration Policy Institute. n.d. "Profile of the Unauthorized Population: United States." www.migrationpolicy.org/data/unauthorized-immigrant-population/state/US.

Miller, Holly Ventura, and J. C. Barnes. 2015. "The Association between Parental Incarceration and Health, Education, and Economic Outcomes in Young Adulthood." *American Journal of Criminal Justice* 40(4):765–84.

Morales Hernandez, Martha. Forthcoming. "Emotional Rollercoaster": How Immigration Policy and Agency Shape Mental Health Among Undocumented College Students." *Journal of Health and Social Behavior.*

Morales Hernandez, Martha, and Laura E. Enriquez. 2021. "Life after College: Liminal Legal Status and Political Threats as Barriers to Undocumented Students' Career Preparation Pursuits." *Journal of Latinos and Education* 20(3):318–31.

Muñoz, Susana M., Darsella Vigil, Elizabeth M. Jach, and Marisela M. Rodriguez-Gutierrez. 2018. "Unpacking Resilience and Trauma: Examining the "Trump Effect" in Higher Education for Undocumented Latinx College Students." *Association of Mexican American Educators Journal* 12(3):33–52.

Nájera, Jennifer R. 2024. *Learning to Lead: Undocumented Students Mobilizing Education.* Duke University Press.

National Association of Colleges and Employers. 2019. "NACE Job Outlook." https://ww1.odu.edu/content/dam/odu/offices/cmc/docs/nace/2019-nace-job-outlook-survey.pdf.

National Center for Education Statistics. 2018. "Factors That Influence Student College Choice." Institute of Education Sciences. https://nces.ed.gov/pubs2019/2019119.pdf

Negrón-Gonzales, Genevieve. 2017. "Constrained Inclusion: Access and Persistence Among Undocumented Community College Students in California's Central Valley." *Journal of Hispanic Higher Education* 16(2):105–22.

Ngo, Federick, and Samantha Astudillo. 2019. "California Dream: The Impact of Financial Aid for Undocumented Community College Students." *Educational Researcher* 48(1):5–18.

NILC [National Immigration Law Center]. 2007. "Facts About Immigrants & the Food Stamp Program." www.nilc.org/issues/economic-support/foodstamps/#:~:text=Food%20stamps%20are%20available%20only,been%2C%20eligible%20for%20food%20stamps.

NILC. n.d. "Know Your Rights." www.nilc.org/get-involved/community-education-resources/know-your-rights/.

Nunley, John M., Adam Pugh, Nicholas Romero, and R. Alan Seals. 2016. "College Major, Internship Experience, and Employment Opportunities: Estimates from a Résumé Audit." *Labour Economics* 38:37–46.

Ono, Kent A., and John M. Sloop. 2002. *Shifting Borders: Rhetoric, Immigration, and California's Proposition 187.* Temple University Press.

Orrenius, Pia M., and Madeline Zavodny. 2015. "The Impact of E-Verify Mandates on Labor Market Outcomes." *Southern Economic Journal* 81(4):947–59.

Ortiz, Anna M., and Alejandro Hinojosa. 2010. "Tenuous Options: The Career Development Process for Undocumented Students." *New Directions for Student Services* 2010(131):53–65.

Passel, Jeffrey S., and D'Vera Cohn. 2015. "Share of Unauthorized Immigrant Workers in Production, Construction Jobs Falls since 2007." Pew Research Center, Washington, DC. www.pewhispanic.org/2015/03/26/share-of-unauthorized-immigrant-workers-in-production-construction-jobs-falls-since-2007/.

Passel, Jeffrey S., and D'Vera Cohn. 2018. "Most Unauthorized Immigrants Live with Family Members." Pew Research Center, Washington, DC. www.pewresearch.org/hispanic/2018/11/27/most-unauthorized-immigrants-live-with-family-members/.

Pastor, Manuel. 2018. *State of Resistance: What California's Dizzying Descent and Remarkable Resurgence Mean for America's Future.* The New Press.

Patler, Caitlin, Jo Mhairi Hale, and Erin Hamilton. 2021. "Paths to Mobility: A Longitudinal Evaluation of Earnings Among Latino/a DACA Recipients in California." *American Behavioral Scientist* 65(9):1146–64.

Patler, Caitlin, and Whitney Laster Pirtle. 2018. "From Undocumented to Lawfully Present: Do Changes to Legal Status Impact Psychological Wellbeing Among Latino Immigrant Young Adults?" *Social Science & Medicine* 199(1):39–48.

Patton, Lori D., ed. 2010. *Culture Centers in Higher Education: Perspectives on Identity, Theory, and Practice.* Stylus.

Pearlin, Leonard I., and Alex Bierman. 2013. "Current Issues and Future Directions in Research into the Stress Process." Pp. 325–40 in *Handbook of the Sociology of Mental Health*, edited by C. S. Aneshensel, J. C. Phelan, and A. Bierman. Springer.

Perrin, Andrew J., and Alanna Gillis. 2019. "How College Makes Citizens: Higher Education Experiences and Political Engagement." *Socius* 5:1–16.

Philbin, Sandy P., and Cecilia Ayón. 2016. "Luchamos por Nuestros Hijos: Latino Immigrant Parents Strive to Protect Their Children from the Deleterious Effects of Anti-Immigration Policies." *Children and Youth Services Review* 63:128–35.

Portes, Alejandro, and Rubén G. Rumbaut. 2001. *Legacies: The Story of the Immigrant Second Generation.* University of California Press.

Portes, Alejandro, and Min Zhou. 1993. "The New Second Generation: Segmented Assimilation and Its Variants." *Annals of the American Academy of Political and Social Science* 530:74–96.

Presidents' Alliance on Higher Education and Immigration. n.d.-a. "Our Mission." www.presidentsalliance.org/about/mission/?fwp_staff_founder=1.

Presidents' Alliance on Higher Education and Immigration. n.d.-b. "Rhode Island." www.higheredimmigrationportal.org/state/rhode-island/.

Reber, Sarah, and Ember Smith. 2021. "College Enrollment Disparities: Understanding the Role of Academic Preparation." Center on Children and Families at Brookings, Washington, DC. www.brookings.edu/wp-content/uploads/2023/01/20230123_CCF_CollegeEnrollment_FINAL1.pdf.

Rendón, María G. 2019. *Stagnant Dreamers: How the Inner City Shapes the Integration of Second Generation Latinos.* Russell Sage Foundation.

Reyes, Daisy Verduzco. 2015. "Inhabiting Latino Politics: How Colleges Shape Students' Political Styles." *Sociology of Education* 88(4):302–19.

Reyes, Daisy Verduzco. 2018. *Learning to Be Latino: How Colleges Shape Identity Politics*. Rutgers University Press.

Rodriguez, Cassaundra. 2019. "Latino/a Citizen Children of Undocumented Parents Negotiating Illegality." *Journal of Marriage and Family* 81(3):713–28.

Rodriguez, Cassaundra. 2023. *Contested Americans: Mixed-Status Families in Anti-Immigrant Times*. New York University Press.

Rodríguez, Cristina. 2008. "The Significance of the Local in Immigration Regulation." *Michigan Law Review* 106(4):567–642.

Rodriguez, Victoria E., Laura E. Enriquez, Cecilia Ayón, and Annie Ro. 2023. "Discrimination and Mental Health Among Undocumented and Mixed-Status College Students: A Mixed Methods Investigation." *Journal of Health and Social Behavior* 64(4):593–609.

Rojas-Flores, Lisseth, Mari L. Clements, J. Hwang Koo, and Judy London. 2016. "Trauma and Psychological Distress in Latino Citizen Children Following Parental Detention and Deportation." *Psychological Trauma: Theory, Research, Practice, and Policy* 9(3):352–61.

Rosales, Rocío. 2020. *Fruteros: Street Vending, Illegality, and Ethnic Community in Los Angeles*. University of California Press.

Rosales, William E., Laura E. Enriquez, and Jennifer R. Nájera. 2021. "Politically Excluded, Undocu-Engaged: The Perceived Effect of Hostile Immigration Policies on Undocumented Student Political Engagement." *Journal of Latinos and Education* 20(3):260–75.

Rubio-Hernandez, Sandy P., and Cecilia Ayón. 2016. "Pobrecitos los Niños: The Emotional Impact of Anti-Immigration Policies on Latino Children." *Children and Youth Services Review* 60:20–26.

Ruth, Alissa, and Emir Estrada. 2019 "DACAmented Homecomings: A Brief Return to Mexico and the Reshaping of Bounded Solidarity Among Mixed-Status Latinx Families." *Hispanic Journal of Behavioral Sciences* 41(2):145–65.

Ryo, Emily. 2018. "Representing Immigrants: The Role of Lawyers in Immigration Bond Hearings." *Law & Society Review* 52(2):503–31.

Ryo, Emily, and Ian Peacock. 2021. "Represented but Unequal: The Contingent Effect of Legal Representation in Removal Proceedings." *Law & Society Review* 55(4):634–56.

Saguy, Abigail C., and Laura E. Enriquez. 2020. "Mobilizing Fearful Constituents." In *Come Out, Come Out, Whoever You Are: Identity Politics in the 21st Century*, by A. C. Saguy. Oxford University Press.

Salazar, Cinthya, Cindy Barahona, and Francesco Yepez-Coello. 2024. "Where Do I Go from Here? Examining the Transition of Undocumented Students Graduating from College." *Journal of Higher Education* 95(6):747–77.

Sallie Mae. 2022. "How America Pays for College: Sallie Mae's National Study of College Students and Parents." www.salliemae.com/content/dam/slm/writtencontent/Research/HowAmericaPaysforCollege2022.pdf.

Sanchez, Ruben Elias Canedo, and Meng L. So. 2015. "UC Berkeley's Undocumented Student Program: Holistic Strategies for Undocumented Student Equitable Success across Higher Education." *Harvard Educational Review* 85(3):464–77.

Sangalang, Cindy C., David Becerra, Felicia M. Mitchell, Stephanie Lechuga-Peña, Kristina Lopez, and Isok Kim. 2019. "Trauma, Post-Migration Stress, and Mental Health: A Comparative Analysis of Refugees and Immigrants in the United States." *Journal of Immigrant and Minority Health* 21(5):909–19.

Sarabia, Heidy, Laura E. Enriquez, Victoria E. Rodriguez, Laura Zaragoza, and Sonia Tinoco. 2021. "What Helps Students Get Help?: An Exploratory Analysis of Factors That Shape Undocumented College Students' Use of Academic Support Services." *Journal of Latinos and Education* 20(3):290–303.

Schmalzbauer, Leah, and Alelí Andrés. 2019. "Stratified Lives: Family, Illegality, and the Rise of a New Educational Elite." *Harvard Educational Review*:635–60.

Seif, Hinda. 2004. "'Wise Up': Undocumented Latino Youth Mexican American Legislators, and the Struggle for Education Access." *Latino Studies* 2(2):210–30.

Shuford, Bettina. 2011. "Historical and Philosophical Development of Multicultural Student Services." Pp. 29–37 in *Multicultural Student Services on Campus: Building Bridges, Re-Visioning Community*, edited by D. Lazarus Stewart. Stylus.

Siegel, M., C. Assenmacher, N. Meuwly, and M. Zemp. 2021. "The Legal Vulnerability Model for Same-Sex Parent Families: A Mixed Methods Systematic Review and Theoretical Integration." *Frontiers in Psychology* 12:1–28.

Silva, Meghan R., Whitney L. Kleinert, A. Victoria Sheppard, Kathryn A. Cantrell, Darren J. Freeman-Coppadge, Elena Tsoy, Tangela Roberts, and Melissa Pearrow. 2017. "The Relationship between Food Security, Housing Stability, and School Performance Among College Students in an Urban University." *Journal of College Student Retention: Research, Theory & Practice* 19(3):284–99.

Silver, Alexis. 2018. *Shifting Boundaries: Immigrant Youth Negotiating National, State, and Small-Town Politics.* Stanford University Press.

Simmons, William Paul, Cecilia Menjívar, and Elizabeth Salerno Valdez. 2021. "The Gendered Effects of Local Immigration Enforcement: Latinas' Social Isolation in Chicago, Houston, Los Angeles, and Phoenix." *International Migration Review* 55(1):108–34.

The S.I.N. Collective. 2007. "Students Informing Now (S.I.N.) Challenge the Racial State in California without Shame . . . Sin Verguenza!" *Educational Foundations* 21(1–2):71–90.

Spitzer, Robert L., Kurt Kroenke, Janet B. W. Williams, and Bernd Löwe. 2006. "A Brief Measure for Assessing Generalized Anxiety Disorder: The GAD-7." *Archives of Internal Medicine* 166(10):1092–97.

Strayhorn, Terrell L. 2018. *College Students' Sense of Belonging: A Key to Educational Success for All Students.* Routledge.

Street, Alex, Michael Jones-Correa, and Chris Zepeda-Millán. 2017. "Political Effects of Having Undocumented Parents." *Political Research Quarterly* 70(4):818–32.

Stuber, Jenny M. 2011. *Inside the College Gates: How Class and Culture Matter in Higher Education*. Lexington Books.

Stuesse, Angela, and Mathew Coleman. 2014. "Automobility, Immobility, Altermobility: Surviving and Resisting the Intensification of Immigrant Policing." *City & Society* 26(1):51–72.

Suárez-Orozco, Carola, Dalal Katsiaficas, Olivia Birchall, Cynthia M. Alcantar, Edwin Hernandez, Yuliana Garcia, Minas Michikyan, Janet Cerda, and Robert T. Teranishi. 2015. "Undocumented Undergraduates on College Campuses: Understanding Their Challenges, Assets, and What It Takes to Make an Undocufriendly Campus." *Harvard Education Review* 85(3):427–63.

Suárez-Orozco, Carola, and Guadalupe López Hernández. 2020. "'Waking up Every Day with the Worry': A Mixed-Methods Study of Anxiety in Undocumented Latinx College Students." *Frontiers in Psychiatry* 11:1–14.

Suárez-Orozco, Carola, Marie Onaga, and Cécile de Lardemelle. 2010. "Promoting Academic Engagement Among Immigrant Adolescents through School-Family-Community Collaboration." *Professional School Counseling* 14(1):15–26.

Suárez-Orozco, Carola, Hirokazu Yoshikawa, Robert T. Teranishi, and Marcelo M. Suárez-Orozco. 2011. "Growing up in the Shadows: The Developmental Implications of Unauthorized Status." *Harvard Educational Review* 81(3):438–72.

Talavera, Victor, Guillermina Gina Núñez-Mchiri, and Josiah M. Heyman. 2010. "Deportation in the U.S.-Mexico Borderlands: Anticipation, Experience, and Memory." Pp. 166–95 in *The Deportation Regime: Sovereignty, Space, and the Freedom of Movement*, edited by N. De Genova and N. Peutz. Duke University Press.

Telles, Edward E., and Vilma Ortiz. 2008. *Generations of Exclusion: Mexican Americans, Assimilation, and Race*. Russell Sage Foundation.

Terriquez, Veronica. 2015. "Dreams Delayed: Barriers to Degree Completion Among Undocumented Community College Students." *Journal of Ethnic and Migration Studies* 41(8):1302–23.

Terriquez, Veronica. 2017. "Legal Status, Civic Organizations, and Political Participation Among Latino Young Adults." *Sociological Quarterly* 58(2):315–36.

Terriquez, Veronica, and Oded Gurantz. 2015. "Financial Challenges in Emerging Adulthood and Students' Decisions to Stop out of College." *Emerging Adulthood* 3(3):204–14.

Terriquez, Veronica, and Hyeyoung Kwon. 2015. "Intergenerational Family Relations, Civic Organisations, and the Political Socialisation of Second-Generation Immigrant Youth." *Journal of Ethnic and Migration Studies* 41(3):425–47.

Terriquez, Veronica, and Ruth Milkman. 2021. "Immigrant and Refugee Youth Organizing in Solidarity with the Movement for Black Lives." *Gender & Society* 35(4):577–87.

Thoits, Peggy A. 2011. "Mechanisms Linking Social Ties and Support to Physical and Mental Health." *Journal of Health and Social Behavior* 52(2):145–61.

Turney, Kristin, and Rebecca Goodsell. 2018. "Parental Incarceration and Children's Wellbeing." *The Future of Children* 28(1):147–64.

UCOP [University of California Office of the President]. 2007. "Major Features of the California Master Plan for Higher Education." www.ucop.edu/acadinit/mastplan /mpsummary.htm.

UCOP. 2013. "President Napolitano Earmarks Aid for Students, Researchers." http:// link.ucop.edu/2013/11/01/president-napolitano-earmarks-aid-for-students -researchers/.

UCOP. 2016. "UC President Napolitano Announces Multiyear Support for Undocu- mented Students." www.universityofcalifornia.edu/press-room/uc-president-napol itano-proposes-multi-year-support-undocumented-students.

University of California. n.d.-a. "Blue and Gold Opportunity Plan." https://admission .universityofcalifornia.edu/tuition-financial-aid/types-of-aid/blue-and-gold-oppor tunity-plan.html.

University of California. n.d.-b. "California Dream Loan Program." https://admission .universityofcalifornia.edu/tuition-financial-aid/types-of-aid/dream-loan-program .html.

University of California. n.d.-c. "Firstgen." www.universityofcalifornia.edu/student -success/firstgen.

University of California. n.d.-d. "Undocumented Student Resources." https://undoc .universityofcalifornia.edu/.

University of California Immigrant Legal Services Center. n.d. "University of Califor- nia Immigrant Legal Services Center." https://ucimm.law.ucdavis.edu/.

University of Hawai'i. 2014. "Board of Regents Policy 6.209." www.hawaii.edu/policy/?ac tion=viewPolicy&policySection=rp&policyChapter=6&policyNumber=209.

USCIS [US Citizenship and Immigration Services]. 2018. "Consideration of Deferred Action for Childhood Arrivals (DACA)." www.uscis.gov/archive/consideration -deferred-action-childhood-arrivals-daca

USCIS. 2020. "Green Card for Immediate Relatives of U.S. Citizen." www.uscis.gov /green-card/green-card-eligibility/green-card-for-immediate-relatives-of-us-citizen.

USDA [United States Department of Agriculture]. 2012. "U.S. Household Food Security Survey Module: Six-Item Short Form." www.ers.usda.gov/media/8282 /short2012.pdf

USDA. 2022. "Definitions of Food Security." www.ers.usda.gov/topics/food-nutrition -assistance/food-security-in-the-u-s/definitions-of-food-security/.

Valadez, Mercedes, Cecilia Ayón, Laura E. Enriquez, and Julián Jefferies. 2021. "Legal Vulnerability and Campus Environment: Assessing Factors That Affect the Aca- demic Engagement of Undocumented College Students." *Journal of Latinos and Education* 20(3):276–89.

Valdez, Carmen R., Kevin M. Wagner, and Laura P. Minero. 2021. "Emotional Reac- tions and Coping of Mexican Mixed-Status Immigrant Families in Anticipation of the 2016 Presidential Election." *Family Process* 60(2):623–38.

Valdez, Zulema, and Tanya Golash-Boza. 2020. "Master Status or Intersectional Iden- tity? Undocumented Students' Sense of Belonging on a College Campus." *Identities* 27(4):481–99.

Valdivia, Carolina. 2021. "'I Became a Mom Overnight': How Parental Detentions and Deportations Impact Young Adults' Role." *Harvard Educational Review* 91(1):62–82.

Vaquera, Elizabeth, Elizabeth Aranda, and Isabel Sousa-Rodriguez. 2017. "Emotional Challenges of Undocumented Young Adults: Ontological Security, Emotional Capital, and Well-Being." *Social Problems* 64(2):298–314.

Vasquez, Jessica M. 2011. *Mexican Americans Across Generations: Immigrant Families, Racial Realities*. New York University Press.

Vega, William A., Michael A. Rodriguez, and Elisabeth Gruskin. 2009. "Health Disparities in the Latino Population." *Epidemiologic Reviews* 31(1):99–112.

Velarde Pierce, Sharon, Alein Y. Haro, Cecilia Ayón, and Laura E. Enriquez. 2021. "Evaluating the Effect of Legal Vulnerabilities and Social Support on the Mental Health of Undocumented College Students." *Journal of Latinos and Education* 20(3):246–59.

Washington Post Staff. 2015. "Full Text: Donald Trump Announces a Presidential Bid." *Washington Post*. June 16. https://colorustrumped.com/wp-content/uploads /notation-trumps-candidacy-announcement.pdf.

Waters, Mary C., and Marisa Gerstein Pineau, eds. 2015. *The Integration of Immigrants Into American Society*. National Academies Press.

Ybarra, Megan, and Isaura L. Peña. 2016. "'We Don't Need Money, We Need to Be Together': Forced Transnationality in Deportation's Afterlives." *Geopolitics* 22(1):34–50.

Yoshikawa, Hirokazu. 2012. *Immigrants Raising Citizens: Undocumented Parents and Their Young Children*. Russell Sage Foundation.

Zayas, Luis H. 2015. *Forgotten Citizens: Deportation, Children, and the Making of American Exiles and Orphans*. Oxford University Press.

Zepeda-Millán, Chris. 2017. *Latino Mass Mobilization: Immigration, Racialization, and Activism*. Cambridge University Press.

INDEX

Page numbers in italics indicate Figures and Tables

ABOUT THE AUTHORS

LAURA E. ENRIQUEZ is Associate Professor of Chicano/Latino Studies at the University of California, Irvine.

ZULEMA VALDEZ is Associate Vice Chancellor and Professor of Sociology at the University of California, Merced.

ANNIE RO is Associate Professor of Health, Society, and Behavior at the University of California, Irvine Wen School of Population & Public Health.

CECILIA AYÓN is Professor of Public Policy at the University of California, Riverside.

JENNIFER R. NÁJERA is Professor of Ethnic Studies at the University of California, Riverside.